THE LOYALISTS IN NORTH CAROLINA DURING THE REVOLUTION

To My Wife

HARRIET KING DEMOND

THE LOYALISTS IN NORTH CAROLINA DURING THE REVOLUTION

by

ROBERT O. DeMOND

ARCHON BOOKS
HAMDEN, CONNECTICUT
1964

PREFACE

THE PART played by the Loyalists in the struggle of the American colonies with Great Britain has been generally neglected by both American and English historians. My interest in the Loyalists was first aroused when I was an undergraduate student of Professor A. C. Flick at Syracuse University. This interest continued, and when my graduate study was resumed at Duke University in the summer of 1934 the present study was begun under the encouragement of the late Professor William K. Boyd.

North Carolina probably contained a greater number of Loyalists in proportion to its population than did any other colony. In spite of this fact Loyalist writers have scarcely mentioned the colony in their treatment of the Loyalists. This is the more surprising when one considers that these Loyalists, unaided by British troops, accomplished more than did the Loyalists of any other colony, and that North Carolina furnished in Colonel John Hamilton the most important Tory leader of the Revolution. This neglect may have resulted from the fact that at the time of the Revolution North Carolina lacked large towns and her newspapers were few. So chaotic became the condition of the state that during the latter period of the war no newspaper was published at all.

The attempt has been made in this study to bring together all of the available source material which concerns this topic and to present it in such a way as to give the reader a realization of the part played by this important group of people. Any study which sets forth the great extent of the activities and efforts of the Tories, incidentally increases the praise which should be given the Patriots who not only put down this rising from within, but also drove the British forces from the state.

It is difficult to thank all of the individuals and societies to whom I am indebted for helpful services and advice. Especial thanks should be given to William P. Martin of the Library of Congress; to Robert W. Bingham, Director of the Buffalo Historical Society; to Miss Mabel Ross, Research Librarian of the Grosvenor Library, Buffalo; to A. R. Newsome and C. C. Crittenden of the North Carolina Historical Commission; and to J. P. Breedlove for the loan of books from the Duke University Library. Most of all I am indebted to the late Professor William K. Boyd for aid and encouragement. Professor Richard H. Shryock has read all of the manuscript and offered many constructive criticisms. Largely on account of his aid this study has been brought to completion.

R. O. D.

State Teachers College
Buffalo, New York
June, 1940.

CONTENTS

	PAGE
PREFACE	vii

CHAPTER

I. MOTIVATION FOR REVOLT	3
II. DISSENTING ELEMENTS	34
III. COMMITTEES OF PUBLIC SAFETY	62
IV. MILITARY ACTIVITIES OF THE LOYALISTS IN THE EARLY PART OF THE REVOLUTION	84
V. SUFFERINGS OF THE LOYALISTS	108
VI. FINAL STRUGGLE BETWEEN PATRIOTS AND LOYALISTS	124
VII. ANTI-LOYALIST LEGISLATION	153
VIII. CONFISCATION OF PROPERTY AND DEBTS OF THE LOYALISTS	170
IX. EXODUS OF THE LOYALISTS	181
X. COMPENSATION AND PENSION ALLOWED TO LOYALISTS	202

APPENDICES

Appendix A	217
Appendix B	240
Appendix C	251
Appendix D	256
BIBLIOGRAPHY	262
INDEX	269

THE LOYALISTS IN NORTH CAROLINA DURING THE REVOLUTION

CHAPTER I

MOTIVATION FOR REVOLT

THE RELATIVELY RURAL and isolated nature of the North Carolina population taught the people self-reliance and independence long before the Revolution. They had moved into North Carolina with the belief that it lay beyond the limits of Virginia and that they would therefore escape the payment of quit rents.[1] Separated from the settlements to the north by numerous waterways, the Carolinians had little contact with their Virginia neighbors. Temporarily they were ignored by the latter, and lived independently of any outside control.

When Governor Berkeley saw that the settlement was likely to succeed, he secured for himself and his associates a grant to the land. The government was a real democracy, for the people met in general session instead of acting through representatives. One of their first acts was to petition the Lords Proprietors that they be permitted to hold their lands under the same terms and conditions as existed in Virginia. By an agreement known as the "Great Deed" the rent became a farthing an acre, payable in commodities at a fixed point.[2]

The first dissatisfaction came in 1672 with an act to regulate prices. One provision declared that rum should not be sold for more than twenty-five pounds of tobacco a gallon. Dealers would not bring rum to sell at this small profit, and trade was lost to the colony.[3] The next year the law was repealed. The people at this time also refused to accede to a law which increased their rent from one farthing per acre to one penny's worth of silver. Governor Carteret, being unable to solve the problem, left for England.

The residents of North Carolina asserted their rights and quarreled with their governors almost from the beginning.

[1] *The Colonial Records of North Carolina* (hereinafter cited as *Col. Rec. of N. C.*), ed. William L. Saunders (10 vols.; Raleigh, 1886-1890), I, 100.
[2] *Ibid.*, I, 175-176.　　　　[3] *Ibid.*, I, 219.

John Jenkins, who was appointed governor in 1673, when the colony was only nine years old, was turned out by the people in 1676.[4] Thus early did the Assembly assert its power over the executive branch. In 1672 Parliament placed a duty of one penny a pound on tobacco shipped from one colony to another. Since tobacco was the staple in which payments were made, it was the basis of bills of credit, and this tax lessened the value of tobacco as a medium of exchange in intercolonial trade.[5] When, in 1677, the people returned from a successful Indian war, they demanded that the export tax on tobacco from one colony to another should not be collected. This was rebellion, not against the Proprietors, but against the laws of England.

The next governors, Miller and Eastchurch, were deposed by the Culpepper Rebellion, the original purpose of which had been to thwart the enforcement of the Navigation Laws and custom duties. This led the Lords Proprietors to declare, in 1676, that the North Carolinians did not understand their own interests and would not regard the wishes of the Proprietors.[6] The fourth governor to be deposed was Seth Sothel, whom the Assembly impeached and expelled in 1689.[7] The first recorded act (1665) of the Albemarle Assembly was a petition to the Lords Proprietors in which they protested against the quit rents and allotments of land and requested that they might receive the same treatment as did the settlers of Virginia. This petition was favorably received; in 1668 the Lords Proprietors allowed them to hold lands under the same terms and conditions as the people of Virginia, by which agreement the rent became a farthing an acre and was payable in commodities at a fixed price instead of one penny an acre in silver as formerly. This concession, later known as the "Great Deed," was greatly cherished by the freemen and the General Assembly.

The people were now well satisfied, for in addition to the concession of the "Great Deed" the government under the Fundamental Constitutions, established in 1669, provided for

[4] *Ibid.*, I, Preface, p. xvii.
[5] Samuel A'Court Ashe, *History of North Carolina* (2 vols.; Greensboro, 1908-1925), I, 117.
[6] *Col. Rec. of N. C.*, II, Preface, p. x.   [7] *Ibid.*, I, 362.

biennial sessions of the legislature without any summons from the governor. In a period of twenty-five years the Albemarle Colony had been ruled by twelve governors, four of whom the people had deposed by force. The Revolution in England at this time may have encouraged the revolutionary spirit in North Carolina that caused Governor Nicholson to describe his subjects as "a very mutinous people."

Governor Burrington, after ten years of association with the people of North Carolina, in writing to the Board of Trade, declared:

> The inhabitants of North Carolina are not industrious but subtle and crafty to admiration, always behaved insolently to their Governors, some they have imprisoned, drove others out of the country, at other times set up two or three supported by men under arms. All the Governors that were ever in this Province lived in fear of the people (except myself) and dreaded their Assemblys. The people are neither to be cajoled or outwitted, whenever a Governor attempts to effect anything by these means he will lose his labor and show his ignorance. . . . They insist that no public money can or ought to be paid out but by a claim given to and allowed by the House of Burgesses.[8]

Governor Burrington's statement was no exaggeration. From the division of the Province in 1688, when Albemarle became North Carolina, to the taking of the colony by the King in 1731 there were sixteen governors. The first of these, Philip Ludwell, brought peace and prosperity to the colony for a while. He was allowed to depart widely from the instructions of the Grand Model and to govern more in accordance with the charter from the Crown.[9] The interest of the governor, who was often a proprietor, was likely to be the same as that of the people, and it was only when the governor attempted to enforce trade regulations and custom dues in the interest of the Crown that the people rebelled.

With the purchase of the rights of the Proprietors by the

---

[8] *Ibid.*, II, Preface, p. xi. In some of these early quotations the spelling has been modernized and occasionally a word changed to conform to modern usage. In no case has the meaning or interpretation of the original been altered.

[9] *Ibid.*, I, 381.

Crown in 1729, a new period in the development of the colony began. Since Burrington, the new governor, did not arrive until two years later, the legislators, although they knew the rights of the Proprietors had been sold to the King, decided to hold their regular session in November, 1729, and to pass a money bill which they knew would not be allowed under the new government. Sir Richard Everard, the governor, was bribed by a gift of £500 to give his consent to a bill providing for an issue of paper money amounting to £40,000.[10]

Events proved that the people were not mistaken in this plan. Among the first instructions to Governor Burrington for the government of the colony was a clause which forbade his giving his consent to any bills of credit to be struck or issued in lieu of money unless the act contained the provision that it should not take effect until approved by the Crown.[11]

The British Government was anxious to know the financial status of the colony that it had recently secured, and required Governor Burrington to report the amount of paper bills current in the colony, on what fund and at what discount they were current. He reported that £40,000 had been issued in 1729 and that £10,000 of this amount was to exchange the old bills then current. In his report Burrington expressed his opinion that the laws made in 1729 ought to remain in force until His Majesty's pleasure thereon could be known.[12] He advised against destroying the paper money unless some other provision was made. This currency became the medium of exchange in the colony, and although the validity of the act was questioned, it was never repealed.[13]

Each new governor introduced a fresh quarrel. Governor Johnston attempted to limit the number of representatives in the Assembly to two members from each county and one from each town and thus alienated from him the counties in the north that had been entitled to five. His chief reason for doing this was the fact that he could not control the representatives from this northern region as easily as he could those from the

[10] Ashe, *op. cit.*, I, 210.   [11] *Col. Rec. of N. C.*, III, 95.
[12] *Ibid.*, III, 145-146.   [13] Ashe, *op. cit.*, I, 219.

southern counties. Because the north had a majority in the
Assembly and could thereby thwart his plan, Governor Johnston decided to call a meeting of the Assembly at Wilmington,
which was designated as the new capital. The representatives
of the northern counties found it almost impossible to attend
on account of the distance. In this Assembly, composed almost
entirely of southern members, Governor Johnston secured his
law for equal representation. The Assembly met at Wilmington, and from 1746 to 1754 the counties from the north had
no representation, for they would not consent to less than five.
Finally, in 1754, the Crown disallowed the act which provided
for equal representation. Until 1775 legislative apportionment
was the same as it had been previous to 1746.[14]

When the Crown assumed control in North Carolina, the
lower house or assembly had been in operation for over half a
century and felt itself entitled to certain privileges granted
it by the Proprietors. Its control of supplies gave it certain
powers over the governor and council. No bill could be passed
to which the lower house did not give its consent. It claimed
and deserved a share in the administration of the land policy
of the colony. For this privilege it went back to the grant of
1668 which gave lands at a very low rate.[15] The lower house
was consulted when the governor needed salaries and supplies
in response to requests from the Crown.[16] The assembly,
which was made up largely of justices, desired that justices
should be appointed to hold office during good behavior.
During the administration of the first royal governor it passed
the following resolution: "Resolved by the committee that the
House be moved to address his Excellency the Governor that
no magistrate in this Province be removed from his office, without complaint for malfeasance in his office, and he be convicted
of the same upon hearing before the Governor and Council."[17]
Governor Burrington answered that he never had removed a
justice without cause and that he never intended to. But he
could not sign such a bill, since it was contrary to his instructions

[14] *Col. Rec. of N. C.*, V, 231 f.   [15] *Ibid.*, IV, 246.
[16] *Ibid.*, IV, 550-555.   [17] *Ibid.*, IV, 237.

which provided for their holding office only during his pleasure.[18] Thus for the most part while the governors in accordance with their instructions were not permitted to appoint justices during good behavior, in order to avoid the evil consequences of dismissal without cause, they were usually accorded a trial.[19]

The power of assessing taxes was given to the justices of the county court by the assembly. The sheriff collected the taxes, and there was a close connection, as will be shown later, between sheriff, justices, and assembly with the latter possessing ultimate power. The undemocratic but effective county court assumed more and more power as time passed. Its officers represented the wealthy property-owners of the county, a small group who kept themselves in power year after year.

This system by which a small group secured and maintained control of the government is sometimes spoken of as the "Court House Ring." The influence of the "Court House Ring" removed the government from the hands of the people and created a self-perpetuating oligarchy. The county was the all-important administrative unit in the affairs of the people. Whatever group controlled these county offices controlled the county. The justices of the peace who controlled the local government were appointed by the governor upon nomination of the assemblymen from each county, who were usually justices themselves and who renominated one of their number. Bute County from 1764 to 1775 had seven members in the Assembly, all of whom were justices. Carteret County from 1725 to 1775 had eighteen members, and all but one were justices. Granville from 1746 to 1776 had nine members and all were justices.[20] The sheriffs to a very large extent had charge of the elections at which assemblymen were elected, and the assemblymen were usually justices.

The sheriff was appointed by each precinct court in the Province.[21] To be eligible for nomination, he had to be a justice of peace of the county. Thus the members of the court

---

[18] *Ibid.*   [19] *Ibid.*, IV, 682-683.
[20] Julian Parks Boyd, *The County Court in Colonial North Carolina* (an unpublished Master's thesis, Duke University), p. 178.
[21] *Col. Rec. of N. C.*, XXIII, 122-127.

nominated one of their own number. Sometimes they did not bother to nominate three men but only one, and then the nomination was equivalent to appointment.[22] Since the assembly was made up of sheriffs, clerks of court, justices of peace, and other members of the county court party, a quarrel with this party meant a quarrel with the assembly. The Board of Trade in 1770 wrote Governor Tryon that the chief representative of the Crown in the county ought to be nominated by the Crown, as was the case in England,[23] and the Board threatened to recommend repeal of the act which gave this privilege to the county court.

When Governor Martin replied to this letter, he explained to the Board of Trade that this act giving the appointment of sheriffs to the justices was so great a favorite with the Assembly, which was composed of justices of peace, that they would never consent to its alteration.[24] Later Governor Martin wrote that the sheriffs were generally leaders in the Revolution. Too late it was realized that a mistake had been made when the Crown had allowed the choice of the chief executive officer of the county to come under the control of the assembly. This, as we have seen, led eventually to a weakening of the control of the royal governor over the colony. This "Court House Ring" system was not democratic, for it was controlled by slave-owners and landowners who made up the aristocracy. By this system the assembly controlled the county officials and debarred a large number of the inhabitants from any part even in local government. Likewise, it took the control of government from the hands of the governor. The result was a chronic and bitter controversy between the assembly and governor at each meeting of the legislature.

Against England's commercial policy of 1660, which was formulated for the benefit of the mother country, North Carolina offered no protest, perhaps on account of the paucity of her activities. Her opposition to the acts of trade of the eighteenth century was slight, if any, for she was little affected

[22] Julian Boyd, op. cit., p. 180.
[23] Col. Rec. of N. C., VIII, 266.   [24] Ibid., IX, 1158 f.

by them, and to evade them was easy. Acts prohibiting the exportation of manufactured articles worried her not at all, for her manufactures were quite undeveloped.[25] In a letter to Lord Halifax in January, 1764, Governor Dobbs averred that illicit trade was scarcely known to his colony: there had been but three inquiries of ships in the colony for illicit trade for nine years. He thought that this was the best record of any English colony in America.[26] The members of the Assembly, opposing the Sugar Act of 1764, protested to Governor Dobbs:

> And though it is with the utmost concern we observe our commerce circumscribed in its most beneficial branches diverted from its natural channels and burdened with new taxes, and impositions laid on us without our privity and consent and against what we esteem our inherent right, and exclusive privilege of imposing our own taxes; yet under these unhappy circumstances your Excellency may be assured that nothing shall be wanting on our part, to rid the trader as far as in our power, of the heavy expenses attending the exportation of our commodities, and to remove as far as possible every incumbrance with which the commercial interest of this province is clogged.[27]

Here was a protest because the tax was levied upon them without their consent. They considered this act an invasion of their rights. This objection foreshadowed their opposition to the Stamp Act, which came the following year.

One of the Imperial Acts of the mother country which did much to stir up agitation in Virginia and which was of small importance in North Carolina, was the Proclamation Act of 1763. This act prohibited the purchase and settlement of the Indian land west of the Appalachian Mountains. Since the settlement of North Carolina had scarcely reached this prohibited line in 1763, the inhabitants were not irked by a ruling which did not affect them. Not so, however, in Virginia. As the land in Virginia became exhausted from the raising of tobacco, the planters ever needed fresh lands. Land speculation was rife, and the people looked longingly to the forbidden lands beyond the mountains.

[25] *Ibid.*, VII, 129.
[26] *Ibid.*, VI, 1020-1023.   [27] *Ibid.*, VI, 1261.

George Washington and Captain William Crawford with the aid of Governor Dunmore were the leaders of a group who had over two hundred thousand acres surveyed and appropriated after the Treaty of Fort Stanwix. Governor Dunmore, in 1774, was reprimanded by Lord Dartmouth for having allocated bounty lands to the soldiers west of the mountains after 1763. Patrick Henry, Hugh Innes, and other soldiers and speculators held unsurveyed claims to lands which could not be located until there was a change in the royal policy.

During the Revolutionary War, Patrick Henry, Thomas Jefferson, Henry Lee, George Washington, and others secured grants which previously the British ministry had denied them. All those who desired land west of the mountains must have rejoiced at this change of policy.[28]

With the passage of the Stamp Act, North Carolina for the first time offered a serious threat of resistance. Tryon became governor the month after the act was passed, and found the colony much excited. When he asked Speaker of the House Ashe what the people would do about the Stamp Act, he received the answer, "Resist with blood and death." Having been ordered by the home government to prorogue the House if there seemed any danger of action, he did so at once.[29]

In October two mass demonstrations in opposition to the act were held in Wilmington, and when Dr. Houston, the stamp agent, arrived in November, he was compelled to resign at once. Immediately Governor Tryon attempted to placate the irate citizenry, and at a dinner given to fifty leading men he promised them that the colony would be favorably treated. In order to persuade them to accept the act in principle, he offered to pay the whole duty on certain instruments. The next morning the people thanked him for his generosity, but added: "We cannot assent to the payment of the smaller stamps; an admission of the part would put it out of our power to refuse with any propriety a submission to the whole; and as we can never consent to be deprived of the invaluable privilege of a trial by

[28] Isaac Samuel Harrell, *Loyalism in Virginia: Chapters in the Economic History of the Revolution* (Durham, 1926), pp. 6-22.
[29] *Col. Rec. of N. C.*, VII, 118.

jury which is one part of the act, we think it more consistent as well as securer conduct to prevent to the utmost of our power the operation of it."[30] In December, 1765, Governor Tryon wrote Conway that the merchants of Wilmington had been as assiduous in obstructing the reception of the stamps as any of the inhabitants, and that no vessels had left the river since the receipt of the stamps. The Governor explained that there was not enough specie in the colony to pay for the stamps that the five superior courts alone would require in one year.[31] At this time Governor Tryon was not anticipating any serious opposition to the act, for he believed that the King's authority would meet with a ready acquiescence in the Southern Provinces, without the necessity of any armed force.[32]

Not only were the merchants of the seaports ruined by the stagnation of trade, but also those further inland. In January, 1766, a trader at Cross Creek complained because he could neither ship nor sell for money goods which he had sent down to Wilmington. He especially complained because Cape Fear was the only port in America that was closed. He expressed his surprise that the people tamely submitted, and boldly declared: "Rouse for shame, act the man, open your Port, and Courts, arrest the men who have made illegal seizures and been detaining those vessels and put them under pain of military discipline if they dare to seize any more."[33] This statement appeared in the North Carolina Gazette, which was printed by Alexander Stewart, His Majesty's printer for the Province. Governor Tryon suspended him from office for giving publicity to such an inflammatory expression.[34]

In November, 1765, the stamps arrived at Brunswick on board the sloop of war Diligence, accompanied by the Viper. The news spread quickly throughout the Province, and armed men from New Hanover and Brunswick counties hurried to Brunswick. Hugh Waddell and John Ashe assumed the leadership and prevented the stamps from being landed.

[30] Ibid., VII, 129.   [31] Ibid., VII, 144.
[32] Alfred Moore Waddell, "The Stamp Act on the Cape Fear," North Carolina Booklet (Raleigh, 1901), I, No. 3, p. 9.
[33] Col. Rec. of N. C., VII, 168a.   [34] Ibid., VII, 187 f.

Two ships, the *Dobbs* and the *Patience,* had arrived from
St. Christopher and Philadelphia, respectively. Their clearance
papers were not made out on stamped paper as the recent Stamp
Act required. Captain Lobb of the armed sloop *Viper,* who had
anchored in the Cape Fear River to see that the Stamp Act
was enforced, seized the two ships. In spite of the fact that
the officers of the two ships protested, the seizure was made on
the grounds that they had been unable to secure the stamped
paper at the ports from which they had sailed.

Several hundred men gathered at Wilmington from the
surrounding counties and plighted their faith and honor that
they would at any risk whatever, and whenever called upon,
unite and truly and faithfully assist each other to the best of
their power in preventing entirely the operation of the Stamp
Act. John Ashe, Alexander Lillington, and Colonel Thomas
Lloyd were chosen to direct the movement, while General
Hugh Waddell was put in command of the body of men. They
were determined to liberate the two ships which were being held
for want of stamps.[35]

Cornelius Harnett and Maurice Moore, before proceeding
to Brunswick, sent a letter to Governor Tryon warning him
that they were coming to secure a redress from their grievances.
This they hoped might be done in a peaceable manner. He
was informed that he was not to be harmed, and a guard was
offered him. This offer, however, Tryon haughtily refused.
The insurgents under the command of their leader boarded the
King's ship *Diligence* at Wilmington and demanded the surrender of the vessels seized for stamps. The ship *Dobbs* was
given up by the King's officers, but Captain Lobb promised
Governor Tryon that he would hold the *Patience* as a matter
of principle. When Tryon found that the ship had been surrendered, he was much chagrined and remarked: "I could not
help answering I thought the detaining of the Patience became
a point that concerned the honor of government and that I
found my situation very unpleasant, as most of the people by

[35] Robert D. W. Connor, *North Carolina: Rebuilding an Ancient Commonwealth* (4 vols.; Chicago and New York, 1929), I, 324-325.

going up to Wilmington in the sloops would remain satisfied and report through the province that they had obtained every point they came to redress."[36]

All officers who were responsible for the enforcement of the act were now gathered and compelled to take an oath never to perform any duty in connection with the enforcement of the act. From that day the Stamp Act was a dead letter in North Carolina: "It is well worthy of observation that few instances can be produced of such number of men being together so long and behaving so well; not the least harm or disturbance, nor any person even disguised with liquor, during the whole time of their stay at Brunswick. Neither was there any injury to any person, but the whole affair conducted with bravery and spirit, worthy the imitation of all the Sons of Liberty throughout the continent."[37] Business was carried on in the Cape Fear section as if no Stamp Act had ever been passed.

Dr. William Houston, the stamp master, who had been obliged to resign, returned to Wilmington in April and was compelled to give up both his commission and his instructions. On April 21 he wrote to Governor Tryon that he was much cast down by the treatment he had received and knew not what he was doing.[38] Governor Tryon, writing to Secretary Conway at this time, reported that the inhabitants in the back country were quiet and not one of them was an advocate of the stamp duty. This demonstrated how solidly the Province was opposed to it. In the same letter he announced the fact that he had removed Maurice Moore from the office of assistant judge for the district of Salisbury on account of his conduct in opposition to the Stamp Act.[39] He was the only one in North Carolina to be punished.

The town of Wilmington furnished the leaders for the opposition to the Stamp Act in North Carolina. They were assisted by the people of New Bern, Brunswick, and Edenton. It was natural that the opposition should center itself in the Cape Fear section, for here was centered the trade of the colony. Many of the gentlemen of New Hanover, Duplin, and Bladen

[36] *Col. Rec. of N. C.*, VII, 173.   [37] *Ibid.*, VII, 168c-178.
[38] *Ibid.*, VII, 198.   [39] *Ibid.*, VII, 199-200.

counties helped to swell the mob that waited upon Governor
Tryon and later demanded the surrender of the seized ships.[40]
Governor Tryon believed that the majority of the group were
compelled to join or were ignorant of what their grievances
were. He did not think this true of the leaders, however. The
great mass of the people, including those of the back country,
were largely unaffected by the stamp duty and took little interest in it.

On March 18 the act was repealed, and the news of its
repeal, reaching North Carolina in June, was received with uni-
versal rejoicing. Many towns celebrated the event, but Tryon's
failure to convene the legislature prevented any action on the
part of the Province as a whole. The Mayor and Corporation
of Wilmington, which had recently been in arms against the
Governor, sent him a congratulatory letter on the repeal of the
act and expressed their gratitude to the Supreme Legislature
of Great Britain for protecting them in their liberties and releasing them from a burden they were unable to bear. In the
closing paragraph the writers could not resist a parting shot
at the Governor for his treatment of them and attributed it
to the fact that he had been misinformed in regard to their
actions. But then they closed by saying: ". . . it ever has been
our constant endeavor, as far as our influence extended, to
promote the ease and happiness of your Excellency's Administration." This letter brought forth a stinging reply from the
Governor.[41] He expressed the hope that the repeal of the act
would result in that cheerful obedience to the legislative authority of Great Britain on which their prosperity depended.
In regard to his having been misinformed he averred that his
opinion was based on their behavior which had come immediately under his observation.[42]

This letter was answered by the Mayor and gentlemen of
Wilmington, who disclaimed any intentional disrespect to His
Excellency which he had seemed to gather from their former
letter.[43] Thus were cordial relations once more established be-

---

[40] *Ibid.*, VII, 168c.   [41] *Ibid.*, VII, 223.   [42] *Ibid.*
[43] This letter had several signatures which we may judge to be the
names of the group so often mentioned as the gentlemen of Wilmington.
They were Marmaduke Jones, John Lyon, Mons. John De Rosset, Thomas

tween the Governor and his people. When the Assembly convened in November, the members complained because he had not convened them sooner, and expressed their resentment at having been called rioters and rebels. At the same time they expressed thanks for so excellent a governor and promised him their support.[44] The leading men of the Assembly were those who had led the opposition to the Stamp Act: Ashe, Harnett, and Moore.

The Assembly showed its regard for the Governor by voting £5,000 for the erection of a house for him, and taxes were levied to meet the expenditure.[45] At the December meeting of the legislature an additional £10,000 (which was to be raised by a poll tax) was voted for finishing the Governor's mansion.[46]

The rejoicing over the repeal of the Stamp Act was short lived, for in 1767 under the Townsend Duty Act a new set of duties was imposed on lead, glass, paper, and tea imported into the colonies. This act did not arouse the ire of the North Carolinians as much as it did that of the Virginians and of the people of Massachusetts. On April 1, when the Assembly received a letter from the Massachusetts Assembly concerning the act, the North Carolina Assembly had not as yet taken any action in regard to it. The purpose of the letter was to assure harmonious action by all the colonies against the act, and to point out to all the colonies what the Massachusetts Legislature considered to be the injustice of it.[47]

When Lord Hillsborough received a copy of this letter, he hastened to notify Governor Tryon and urged him to use his influence to prevail upon the Assembly of North Carolina to

---

Lloyd, Frederick Gregg, Cornelius Harnett, John Ansiam, James Moran, Richard Eagles, Obadiah Holt, Alexander Duncan, John Burgwin, John Dubois, William Purviance, William Campbell, George Parker, Anthony Ward, Henry Toomer, William Wilkerson. They also expressed their loyalty to the King and their abhorrence of an article in the *Barbados Gazette* of April 19 which cast aspersions at their governor. His reply was all that Wilmington people could have desired. He expressed his willingness to forget every impropriety of conduct that had been shown by the people of Wilmington and thanked them for their approbation of his general conduct (*ibid.*, VII, 242-243).

[44] *Ibid.*, VII, 347-350.
[46] *Ibid.*, XXIII, 711, 723.
[45] *Ibid.*, XXIII, 664.
[47] *Ibid.*, VII, 688.

take no notice of it and to treat it with the contempt that it deserved. Then, as if by apology for having even suggested that North Carolina might be disloyal, he added: "The repeated proofs which have been given by the Assembly of their reverence and respect for the laws and of their faithful attachment to the Constitution leave little room in his Majesty's Breast to doubt of their showing a proper resentment of this unjustifiable attempt to revive those distractions which have operated so fatally to the distraction of this Kingdom and the Colonies, and accordingly his Majesty has the fullest confidence in their affections."[48] He then warned Governor Tryon, however, that if after his strongest endeavors there should appear in the Assembly a disposition to receive or countenance the seditious paper, to prorogue or dissolve the legislators at once.

The North Carolina Assembly evidently showed no disposition at this time to support Massachusetts, for Governor Tryon did not find it necessary to take any precipitate action to prorogue the Assembly. In December, 1768, Governor Tryon was able to write to the Earl of Hillsborough that the temper and moderation of the legislature had enabled him to go through the business of government.[49] On the last day of the session, December 5, the Assembly prepared a humble petition and remonstrance to the King, in which they merely remonstrated against the present tax because they were not represented in the British Parliament. At the same time they protested their subordination to the Parliament of Great Britain.[50]

Not all of the members of the Assembly were satisfied with the mild protest to the King or with the lack of co-operation with the other colonies. Samuel Johnston declared that the Assembly acted with great pusillanimity at this time in merely protesting to the King.[51] John Harvey, in his reply to the letter of Massachusetts, assured them that North Carolina supported them in every respect. This message greatly encouraged Massachusetts, and they now declared that all the colonies were united.[52]

[48] Ibid., VII, 712.
[49] Ibid., VII, 880-881.
[51] Ibid., IX, 9.
[50] Ibid., VII, 982.
[52] Connor, North Carolina, I, 333.

Governor Tryon was especially annoyed at an address to the King resolved upon November 2, 1769, in which the Assembly protested against the carrying of people from America to be tried for treason.[53] It was decided to entrust this petition to the agent of the colony in England for presentation to the King and people of England after having it printed and published in the English newspapers.

When Governor Tryon learned of these resolves he dissolved the Assembly. In reporting the affair to the Earl of Hillsborough he wrote that these resolves were similar to the ones drafted by Virginia and that North Carolina appeared to be in closer union with Virginia than with any other colony and, he believed, would pursue the same conduct as that colony.[54] In his reply to the Assembly he declared: "I find some resolves upon your journals . . . resolves, that after the assurance I had given you in my speech, have sapped the foundation of confidence and gratitude, have torn up by the roots every sanguine hope I entertained to render this province further service, if in truth, I have rendered it any, and made it my indispensable duty to put an end to this session."[55] So great was Tryon's influence over the Assembly that it immediately apologized for what it had done, again expressed its full confidence in him, and thanked him for all he had done for the colony, closing with the words that he deserved the blessings of posterity.[56]

This sudden dissolving of the Assembly was a shrewd move on the part of the Governor to prevent the Assembly from adopting any association against the importation of British goods. All the other colonies had adopted such agreements, and Governor Tryon thought it important to prevent the formation of a united front. Immediately after it was dissolved the Assembly repaired to the courthouse, where John Harvey was chosen moderator. Sixty-four of the seventy-seven members of the Assembly attended this extralegal gathering. After a two-day discussion they agreed upon a complete plan of nonimportation and recommended it to the people to show their support of

[53] *Col. Rec. of N. C.*, VIII, 122.   [54] *Ibid.*, VIII, 152.
[55] *Ibid.*, VIII, 134.   [56] *Ibid.*

nonimportation on the part of the other colonies. North Carolina was the last colony to adopt the association.[57]

Fortunately for the enforcement of the association, the patriot Cornelius Harnett was one of the leading merchants of the Province and champion of the Sons of Liberty of North Carolina. The Sons of Liberty represented the towns of Wilmington and Brunswick and the six counties of the Cape Fear and were determined that nonimportation should be obeyed in that section. Since the merchants in this section imported most of the goods for the colony, success or failure here largely determined the action for the entire colony.[58] The policy of nonimportation as a weapon against the Stamp Act had not been successful because it had not been enforced. Hence the Loyalists ridiculed the attempt of the colonies to revive it at this time as a weapon against the Townsend Act. Since the time of the Stamp Act, however, the sentiment of union had grown to such an extent that the leaders of the Cape Fear were able to secure better co-operation of the people in the enforcement of the measure.[59]

It is difficult to discover just how successful were the leaders of the association in the Cape Fear section in enforcing nonimportation. In February, 1771, Governor Tryon declared: "Notwithstanding the boasted association of people who never were in trade, and the show patriotism of a few merchants to the Southward of the province, the several ports of this province have been open ever since the repeal of the Stamp Act for every kind of British manufacture to the full extent of the credit of the country."[60] Meetings were held in Wilmington in 1770, which were attended by the leading inhabitants of the Cape Fear section. It is probable the merchants had generally ignored nonimportation, since efforts were now made to enforce it. Merchants who purchased wines and other forbidden articles were threatened with the publication of their names.[61]

[57] Robert D. W. Connor, "Revolutionary Leaders of North Carolina," North Carolina State Normal and Industrial College, *Historical Publication* (High Point, N. C., 1916), No. 2, pp. 34-35.
[58] *Ibid.*, No. 2, p. 56.   [59] Connor, *North Carolina*, I, 335.
[60] *Col. Rec. of N. C.*, VIII, 496.
[61] Arthur Meier Schlesinger, *The Colonial Merchants and the American Revolution, 1763-1776* (New York, 1918), pp. 208-209.

As late as December, 1774, Andrew Miller was not suffering from the boycott that had been declared against him for his refusal to sign the association. Willie Jones, the Patriot, as well as his brother who was a colonel in the American forces, were both trading with him and ordering goods at that time. In a letter to Thomas Burke, Miller stated that he had not lost one customer through his refusal to sign the association.

The opposition to the Townsend Act in North Carolina does not seem to have sprung as much from any grievances that North Carolinians were suffering as from sympathy for the other colonies. The people thought that the cause of Boston was the cause of all and that the overthrow of legislative government in one colony would lead to its overthrow in all the colonies.

In contrast to the opposition in North Carolina, that in Virginia was general, though more mild and dignified in the Tidewater than in the Piedmont. A young capable leader in the person of Patrick Henry appeared in the House of Burgesses in 1765 to represent this more radical upland section. He immediately took the lead in opposing the Stamp Act. The planters of the Tidewater also were opposed to the act, but were unwilling to support Henry's violent resolutions which openly and indignantly denied England's right to tax the colony.[62] After a debate of two days amended measures passed the House.[63]

When Commissioner Mercer brought the first consignment of stamps to Williamsburg for sale, the people of the town arose and demanded that he resign. These people were the best citizens of Williamsburg and the planters of the neighborhood. The inhabitants of the western counties under the leadership of Henry had led the opposition to the act. The planters of eastern and southern Virginia were now united against the act and carried all the other classes with them.[64] Sentiment was now unanimous from the coast to the mountains.[65] In contrast, oppo-

[62] Hamilton James Eckenrode, *The Revolution in Virginia* (New York, 1916), p. 18.
[63] *Ibid.*, p. 19.   [64] *Ibid.*, p. 26.
[65] William Wirt, *Sketches of the Life and Character of Patrick Henry* (Ithaca, N. Y., 1850), p. 59.

sition in North Carolina was confined to the Cape Fear area
and the few other trading counties under the leadership of the
merchants.

The Southern Provinces lagged far behind those in the North
in adopting the association for the nonimportation of British
goods in opposition to the Townsend duties. In Virginia the
planters led the movement, and it was only with great difficulty
that the merchants could be persuaded to co-operate. George
Washington claimed that it could be made successful only by
persuading people to buy no imported articles from the merchants except certain enumerated ones.[66] It was never well
enforced in Virginia.[67]

In South Carolina the association was sponsored by the
planters and by the mechanics and working men in Charleston
in opposition to the merchants. The latter were soon compelled
to join, and nonimportation was better enforced here than in
any other Southern province.[68] Likewise, in Georgia the merchants did everything possible to head off the association, but
in vain. The majority of the people had no interest in the
movement after it had been adopted, and it was speedily disregarded.[69] This attitude of Georgia was not important, since
the trade of that colony was insignificant. North Carolina
was the only Southern province where the movement in favor
of the association was led by merchants. Here the action was
not unanimous, for those merchants who afterwards became
famous as Loyalists at no time signed the agreement.

When Martin succeeded Tryon as governor of North Carolina in August, 1771, and called a meeting of the Assembly in
November, no question of unjust taxation or navigation laws
arose to plague the meeting. The obstacle against which the
Governor was to go down in defeat and with him royal government in North Carolina was the local controversy with the
Assembly over money matters and the establishment of courts.

---

[66] W. C. Ford (ed.), *George Washington, Writings, Being His Correspondence, Addresses, Messages, and Other Papers, Official and Private* (14
vols.; New York, 1889-1893), II, 263-267.
    [67] Schlesinger, *op. cit.*, p. 199.
    [68] *Ibid.*, pp. 142-146.   [69] *Ibid.*, p. 209.

In order to understand the financial chaos which confronted Governor Martin when he took office, it is necessary to recall the money situation previous to this time. From the beginning it was the intention of the Crown not to permit the issue of bills of credit without the consent of the Crown officials in England. How difficult it was to enforce this restriction is shown by a brief sketch of the issue of paper money in North Carolina previous to 1729.

The first issue of paper money of £4,000 in 1712 was to pay for a war with the Tuscaroras. It was made legal tender and forced upon the colonists. This was followed by an issue of £8,000 in 1713. The Proprietors were forced to accept this in payment of quit rents and suffered thereby, as its value quickly depreciated. In 1714-1715, £24,000 more were issued. A law was passed which stipulated that anyone refusing to accept the money would be punished by a forfeiture of twice the amount he had rejected.[70] This money soon depreciated 40 per cent in North Carolina and was practically worthless outside. Such was the fiscal condition as inherited by Burrington, the first Royal Governor.

In 1735, bills were issued to the amount of £52,500, of which £40,000 were to redeem those of 1729. This meant that none of the issue of 1729 had been redeemed as provided for by law. Again in 1748, £21,350 were issued, and one pound of this was declared to be worth seven and one-half pounds of the old paper money; this was outright repudiation.[71] New issues in 1754, 1760, and 1761 made a grand total of £93,350 for the four issues. In 1764 an act was passed by Parliament which forbade any further issue of bills of credit by an American province.

Although this act put an end to the issuing of bills of credit in North Carolina, it did not put an end to the need of currency, and the colony soon found means to circumvent the law. This was accomplished by means of debenture notes. In 1768 the colony asked that it be allowed to issue £30,000 in bills, although

---

[70] *Col. Rec. of N. C.*, III, 177-179.   [71] *Ibid.*, XXIII, 293-294.

it knew there was an act of Parliament to the contrary. Governor Tryon compromised with the colony by permitting the issue of £20,000 of debenture notes, since the colony was £4,844 in debt for the Regulator campaign and he needed money to finish the building of his palace at New Bern. These debenture notes were not forced on the public by making them legal tender.[72] The English merchants protested against allowing the colony to pass acts which permitted the issuance of paper money that passed as legal tender. Currency rapidly depreciated in value,[73] but the debenture notes, not being legal tender, could not be forced upon the English merchants in payment of goods, and thus their opposition ceased. The North Carolinians accepted the issuance of debenture notes in lieu of legal tender paper only after they were unable to procure the latter. Naturally they wished for a currency in which they could pay their English creditors as well as those within the colony.

When Josiah Martin became governor of the Province, he found the fiscal affairs in such a condition that he asked for a further issue of paper money with which to take up the unredeemed bills of credit and also to pay off the floating debt of the colony. Permission was granted on condition that these new bills should not be legal tender. Accordingly, debenture notes to the extent of £60,000 were issued with the assurance that they would be redeemed by the Assembly.[74] This was a special tax of two shillings upon each taxable in the Province, which was to be collected for ten years and no longer.

Governor Martin described the strife over money at this time in a letter to Lord Hillsborough: "A great part of the time of this session, my Lord, was consumed in the most disorderly speculations such as I am informed are constantly the offspring of a necessity to raise money in this country."[75] The people from the Southern districts who were in debt, and many of whom had participated in the Regulation War, were in favor

[72] Charles Lee Raper, *North Carolina: A Study in English Colonial Government* (New York, 1904), pp. 143-144.
[73] George Louis Beer, *British Colonial Policy, 1754-1765* (New York, 1907), p. 182.
[74] *Col. Rec. of N. C.*, IX, 76.   [75] *Ibid.*, IX, 76.

of the new issue. It was voted to set aside a part of the money to indemnify them for their service against the Regulators.

In December of the same year in which the act had been passed the Assembly decided that enough money had been collected to redeem all of the old issues of money, and brought in a bill that none of these special taxes should be collected in the future. The Governor declared that the bill was teeming with fraud and rejected it. The Assembly then prepared resolutions discontinuing the tax and indemnifying the sheriffs for noncollection. When the Governor became aware of this, he dissolved the Assembly before the resolutions could be entered on the journal. Not to be thwarted, Speaker Caswell communicated the substance of the resolve to the treasurer as an order from the Assembly. The enraged Governor thereupon ordered the sheriffs to make collections as usual under the pain of being sued upon their bonds for noncollection.[76] In some cases the sheriffs feared the Governor, and collections were made as before. The dispute between the Governor and the Assembly continued, and at the meeting in December, 1773, the legislature was prorogued when a similar bill was introduced.

When the Assembly met again, in March, 1774, another bill for discontinuing the taxes was passed and rejected by the upper house. This time the Assembly placed the following resolution on its journal: "That the taxes in question had long since had their effect; that the assembly had frequently passed bills to repeal the act under which they were collected, and that their not being able to obtain a law for that purpose was a great grievance to the people; that the Treasurer issue orders to the collectors not to receive the said taxes from any person for the year 1774 or any subsequent year; that the Assembly considered it their duty to indemnify any person from all damages incurred in obedience to these resolutions, and that the public faith stood engaged to make good any deficiency appearing on the final settlement by reason of the noncollection of the said taxes."[77] The Governor, on learning of the resolves, dissolved the legis-

[76] Raper, op. cit., p. 202.
[77] Col. Rec. of N. C., IX, Preface, p. xviii.

ature by formal proclamation. The situation remained unchanged until the overthrow of royal authority in the colony.

The money question was the one thing on which Governor Martin and the Assembly were arrayed against each other from the beginning of his administration and in regard to which neither would yield. Time increased the bitterness rather than healed it. The people naturally agreed with the Assembly that they ought not to pay these special taxes. They could not be expected to feel any loyalty to a governor who was attempting to compel them to pay taxes in opposition to the expressed wishes of their elected representatives.

In Virginia, as in North Carolina, finance was of prime importance in bringing on the war with the mother country. During the Seven Years' War, Virginia had authorized £450,000 of paper, and the planters were deeply in debt. By 1774 only £54,791 of this money was outstanding.[78] The Virginians suffered for want of a circulating medium and clamored for paper money. The balance of trade with England was against Virginia, and in 1775 Virginia exchange was 30 per cent under par in London. Within a few months all the bullion in the Virginia treasury went to London. These conditions furnished fertile soil for revolutionary propaganda.[79] The financial condition of the individual planter in Virginia was even worse than that of the government. In 1791, of the £4,930,650 due to British merchants, almost one half was owed by Virginians. As early as May, 1774, Thomas Jefferson and Patrick Henry proposed to the Virginia Assembly that all payments on British debts should stop.[80] This was practically accomplished by the Sequestration Law of 1777.

The leading families in Virginia were hopelessly in debt to their English creditors. To mention only a few, Thomas Jefferson was indebted to English and Scotch firms to the amount of £10,000; Archibald Cary owed a like amount. After the sequestration by the state of debts due to British merchants, Patrick

[78] Harrell, op. cit., p. 24; William and Mary College Quarterly, XX, 228.
[79] Harrell, op. cit., p. 25.
[80] Journals of the House of Burgesses of Virginia, 1773-1776, p. 139; Harrell, op. cit., pp. 26 f.

Henry, Burr Harrison, Edmund Pendleton, George Webb, William Blunt, William Harrison, Joseph Jones, the Balls, the Lees, the Flemings, and the Marches, all paid their debts in depreciated currency. In addition to these well-known Virginians, over five hundred other debtors discharged their debts to British merchants in cheap paper money.[81] The attitude of this large class of influential Virginians in regard to independence must have been affected by their economic condition. The rapid contraction of currency to meet the demands of the British trading interests and the ruinous trend of Virginia exchange accentuated the diverse economic interests of the colony and the mother country. The planters were hopelessly in debt to the British merchants. Current political theories in the colonies and the economic interests of the planters were in harmony.[82]

South Carolina had her own private quarrels with the mother country. One of these which assumed important proportions was the decision of the South Carolina House of Commons to remit £1,500 sterling to Great Britain for the support of the constitutional rights and liberties of the people of Great Britain and America. This money was needed to pay the debts of John Wilkes, a member of the opposition in Parliament, who had suffered much at the hands of the government because of his espousing freedom of speech and other constitutional rights.[83] This right of the lower house to control appropriations was a standing cause for argument between the governor and council on one side and the lower house on the other, and contributed to the support of revolutionary measures in the state. Royal officers remained unpaid since no tax bills were passed. In October, 1771, the colonial treasurers were sent to jail by the Commons when they refused to advance money without the consent of the governor and the council.

The attempt of Governor Martin to come to an agreement with the Assembly in the establishing of courts for the Province proved equally as difficult as had the financial question. The

---

[81] Harrell, op. cit., pp. 27 f.   [82] Ibid., p. 29.
[83] David Duncan Wallace, The History of South Carolina (4 vols.; New York, 1934), II, 90 f.

right to attach property of debtors who absconded had existed from the beginning of the colony. As the colony grew, British merchants began to carry on business there by means of agents without ever coming there themselves. Likewise, men in England came to own large tracts of land. Neither of these groups could be sued by their Carolina creditors in the colonial court, but the action for the recovery of any debt against such individuals had to be brought in British courts.[84] In 1768, in order to overcome this injustice, a system of courts was established which enabled creditors to proceed by attachment against nonresident debtors. The authorities in England were opposed to the law, but allowed it to stand with the thought that when the court was renewed this part of the law would be left out. Hence, when the law came up for renewal in 1773, Governor Martin was instructed not to sign it unless this provision was left out. The Assembly insisted that it remain, and thus Governor Martin, the English authorities, and the British merchants were lined up against the Assembly and the creditors of the British merchants. Governor Martin saw the justice of the claims of the Assembly and thought that North Carolina at least ought to be on the same footing as the other colonies in America.

Since the Court Law of 1768 was about to expire and the new law would not be operative until approved by the King, two other bills were introduced to extend the life of the former Court Law for six months or until the next session of the Assembly. These were amended in the council to conform to the instructions of the Governor by leaving out the foreign attachment clause. A bill for the continuance of the inferior courts was also passed by the council, but both were vetoed by the Governor. Thus both were defeated, and at the expiration of the legislature the Province was without courts.[85] On March 6 the Assembly was prorogued for three days, but since at the expiration of that time there was not a quorum, it was dissolved.[86]

The colony was now without any general courts, and the

[84] *Col. Rec. of N. C.*, IX, Preface, p. xx.
[85] *Ibid.*, IX, 558, 600.   [86] *Ibid.*, IX, 596.

minor ones in operation were very limited in their jurisdiction. There was no way to punish criminals and crime increased. There were but five provincial laws in force; action for debts had to be brought before a single magistrate, and few were punished. The people were greatly distressed but preferred this temporary evil to giving up the right of attachment. Josiah Quincy, Jr., who was traveling in the Province at this time, remarked that there were no courts in the Province and no laws in force by which any could be held. This resulted in a condition that determined him not to remain long in Edenton.[87]

Governor Martin had authority under the King's instruction to establish courts by oyer and terminer, and this he proceeded to do. The cases of men who were in jail were tried, and a very good effect in maintaining order was reached. The legality of these courts was questioned, and this widened still further the breach between the Governor and the people.[88] In December a meeting of the Assembly was called at New Bern. The question of the establishment of courts came up, and because neither party had changed their minds since the previous session, nothing was accomplished. The Assembly declared that the Governor had no right to establish courts of oyer and terminer, and refused to defray the expense. The council stood with the Governor, and no court bill was passed.

If nothing was accomplished in regard to courts, definite steps were taken to align North Carolina with the other colonies in protesting against their grievances. Johnston, Horne, and Harnett were appointed a committee to answer the letters and resolutions which the Speaker had received from Massachusetts Bay, Virginia, Rhode Island, Connecticut, and the counties of the Delaware. Two days later the committee reported to the Assembly as follows:

That the vigilance which the Honorable House of Burgesses of Virginia have displayed in attending to every encroachment upon the rights and liberties of America, and the wisdom and the vigor with which they have always opposed such encroachments are worthy the imitation and merit of all their sister Colonies, and in no one

[87] Ibid., IX, 610-613, 625, 686.   [88] Ibid., IX, 686-687.

nstance more particularly than in the measure proposed for appointing Correspondence Committees in every Colony, by which such harmony and communication will be established among them, that they will at all times be ready to exert their united efforts, and most strenuous endeavours to preserve their just rights and liberties of the American Colonies, which appear of late to be so systematically invaded that we heartily concur with their spirited Resolves.[89]

A Standing Committee of Correspondence of nine members was appointed.[90] Five of these were to be a committee whose duty it was to keep in communication with the other colonies, and the committee was especially instructed to inform itself in regard to a court in Rhode Island, whereby persons accused of crime in America were to be transported across the sea for trial. When Governor Martin saw nothing was being accomplished, he summoned the Assembly to be prepared for prorogation. Before leaving they appointed a committee to prepare an address to the King in regard to the court law and requested that it be sent by Governor Tryon of New York, of whose good intentions to this colony they were assured. Governor Martin declared that this scheme was the work of a small group, and all but the immediate continuers of it looked back with shame and indignation to the unmerited insult which thus bound him.[91]

This Assembly had met primarily for the purpose of establishing a court law. The leaders, by the appointment of a Committee of Correspondence who were directed to co-operate with the leaders in other colonies, definitely aligned North Carolina with the other colonies in opposition to England. Josiah Quincy on his visit to North Carolina early in 1773 spent the night with Cornelius Harnett and discussed with him and Robert Howe the plan of a continental correspondence. Thus the idea was not new to them at the time when it was finally formed.[92] Henceforth the Assembly was certainly arrayed on the side of the Revolution.

When the Assembly again met in New Bern, in March,

[89] *Ibid.*, IX, 740.
[90] This committee was composed of John Harvey, Robert Howe, Richard Caswell, Edward Vail, John Ashe, Joseph Hewes, Cornelius Harnett, William Hooper, and Samuel Johnston.
[91] *Col. Rec. of N. C.*, IX, 800. [92] *Ibid.*, IX, 610.

1774, there were no courts, either civil or criminal, in existence in the colony. All attempts to establish superior courts had failed on account of the attachment clause. For the first time the council now began to vote with the Assembly on the court question, and a system of inferior courts of oyer and terminer were established.[93] The benefits which might have been received from these courts were largely nullified by the actions of Judge Maurice Moore, of Wilmington, who questioned the legality of the law and of the commission of the judge. This may have been an act of retaliation on his part against the Assembly for having destroyed the court of which he had been declared the judge by Governor Martin a short time previous.

After the legislature was prorogued, it was learned that the Governor did not anticipate calling another assembly until he was assured of an improvement. There were few courts in the colony and no assembly. The Committee of Correspondence kept in touch with the progress of the colonies in the North and individually always expressed sympathy to the people of Boston regarding the closing of the port. They declared that if the Governor refused to call the Assembly for July 26 they would do so themselves. The same junto that made up the first Committee of Correspondence sent out a circular letter to the towns calling for a convention. The citizens of Wilmington, New Bern, Halifax, and various other towns and counties responded and met to choose delegates to represent them at a general convention to be held in New Bern on August 25, 1774.[94] These individual meetings adopted resolutions expressing their sympathy for the people of Massachusetts and condemning the action of Great Britain in taxing them without their consent. The Committees of Correspondence became the Committees of Safety and gradually took on the control of the government.[95] At the convention in New Bern, Hooper, Hewes, and Caswell were appointed delegates to the Continental Congress in Philadelphia. Stringent provisions for nonimportation and exporta-

---

[93] *Ibid.*, XXIII, 931.   [94] *Ibid.*, IX, 1016-1040.
[95] *Ibid.*, IX, 1050-1061, 1898; II, 13.

tion to Great Britain were drawn up, and a committee was provided for each county to see that these resolves were enforced.

A study of the six pages of the resolutions adopted on the last day of the session reveals the fact that the most of them related not to complaints directly affecting North Carolina but rather in regard to those directed against the other colonies, especially Massachusetts. Typical of them was the following:

Resolved that the inhabitants of Massachusetts Province have distinguished themselves in a manly support of the rights of America in general, and that the cause in which they now suffer is the cause of every honest American which the Constitution holds forth to them. That the grievances under which the town of Boston labors at present, are the effect of a resentment levelled at them for having stood foremost in an opposition to measures which must eventually have involved all British America in a state of abject dependence and servitude.[96]

The people of the colony, suffering little from the aggressive action of the Crown, apparently employed the outrages committed on the people of Massachusetts and of Boston, in particular, as a ground for discontent and rebellion.[97]

This convention, which was called primarily for the purpose of securing united action with the other colonies and to elect members of the Continental Congress, laid the foundations for a truly revolutionary government when it recommended that at future meetings the counties and towns should be represented. A definite step toward independent government had been taken.[98] The committees which were recommended for each county to enforce the resolves of Congress acted as Committees of Correspondence and were set up almost at once. By November the Committee of Safety for Wilmington was already exerting authority.

It must not be supposed that Governor Martin had allowed this Congress to meet without his opposition. On August 12 he called a meeting of the council and gravely asked their advice

[96] *Ibid.*, II, 104 f.
[97] Joseph Seawell Jones, *Defense of the Revolutionary History of the State of North Carolina* (Raleigh, 1834), p. 143.
[98] Ashe, *op. cit.*, p. 423; *Col. Rec. of N. C.*, IX, 1047.

as to the best means of prohibiting the proposed meeting. The council advised him to issue a proclamation forbidding the people to attend.[99] In compliance with this advice the proclamation was issued on August 13, and the officers of the Province were commanded to use their influence to stop the meeting. The people were no longer frightened by a flow of words, and to Governor Martin's chagrin all of the members of this council except James Hassell attended the Congress and appeared to be on terms of greatest intimacy with the members.[100] This Congress, which had been called primarily to adjust local grievances, proceeded to establish a real revolutionary government.

Governor Martin convened the last Colonial Assembly in North Carolina at New Bern on April 4, 1775. John Harvey called a congress to meet at the same place April 3. Both bodies contained practically the same members. Little was accomplished. The Assembly openly defied the Governor by declaring its support of the Continental Congress and the Revolutionary Congress in the State and the Continental associations. For this it was dissolved. This was the last royal assembly to be presided over by Governor Martin in North Carolina.[101] Early in June he sought safety within the walls of Fort Johnson, and later boarded His Majesty's sloop *Cruizer*. With royal government at an end, order was maintained by the committees of safety and provincial congresses until a state constitution was adopted in December, 1776.

In summarizing the cause of revolt in North Carolina it is evident that local grievances and not the Imperial Acts of the British Parliament are the more important. During the Proprietary period there were frequent quarrels between the assembly and the governor, over quit rents and the attempt of the governors to uphold the interest of the Proprietors. When North Carolina became a royal province in 1729, the old local controversy over quit rents continued and new ones developed. Burrington, the first royal governor, was in one continuous quarrel with the Assembly over the payment of quit rents. He

[99] *Ibid.*, IX, 1029.
[100] *Ibid.*, IX, 1056.   [101] *Ibid.*, IX, 1205.

demanded payment in sterling, while the Assembly held out for the time-honored custom of payment in commodities.[102]

From 1759 to 1761 the appointment of a colonial agent in England was a subject of controversy. The lower house insisted on appointing the agent and was supported by Parliament.[103]

The conflicts over quit rents, fees, and the colonial agent were of minor importance in comparison with the judicial and fiscal controversies. These under Governor Dobbs became of serious importance.[104] No solution could be found for a settlement of the controversy, and under Governor Martin the conflict became active. Each meeting of the legislature only served to accentuate the quarrel between the governor and the assembly and often caused the governor to prorogue or dissolve it. The climax came in 1774, when the leaders of the Cape Fear section called a convention to deal with local grievances and ended by going over to the revolutionary cause and laying the foundation of a revolutionary government. All of this action was in behalf of local grievances. The ruling class and the members of the legislature, in alliance with the justices, led North Carolina, step by step, to join the other colonies in the Revolutionary movement. However, there were other elements in the colony not represented in the ruling class who were apt to take another point of view in the impending struggle.

[102] *Ibid.*, IV, 110-114.
[103] *Ibid.*, VI, 54-56.   [104] *Ibid.*, VI, 246-248.

CHAPTER II

DISSENTING ELEMENTS

THE PRECEDING CHAPTER attempted to make clear that there were two political parties or groups in North Carolina. The governor and council made up the Government party, while the Assembly represented the People's or Popular party.[1] A large number of the people in the state had no part in the Government party and were equally unrepresented in the political machine which controlled the assembly and county offices. Whether this vast group would support the governor and remain loyal to the King or would join in the rebellion was an open question.

Generalizations are dangerous in treating any phase of history and doubly so in writing of the Loyalists. We cannot say that any one section or group was wholly loyal. The Tidewater region, in which lived most of the justices and small officials, in general tended to support the Revolutionary cause. These counties had more than a just share of the representatives, but worked in harmony with the justices, lawyers, and sheriffs of the back counties. Since the Tidewater region was in the majority in the Assembly, this section determined to raise most of the money by poll taxes, which fell especially hard on the people of the back country, where money was scarce.

Dissensions between the two sections led to armed conflict. Governor Tryon, the officers, and the people of the Tidewater and the officers of the back country arranged themselves against the common people of the back country. The remembrance of the struggle between the two sections was fresh in the minds of the people when the Revolution broke out. To understand why so many people in this back country decided to remain loyal to the King, one must have a knowledge of the War of the Regulators.

[1] *Col. Rec. of N. C.*, II, 243.

The grievances of the people known as the Regulators, which resulted in the Battle of Alamance (a struggle between the people and Governor Tryon's forces), are well set forth in Herman Husband's work, *Impartial Relations,* as follows: "Well, Gentlemen, it is not our mode or form of government nor yet the way of our laws, that we are quarrelling with, but with the malpractices of the officers of our county courts, and the abuses we suffer by those that are empowered to manage our public affairs, this is the grievance gentlemen, that demands our serious attention. And I shall show you that most notorious and intolerant sources have crept into the practice of law in this country and I doubt not in other countries; though that does not concern us." Husband, who quoted these words in 1770 to show the complaints of the people in Orange County, took them from an address to the people of Granville County made by George Sims in 1765.[2] Thus these complaints had existed over a long period of time and over a widespread territory.

The causes are briefly summed up under three heads as follows: (1) unlawful exaction of fees by clerks and county registerers of deeds, (2) unlawful exaction of taxes under the color of legislative authority, and (3) directly the unequal distribution of benefits and burdens of the Provincial Government.[3]

One recent writer emphasizes taxes, dishonest sheriffs, and extortionate fees as the cause of the uprising.[4] A still more recent historian believes the background to have been the scarcity of money, taxation, and the land policy of the Granville district.[5] To these might be added religious intolerance.

The leaders of the movement in Granville County were men of intelligence. Thomas Pearson, to whom Sims's address was dedicated, was a justice of the county court and later became a leader of the Regulation movement in the colony. Sims's petition displays his learning and ability.

[2] Archibald Henderson, "The Origin of the Regulation in North Carolina," *North Carolina Booklet* (Raleigh, 1918), Vol. XVII, No. 4.
[3] *Col. Rec. of N. C.,* VII, 90.   [4] *Ibid., Sanders' Introduction,* VII, xiv.
[5] William Kenneth Boyd, *Some Eighteenth Century Tracts Concerning North Carolina* (Raleigh, 1927), p. 177.

Prior to this, petitions had been circulated by Reuben Searcy and others on March 23, 1759. The chief cause of the complaint at this time was the fact that Robert James, Attorney General of North Carolina, had charged exorbitant fees and had prevented the appointment of justices of peace for a part of Granville County.[6] Herman Husband declared that Searcy was prosecuted for libel, but a search of the records fails to show a corroboration of his statement.[7] Opposition to the agents of Granville County developed rapidly. Corbyn and Childs had for several years been exacting exorbitant fees and had remitted little money to Lord Granville. The taxpayers applied to their neighbor, Robert Smith, then attorney general, to know what to do, and were advised to petition either the Earl or the Assembly.[8] Accordingly, the petition was presented to the Assembly, but the chairman became friendly to Corbyn and merely compelled him to produce his table of fees. This angered the people and convinced them that justice was not to be had from the Assembly. In January the petitioners decided on violence, forcibly entered Corbyn's house at Edenton, and carried him to Edgecombe County. He was not released until he promised to return to them all the fees he had unjustly collected.

No attempt was made to punish the rioters at this time. In May, 1759, complaints were made at the session of the council at New Bern that, unless the rioters were placed in jail, there would be no safety in the county.[9] When at last the rioters were placed in confinement, a mob broke down the doors and released the prisoners. The Assembly censured the Governor for his failure to put down the rioters, while he in turn claimed that it was the duty of the other officials, especially the Attorney General, to do this. Previous to this time there had been a feeling of antagonism between the Assembly and Granville's agent, a fact which lends plausibility to the statement made by Governor Dobbs, in his journal, that the Assembly had found it to its interest to make up matters with Corbyn and had changed sides.

[6] Henderson, "The Origin of the Regulation in North Carolina," p. 320.
[7] W. K. Boyd, *op. cit.*
[8] *Col. Rec. of N. C.*, VI, 294.   [9] *Ibid.*, VI, 295.

The movement, which eventually culminated in the Battle of Alamance, had its beginnings in Orange County in 1766. In that year the following paper was read before an inferior court in Orange County:

Whereas that great harm may come of this designated evil, the Stamp Law, while the Sons of Liberty withstand the lords in Parliament, in behalf of true liberty, let no officers under them carry on unjust oppression in our province; in order therefore as there are many evils of that nature complained of in the County of Orange, in private amongst the inhabitants. Therefore let us remove the jealousies out of our minds. Honest rulers in power will be glad to see us examine the matter freely. And, certainly there are more honest men than rogues, yet rogues are harbored among us sometimes almost publicly.[10]

It was then declared that every honest man was willing to contribute to the support of the rulers, and having done this, he was responsible for seeing that the rulers did not abuse that trust.

At this time Governor Tryon had obtained £15,000 from the colony for the building of a new house. This together with the other grievances stirred up another group in Orange County on the west side of the Haw River. These people, first known as the mob, later were termed the Regulators.[11] They were more radical than the former leaders of the movement and were willing to go much further in their demands. Their first complaint was that they were taxed out of proportion to their numbers. They next complained that although they were British subjects, they were not informed of the use which was being made of the taxes. The last paragraph of their complaint was almost revolutionary:

Think not to frighten us with rebellion in this case for if the inhabitants of this province have not as good a right to inquire into the nature of our Constitution, and disbursments of our funds as those of our Mother Country, we think it is arbitrary proceedings that we are debarred of this right. Therefore to be plain with you it is our intent to have a full statement with you in every particular point that is a matter of doubt to us. So fail not to send an ambas-

---

[10] W. K. Boyd, *op. cit.*, p. 259.   [11] *Ibid.*, p. 263.

sador by the bearer. If no answer we shall take it for granted that we are disregarded in this our request again from the public.[12]

When this petition reached the officers of the government, the suppliants were called rebels and insurgents, and threatened with hanging and shooting. The officers did not distinguish between those who had made the first mild request and those who were more radical.

At a meeting on April 4, 1768, Peter Craven and John Howe were sent to request two late sheriffs and a vestryman to meet a delegation of the Regulators and give them a list of taxables for each year, the names of the insolvents, and an account of how the money was to be used which was paid in taxes. This procedure was perfectly legal; therefore the Regulators had committed no act of violence. The officers of the law were bent on continuing their illegal practices and sold a mare, a saddle, and a bridle of one of the Regulators.[13] This aroused the spirit of opposition in the people, and a large group of them rescued the mare and fired their guns at the roof of Colonel Fanning's house. That the Regulators had cause for their anger may be judged from the fact that the total tax sale brought only four or five dollars, or just enough to pay for the tax. This was paid by one of the officers whose money was refunded to him when the horse was taken from him and given to its former owner.[14]

Lieutenant Colonel Grey, who commanded the militia, was ordered by his superior, Colonel Fanning, who was attending court at Halifax, to mobilize seven companies of the militia to put down the riot. The people were so in sympathy with the Regulators that only one hundred and twenty presented themselves with arms.[15]

When Colonel Fanning received the news of how few people were willing to help put down the riot, he decided to go to Hillsboro and take personal command. He learned that reinforcements might be expected from Anson, Mecklenburg, and Rowan counties to aid the Regulators; so he asked for

[12] *Ibid.*, p. 265.
[14] *Ibid.*, VII, 705.
[13] *Col. Rec. of N. C.*, VII, 702.
[15] *Ibid.*, VII, 706-707.

authority to call for aid from other counties besides Anson. To this the Governor gave his consent as did also the council.[16]

In the meantime the discontented of Anson County interrupted the county court and held a meeting at which they nominated one of their own men for the Assembly. Colonel Spenser asked Tryon's advice in the matter, and he was ordered, as Colonel Fanning had been, to arouse the militia and put down the uprising.[17] The Anson Regulators wrote to those in Orange County and asked for advice. The latter warned them against the use of violent action. They[18] petitioned the Governor for a redress of their wrongs and for the removal of the justices of peace in the county, whom they blamed for the most of their injustices.[19] Governor Tryon's letter was more conciliatory than had been his answer to the Regulators of Orange County.

The Regulators were so strong in Orange, Granville, Anson, and Halifax that they sent a completely new set of men to represent them in the legislature, which met in October, 1769. In fact, less than half the old members of the former Assembly returned.[20] Orange County was represented by Herman Husband and John Pryor.[21] The influence of the Regulators was manifested by a set of resolutions which were adopted at this session. The first of these declared that the right of taxation in the colony rested solely with the Assembly. The second declared the right of the colony to petition His Majesty for redress of grievances and to join with other colonies in asking for a redress of the violated rights of America. The third asked that persons accused of treason be allowed trial in the colony where they lived.

Judge Maurice Moore complained to Governor Tryon in March, 1770, that the sheriffs of the counties of his district were unable to collect public tax or private debt among the Regulators. No civil process, he declared, could remedy this evil, since the people would not permit them to be served among them.[22] At the same time a letter arrived from Henry Mc-

---

[16] *Ibid.*, VII, 740.
[17] *Ibid.*, VII, 722-726.
[18] *Ibid.*, VII, 759.
[19] *Ibid.*, VII, 808-809.
[20] Bassett, *op. cit.*, p. 184.
[21] *Col. Rec. of N. C.*, VIII, 106.
[22] *Ibid.*, VIII, 178.

Culloch, agent of North Carolina in England, to James Harvey, in which he expressed hearty approval of the acts committed by the previous Assembly for which they had been dissolved by the Governor. Since these acts were instigated by the Regulators, this statement of an impartial observer went far to vindicate their behavior.

Governor Tryon in his correspondence with Lord Hillsborough kept him constantly informed of the disobedience of these Regulators. At the same time Tryon remarked that if the treasurers were to publish a statement of their accounts as would bear the test of the public, it would go far to allay the discontent. The unrest in Rowan and Orange counties was also laid to conditions which existed in Granville County. There the land office had been closed for five years. During that time many people had been unable to procure lands in the Western settlements; as a result, they had illegally settled upon the vacant land in the county. Naturally they were unwilling to improve and pay taxes on land which they might be called upon to vacate at any time.[23] In Dobbs County, Thomas Blake and John Curlu, two Regulators, were preaching their doctrine and making trouble for the sheriffs. In an attempt to capture them James Lindsay, who was aiding the sheriffs, was killed.[24] Governor Tryon issued a proclamation wherein he offered a reward of £100 for the capture of either of them. The spirit in which the people supported one another showed itself in that neither of them was apprehended.

In the summer of 1770 the Regulators of Orange County presented a petition to Chief Justice Martin Howard and to Associate Judges Maurice Moore and Richard Henderson.[25] In this they complained that though many of the officers had been convicted, they were unable to get their money back, and that the same officers still continued to take illegal fees. In a few words they declared that they were only seeking to obtain unprejudiced justice, to bring to trial all extortionate officers,

[23] *Ibid.*, VIII, 195.
[24] Eli Washington Caruthers, *A Sketch of the Life and Character of the Rev. David Caldwell* . . . (Greensborough, N. C., 1842), p. 171.
[25] *Col. Rec. of N. C.*, VIII, 233-234.

lawyers, and clerks, and to call to proper settlement of their accounts the sheriffs for the years 1764, 1765, 1766, and 1767. If they could not obtain this, they declared that they knew not to what extremes they might be driven.

The meeting of the Superior Court at Hillsboro in September, 1770, seemed to offer the Regulators another opportunity to obtain justice. James Hunter presented their petition to Judge Henderson on the first day of the court. The record of what transpired is preserved in the Orange County Court Records and in letters written by Judge Henderson to Governor Tryon a few days later.[26] Almost as soon as the court began on Monday morning, the town was filled with a great number of people shouting and behaving in a tumultuous manner. They made their way into the court until there was no more standing room and brought with them clubs, whips, and other weapons. Jeremiah Fields, who acted as spokesman of the group, declared that they had come down to see that their cases were tried and that they obtained justice. Various accusations were brought against the court.[27]

The Regulators retired from the courtroom; and evidently they were about to leave the judge to carry on the court when a Mr. Williams, an attorney, started to enter. The sight of this unpopular lawyer was too much for the people, and they fell upon him with clubs and nearly killed him. Their spirits aroused, they next fell upon Colonel Fanning, whom they pulled from the judge's bench, where he had sought sanctuary, and dragged him from the room by his heels. He narrowly escaped with his life. Judge Henderson asserted that he himself was threatened, but James Hunter and other leaders promised him protection if he would continue to hold court. This he promised to do with no idea of keeping his promise, for it was required that no lawyer save His King's Attorney be admitted. The Regulators then proceeded to whip Thomas Hart,

[26] *Ibid.*

[27] They charged the court with injustice and objected to the jurors who had been appointed, and demanded others should be appointed in their stead. The fact that Henderson declared these too tedious to mention, indicates that the people could expect no justice from him.

Alexander Martin, Michael Holt, John Littel (the clerk of the town), and several others. Colonel Grey, Major Lloyd, Francis Nash, John Cooke, Tyree Harris, and others escaped the same treatment by flight. Judge Henderson was then permitted to adjourn the court and was escorted by the multitude to his lodgings. Had they known that before dawn he would break his promise to them and seek safety in flight, they would not have dealt so leniently with him. His only regret seems to have been that he was unable to rescue poor Colonel Fanning from the Regulators and take him with him. Colonel Fanning was permitted to escape the following day on the condition that he was to take the road and run until he was out of sight. They then vented their feelings on his house, the furnishings of which were destroyed.

After Judge Henderson had abandoned the courthouse, the Regulators took charge and held a mock trial and disposed of the cases which were supposed to come up at this time. Seventy-two cases were called and disposed of, and the verdicts solemnly recorded in the courthouse records.[28]

The first case was John McMund *vs.* William Courtney, and the judgment of the court was "damned rogues." In the case of Benjamin Drummond *vs.* John Lambert "the plaintiff may pay the costs." Peter Noay had an action against Edmund Fanning, and the verdict was that "Fanning must pay," and in the case Fanning *vs.* Abraham Smith again the verdict was against Fanning. Case number 21 was Isaiah Hogan *vs.* Herman Husband, and "Hogan pays and be damned." The last five cases were typical of the whole and included the following verdicts: "file and be damned," "the man was sick it is damned roguery," "executed by a damned rogue and bill not sufficient," "negroes not worth a damn," "cost exceeded the whole, plaintiff may pay the costs." Doubtless the Regulators themselves regarded these trials as only a farce, but the judgments were no more one-sided than they would have been under a court controlled by their enemies.

Almost at once depositions and letters began to pour in to

[28] *Col. Rec. of N. C.*, VIII, 236-240.

Governor Tryon in which the writers described the rioting at Hillsboro and begged for his protection. Tryon was much worried by these reports and in a letter to Lord Hillsborough wrote that he had called a meeting of the council to consult them on measures to be taken. When the council consulted the attorney general as to the nature of the acts which were committed at Hillsboro, he observed that they amounted to only a riot or in some cases a misdemeanor. He further declared that they would have to be tried in the county where the acts were committed and that the recent instances in the court showed how ineffectual any process would be.[29]

Richard Henderson soon discovered that he was no more popular with the people of his county of Granville than he had been at Hillsboro. In November he complained to Governor Tryon that his barn and stables with their contents as well as his house had been consumed by fire. The Governor immediately offered a reward of £100 to anyone who would inform on the others.[30]

A mere rumor that the Regulators from Granville County were coming to New Bern to overrun and intimidate the Assembly caused Governor Tryon to write to the officers of the militia in the intervening counties to have regiments in readiness to stop such a movement. A communication from the Regulators at this time is evidence of the fact that they had a high regard for their reputation for honesty.[31] They said that inasmuch as they had been accused of having carried away a certain sum of money from Edward Fanning's house, they wished to clear their good name. The Regulators urged Fanning to send their accusers among them and to point out the accused, and promised to assist in bringing them to justice. When the Assembly met in December there were threats that the Regulators of Bute and Johnston counties would be on hand at Hillsboro to prevent Colonel Fanning from taking a seat in the Assembly. A letter with this news was sent to Governor Tryon, and he was informed that Colonel Simpson had called out the militia in

[29] *Ibid.*, VIII, 252.
[30] *Ibid.*, VIII, 259.   [31] *Ibid.*

order to march to New Bern and maintain order. The council decided to take no chances and retained part of the Craven County Militia, which was then under arms in the city to protect the Assembly.

At this meeting Governor Tryon felt the necessity of listening to the demands of the dissatisfied element of the colony. In his message to the legislature he confined himself to four points, two of which were the results of the demands of the Regulators, namely, the abuses in the conduct of the public funds and the general complaints against public officers and offices. One would think that Governor Tryon had almost been converted by the Regulators when he stated: "Let me recommend to you to make the most scrupulous inquiries into the complaints against public officers and offices in the government, and to provide as well for the redress of those which have an existence as to establish the fees of office in so expressed and determined a manner as will put them beyond a possibility of doubt and abuse. This will give great and just account to the public; you will be furnished with an account of the fees by men on each instrument I have issued that the country may be informed of any conduct in the particular."[32]

The part of his message which dealt with the riots at Hillsboro was a mixture of flattery and cajolery. No one was definitely blamed as to the cause of the riots, but all honest legislators were declared to be in duty bound to put them down and punish the perpetrators. The Assembly had been made to believe that its own rights had been violated by these riots, and was asked to wipe away the unwarranted stains upon an administration that had been forwarding the prosperity and advancement of the community. To placate the back settlers further, Governor Tryon recommended that a seminary be established among them. In their reply to his speech the council promised their utmost support in punishing the guilty for their acts at Hillsboro. The Assembly at this session was in receipt of several depositions from the people who denounced the activities of the Regulators.[33] On the other hand, Herman Husband

---

[32] *Ibid.*, VIII, 283.   [33] *Ibid.*, VIII, 387.

was busy presenting petitions from the various counties complaining of grievances and praying for relief.[34]

In the spring of 1771 Governor Tryon decided to subdue the Regulators by force of arms. He sought an army of two thousand, five hundred and fifty men from twenty-nine counties. Bute County at first refused to furnish a single man, since all of the eight hundred assembled declared themselves on the side of the Regulators.[35] Later some volunteers from the county supported them. General Waddell was placed in command by Tryon, while Caswell, Ashe, and Harnett were all given high rank. The men who but a few years before had been opposing the Stamp Act, and who a few years later were to be leaders in the Revolutionary movement, were now eager to help Governor Tryon subdue a group of their own countrymen who were only struggling for their just rights. In fact, most of the leading men of the east were in the line of march. In addition to those already mentioned, there were Robert Howe, Alexander Lillington, James Moore, Abner Nash, William Lindsay, Willie Jones, John Harvey, Jr., Moses Alexander, Thomas Polk, Samuel Spencer, Griffith Rutherford, Aaron Osborn, and others who were later devoted patriots.[36] The government's forces, well-armed and well-led, about eleven hundred in number, met the Regulators about two thousand in number on May 16, 1771, and easily defeated them. The latter were poorly armed and without experienced leaders.[37] Each side lost the same number killed, while the wounded of the Regulators probably outnumbered those of Tryon.[38]

Governor Tryon was severely censured for hanging one of the prisoners, James Few, on the evening of the victory. An account of his execution appeared in the Community Diary of the Moravians a week later: "A certain young man, a fine young fellow had been captured and when given the alternative of being hanged or taking an oath he chose the former. The Governor wished to spare his life and twice urged him to

[34] Ibid., VIII, 309.
[35] Ibid., VIII, 552.   [36] Ashe, op. cit., I, 368.
[37] Col. Rec. of N. C., VIII, 647-648.
[38] Ibid., VIII, 634.

submit, but the young man refused. The messenger described how the man with the rope around his neck was urged to yield and refused. The Governor turned aside with tears in his eyes as he was swung into eternity."[39] Edmund Fanning, one of Tryon's cohorts, demanded Few's execution on the pretence that he had assisted in tearing down and destroying Fanning's house. The Regulators denied that he had been present.[40] Tryon justified this execution by saying: "This gave great satisfaction to the men, and at this time it was a necessary sacrifice to appease the murmuring of the Troops, who were importunate that public justice should be immediately executed against some of the outlaws that were taken in the action, and in the opposing of whom they had braved so many dangers and suffered such loss of lives and blood, and without which satisfaction some refused to march forward while others declared they would give no quarter for the future."[41] This was surely a poor excuse for such an act.

On the next day Governor Tryon pardoned all those who would submit and take the oath of allegiance except the prisoners and those previously outlawed. By July 4 over six thousand had submitted.[42] After Tryon and his army reached Hillsboro a court-martial was held, and twelve of those convicted of high treason were sentenced to be hanged. The sentence was carried out in regard to six, and the rest were pardoned.[43] The executions took place in the presence of the army and the prisoners. This was doubtless intended to intimidate them. His object having been accomplished, Governor Tryon returned to New Bern, where he was lauded by the leading men of the eastern part of the Province for his bravery and courage. He was now appointed Governor of New York and was succeeded in North Carolina by Josiah Martin.

Governor Martin was not popular with the friends of the former Governor, and when the leaders of the Regulators asked

[39] Ashe, op. cit., p. 772. [40] Col. Rec. of N. C., VIII, 648.
[41] The State Records of North Carolina (hereinafter abbreviated S. R. N. C.), ed. Walter C. Clark (vols. 11-26; Goldsboro, N. C., 1886-1907), XIX, 845.
[42] Col. Rec. of N. C., IX, 9. [43] Ibid., VIII, 635.

him for pardon he was inclined to listen to them. Jeremiah
Field, Ninian Hamilton, Mathew Hamilton, James Hunter,
Thomas Welborn, William Butler, and John Fruit petitioned
for pardon.[44] Martin, anxious to grant pardons, felt compelled
to wait. When, in 1773, the British Government advised an act
of amnesty on the part of the legislature it refused because it
did not make enough exceptions. This treatment naturally inclined the Regulators to be more loyal to England than to the
colony. After the Revolution began, the King authorized the
Governor to grant full pardon to all involved in the Regulation.
Herman Husband was alone excepted.[45]

In the second year of his administration Governor Martin
made an extensive tour through much of the region inhabited
by the late insurgents. In a letter to Lord Hillsborough he
wrote that they came to him in large numbers asking for pardons
and that he dismissed them with sentiments of pity and compassion. He was completely won over to the justice of their cause.
This may have been partly his course to win them over to the
cause of the government by merciful means, a thing Tryon had
failed to do by force. His account was a severe indictment of
Tryon and his officials:

> My progress through this Country My Lord hath opened my
> eyes exceedingly with respect to the commotions and discontents
> that lately prevailed in it. I now see most clearly that they have been
> provoked by insolence and cruel advantages taken of the peoples
> ignorance by mercenary tricking Attornies, Clerks and other little
> Officers who have practiced upon them every sort of rapine and
> extortion by which having brought themselves their just resentment
> they engaged Government in their defence by artful misrepresenta-
> tions that the vengeance the wretched people in folly and madness
> aimed at their heads was directed against the constitution and by this
> stratagem they threw an odium upon the injured people that by
> degrees begat a prejudice which precluded a full redress of their
> grievances. . . .[46]

Having thus been convinced of their innocence, Governor Martin began action to secure pardons for them. They felt that he
was their friend, and naturally supported him later against those
who had attempted their destruction.

[44] *Ibid.*, IX, 14-93.　　[45] *Ibid.*, X, 90.　　[46] *Ibid.*, IX, 330.

On this tour he perhaps visited Colonel William Field and his brothers, who were members of a prominent family. Four men by the name of Field were captured at the time of the Battle of Moore's Creek, one of whom, Jeremiah, is several times mentioned as being a Regulator. He spoke for them at the riots at Hillsboro and was indicted as a Regulator at a Special Court of Oyer and Terminer at New Bern, March 11, 1771.[47] Together with his brother Robert, he was ordered to raise the King's Standard at Cross Creek,[48] and with his brothers, William, Robert, and Joseph, was taken prisoner at Moore's Creek.[49] These people were all anxious to receive pardons and again to live within the law.

The exact number of the Regulators who remained true to England and fought in the Revolution as Loyalists will never be known. When one reads the accounts of the engagements fought within the state the names of the Regulators appear constantly. Only two or three Regulators of prominence were Patriots. One of these, Thomas Persons, became famous as aiding the cause of the colony and later was a member of the provincial council.

So convinced was the Congress at Hillsboro of the need for winning over their former enemies, the Regulators, that a committee was appointed to confer with them. Since this committee was composed of such men as Caswell, Maurice Moore, Locke, the Reverend Mr. Patillo, and others who had been prominently opposed to the Regulators, it is no wonder that they had but slight success in persuading them to fight against their lawful Sovereign.[50] Patillo, a Presbyterian minister, had addressed his congregation on the evils of being a Regulator and at the same time had praised Tryon for his action against them. Moore had sat on the court which had convicted twelve of them of treason and sentenced them to death. It was too much to expect this to be soon forgotten.

The Continental Congress at Philadelphia was not indif-

[47] *Ibid.*, VIII, 241, 245, 531.   [48] *Ibid.*, VIII, 599.
[49] *Ibid.*, X, 169.   [50] *Ibid.*, X, 169.

ferent to the importance of the disaffection of this strong group. Evidently they thought that ministers would be effective in persuading them to break the oath which had been forced on them, for it was voted that two ministers of the Gospel should be sent among them to explain the present dispute. It was also voted that their expenses of forty dollars a month should be paid by the Continental Congress.[51] This was the only instance in which Congress made such an appropriation. All such efforts were fruitless, for wherever the Regulators looked they saw their old enemies in control. They preferred to remain under British rule rather than to change to a government entirely in the hands of their enemies. The result was that in 1775 Governor Martin was able to write to the Earl of Dartmouth that he could depend upon the support of the Regulators, then two to three thousand strong, whenever he should call upon them.[52] This promise would doubtless have been kept if they had not been deceived.

In the early part of 1775, Governor Martin was much heartened by the loyal addresses which came to him from the counties that had been the center of Regulation troubles. The one from Rowan and Surry counties was signed by Samuel Bryan and one hundred and ninety-four men who declared that they expressed the sentiments of a large number who did not sign it. Guilford County, a stronghold of the Regulators, wrote as follows:

His Majesty's most loyal subjects of the County of Guilford and Province of North Carolina beg leave to assure your excellency that we hold an open detestation to all illegal and unwarrantable proceedings against his Majesty's Crown and dignity, and as there is a general dispute between his Majesty and the Colonies of America, past our knowledge to determine what the event may be. We therefore hold a firm attachment to his Majesty King George the Third his crown and dignity. We therefore being an unhappy people, lying under the reflection of the late unhappy insurrection, we have therefore taken this opportunity to show forth our loyalty to his Majesty and his lawful commands and for further confirmation have hereto, subscribed our names as maintaining our rights under legal authority.

[51] *Ibid.*, X, 331.   [52] *Ibid.*, X, 406.

This address was signed by John Fields and one hundred and sixteen men. The strongest address of loyalty came from Anson County, which not only declared His Majesty's Government to be the grand network and guardian of their civil and religious liberties but also expressed abhorrence at this action of the colonies.[53] Governor Martin was much pleased with this profession of loyalty on the part of the Regulators.

Whether these men were Tories because of the fact that they remembered their grievances against their old enemies who were now leading the Revolutionary movement, it is difficult to determine. Many of the former Regulators were not only outside of the office-holding class but were not even voters. Governor Martin appeared to them as a friend and a protector. If he failed to receive from them as much aid as he had anticipated it was due to his blundering and not to want of zeal on the part of the Regulators. The Regulation movement was only one of the important factors which helped to influence the people of North Carolina in their attitude toward independence. Almost as important were race, occupation, and location of settlement.

The Scotch as a race generally remained loyal to the King of England and were the most important single group in North Carolina to do so. The first Scottish Governor of North Carolina who actively encouraged the immigration of his countrymen to the colony was Gabriel Johnston. In September, 1739, three hundred and fifty of his countrymen arrived. That they might be able to induce their friends to come, they asked that some mark of favor be shown to them. Accordingly, it was voted that they should be free from taxation for a period of ten years and that £1,000 should be distributed among the several families. It was further resolved that any group of forty Protestants who would come to North Carolina from the mother country and settle in one township should be free from all taxes for one year. Soon Dugald McNeil, Dan McNeil, Duncan Campbell, Colonel McAllister, and Neil McNeil, whose names portray their origin, were appointed magistrates in Bladen County and were the first

[53] *Ibid.*, IX, 1161-1164.

of their countrymen to hold that office in this country.[54] By 1767, there were eight hundred and ninety-nine white taxables in Cumberland County, most of whom were from Scotland, and they were able to maintain a Presbyterian minister. The next year a sum of money was voted to the Governor to reimburse him for the money he had paid out to several families who had arrived at Brunswick from Scotland the previous year.[55]

By 1770, the trade of North Carolina was largely in the hands of these people who were reported to have come in schools to get rich.[56] In 1771 an act was passed in behalf of several shiploads of Scotch families, who numbered sixteen hundred. During 1772 between six and seven hundred more came to the Cape Fear section. As late as 1775, when the Revolution was well under way, they continued to pour in and probably not less than seven hundred came in that year.

The question may now be raised, what caused the Scotch people for the most part to remain true to the Home Government when the contest with the colonies came? Those who came after 1745, the date of the defeat of the Scotch at Culloden in the war between England and Scotland, were bound by a solemn oath to become good and faithful subjects of King George II of England. Extremely religious people, they felt bound by this oath. They took the view that they owed their lives to the fact that a gracious king had permitted them to migrate to North Carolina, and they were loath to turn against him.

Being accustomed to a government by a king, they could conceive of no other. The revolutionary idea of a democracy was foreign to them, since they were accustomed to obey their superiors.

The leaders were for the most part determined to support their King. Some of them left landed estates in Scotland which they still owned, and to join the Revolution meant forfeiture of their estates. They blamed the poor markets in the colony on the disturbance which their factious neighbors were creating with the mother country. Residing also in North Carolina

[54] Ibid., IV, 8-9.   [55] Ibid., VII, 618.   [56] Ibid., VII, 652.

at this time were many Scottish officers who had fought in England after the defeat at Culloden, and these were now on half pay and subject to call to service. All those whom the common people regarded as their superiors supported the King, and this naturally influenced them to do likewise. Their leaders stressed the fact that all their past efforts against the King had ended in defeat, and this was sure to do likewise. They were told that this was their grand opportunity to show their loyalty to a king who might yet lack entire confidence in them.

The Scotch merchants, like many other merchants of North Carolina and the South, were mostly Loyalists. They carried on trade directly with England, exchanging tobacco, lumber, and other native products for those wares of the mother country.[57] War would destroy this trade and bring them ruin. The merchants of New England, on the other hand, received much of their raw materials from the West Indies, which they manufactured and sent to England. They were gradually ruined by the Navigation Laws and had much more reason to support the side that would free them from this burden than did the merchants of North Carolina.

Conspicuous among the North Carolina merchants was Andrew Miller, a Scotchman of Halifax County, who refused to sign the association against trade with England. The Safety Committee of Halifax County then resolved to have no more trade with Andrew Miller and to recommend that the people of the country adopt the same measure. This move against Andrew Miller was taken in December, 1774, and was one of the first of similar actions in the colony.

Probably the most important merchant in North Carolina, as well as the most valuable Loyalist to the British cause, was John Hamilton, a merchant of the Albemarle section. When the debts of the Loyalists were confiscated in North Carolina, his company lost £14,834.[58] During the war he raised and

[57] Rev. E. W. Caruthers, *Interesting Revolutionary Incidents: and Sketches of Character, Chiefly in the "Old North State," First Series* (Philadelphia, 1854), pp. 50, 61.
[58] MS Papers of the Confiscation Commissioners, 2 boxes (North Carolina Historical Commission, Raleigh).

quipped at his own expense about fourteen hundred Tories to
ight for the British cause. His loyalty to the British Government was proclaimed when he was required to take the test
oath or depart from the state in sixty days. His business as a
merchant in Halifax gave him a wide acquaintance among the
people, who came to have great confidence in his honesty. It
was said that he was a Loyalist because he believed England to
be in the right. His kind treatment of the Whigs who became
his prisoners during the war, won for him their lasting grati-
ude.[59] He led the Tories in numerous engagements in North
Carolina, South Carolina, and Georgia, and after the war was
stationed as British consul at Norfolk.

Of the sixty-eight persons who were designated by name
in the North Carolina Confiscation Act of 1779, forty-five were
merchants.[60] Of all those who sought compensation from England after the war, almost one half were merchants. They came
from almost every city and county in North Carolina and
ranged in importance from James Glass, who was designated
as a small merchant from Edenton, to the great firms of Archibald Hamilton and Company and Samuel Cornell. Their loyalty may have been due to the fact that they were prosperous
under the existing conditions. Thomas McKnight, a merchant,
in a letter to Samuel Johnston observed that, however suitable
independence was to the Northern colonies, it was not adapted
to the South. He added that, while he thought no plans for
independence were harbored in the South, "I cannot help thinking we are gradually and step by step being led into . . . them
as effectively as if we had been originally concerned in the
plan." Incidentally he was prosperous and did not wish to be
disturbed.[61]

Some of the larger merchants, such as Hogg and Campbell
and John Hamilton and Company, bought goods on time from
the British merchants and sold them on credit to the planters.
On their books they had listed the names of hundreds of debtors

[59] Lorenzo Sabine, *Biographical Sketches of the Loyalists of the American
Revolution* (2 vols.; Boston, 1864), II, 511-512.
[60] *S. R. N. C.*, XXIV, 263-264.   [61] *Col. Rec. of N. C.*, X, 249.

at the outbreak of the war. If they joined the Revolution and did not settle their accounts, their credit with the British merchants would be destroyed. Some of them, like Andrew Miller, had conscientious scruples against not paying their honest debts. Other merchants without cash of their own depended entirely upon their credit with the British merchants for the financing of their trade.[62]

Although the majority of the merchants of North Carolina supported the Loyalist cause, a large number in the Cape Fear region were leaders in the rebellion. Conspicuous among this number were Cornelius Harnett, Robert Hogg, Thomas Ogden, David Barrows, Joseph Hewes, Robert Smith, and Joseph Blount. These names were offset by such men as John Cruden, Hogg and Campbell, George Hooper, James Glass, Hogg and Clayton, and Samuel Cornell in the same region who supported the cause of the King. The merchants of Cross Creek were almost unanimous in their support of the King.[63] Those of the Albemarle region were also generally loyal, probably on account of the fact that many of them were under the control of British merchants because of their debts.[64] The middle-class Scotchman was accustomed to following the leadership of the wealthier class, and when this element declared for the King, he unhesitatingly followed.

The Germans were also an important racial element in North Carolina, but were of much less importance than the Scotch in the Revolution. Many of them entered the colony by way of the back country from Pennsylvania in search of lands. They settled chiefly in Forsyth, Guilford, Randolph, Davidson, Stokes, Rowan, Cabarrus, Stanley, Lincoln, Gaston, Catawba, and Burke counties, these bordering the frontier from Virginia to South Carolina.[65] These were the counties which were prominent in the War of the Regulation. In this war a large number of the Germans supported the Regulators.[66]

[62] S. R. N. C., V, 203.
[63] Adelaide Fries (ed.), Records of the Moravians in North Carolina (2 vols.; Raleigh, 1922), III, 1055-1058.
[64] Charles Christopher Crittenden, The Commerce of North Carolina 1763-1789 (New Haven, 1936), p. 118.
[65] Col. Rec. of N. C., VIII, 729.   [66] Ibid., VIII, 730.

When the Revolution continued, many of them remained loyal to the King; as a result of their activities, they suffered the confiscation of their estates. Of the one hundred and eighty-two people summoned before the Rowan County Inferior Court in 1783 to show cause why they should not have their estates confiscated, one fifth were German.[67]

The Moravians, a religious sect, which was made up largely of Germans and which somewhat resembled the Quakers, had settled in North Carolina just previous to the war. Since it was contrary to their religious principles to take either an oath or to serve in the army, they found themselves in a difficult position. They claimed exemption also because of the "conscientious objections," and it was granted them. In lieu of this service large fines were collected from them at the beginning of the war, and later they were taxed threefold.[68] Their neutral stand, though it was a friendly neutrality as far as the Patriots were concerned, gave both the Whigs and Tories an excuse for preying on them. The Tories claimed the Moravians were in sympathy with the Continental forces, while the committees of safety accused them of secretly aiding the Royal party.[69] Although the Moravians always supplied the demands of the Whig soldiers by giving them everything they demanded and accepted in payment worthless money or promises to pay, they frequently found themselves in difficulties. At one time a band of Whig militia robbed and pillaged the people so badly that they were left like a conquered enemy. In fact, they suffered much more from this class than they did from the Tories.[70]

Certain professional as well as racial groups were inclined to remain loyal to the King. Chief among these may be mentioned the clergy. Especially was this true of some of the Episcopalians, who sacrificed their goods to their loyalty and died in poverty. They, recognized as being among the ablest

[67] Rev. Jethro Rumple, *A History of Rowan County, North Carolina* (Salisbury, 1881), pp. 168-170.
[68] *Col. Rec. of N. C.*, VIII, 729.   [69] *Ibid.*, VIII, 730.
[70] Adelaide L. Fries, *The Moravian Church, Yesterday and Today* (Raleigh, 1926), p. 168.

people in the colony, were often allowed to remain.[71] The Reverend John McLean and the Reverend William McKenzie were among those who petitioned for aid from England on account of their loyalty. The Reverend John Wills, minister from New Hanover, was suspended for his loyalty and wrote for aid to the Archbishop of Canterbury, who gave him £50 out of funds for distressed American clergymen. While General Campbell was absent from his troops before the Battle of King's Mountain, the Reverend Mr. McCrea of the old established church visited the camp and attempted to discourage the men from fighting, warning them that they would be murdered like bees. General Campbell respected McCrea's age too much to punish him, but as an example of what he intended to do to Cornwallis, Campbell ordered the clergyman to prostrate himself on his belly in the road, where every soldier stepped over him on the march.[72]

Certain other groups and officials were definitely aligned on the side of the King. Most important among these were the Crown officials. Of the members of the Governor's Council, which met in December, 1774, John Rutherford, Lewis De Rosset,[73] Martin Hassel, and Samuel Cornell were Loyalists.[74] These four were also among those who made claims to England for loss of property or salary. William Brimmage, Deputy Attorney for the Crown, was a Tory leader and was arrested for conspiracy.[75] James Cotton, a surveyor of Anson County, was made a prisoner for his support of government, as was Captain Robert Cunningham.[76] They were among the leading men of the colony and persuaded large numbers of the country people to take up arms for the King.

The members of the council were often men who had served in the Assembly or held some other office in the colony. The record of Lewis De Rosset serves as an example. He had been

---

[71] Joseph Kelley Turner, *A History of Edgecombe County, North Carolina* (Raleigh, 1920), p. 89.

[72] Lyman C. Draper, *King's Mountain and Its Heroes* (Cincinnati, 1881), p. 396.

[73] *Col. Rec. of N. C.*, XIX, 887-888.   [74] *Ibid.*, X, 236.

[75] *Ibid.*, XXVII, 538-539.   [76] *Ibid.*, XI, 290.

ne of North Carolina's most useful and prominent citizens and
vas held in respect and confidence by the common people as
vell as by the Governor. He was a member of the lower house
f the General Assembly in 1751 and was chairman of the pub-
ic accounts as well as justice of peace for several years. From
752 to the Revolution he was a member of the council and in
754 was made commissioner to prepare and emit £40,000 of
roclamation money. In addition, he was also receiver general
f the King's quit rent, which office he resigned in 1761. Some
f the measures which he introduced for the state's good were:
"For leave to build St. James Church, also one at Brunswick;
egulating exports on the Cape Fear; also appointing inspec-
ors; a petition for the establishment of a post office in the prov-
nce and also of a quarantine." He was adjutant general on
Jeneral Waddell's staff in 1771 and lieutenant general under
Tryon in 1768.[77]

Loyalism in North Carolina may be traced by sections and
ounties as well as by races and classes. The counties of Surry,
Juilford, Orange, Rowan, Randolph, Chatham, Cumberland,
Anson, Brunswick, and Montgomery made up a section which
vas strong in its support of the King.[78]

One careful student of these times has estimated that a
najority of the people of Cumberland County were Tories.[79]
Others have placed their number as large as two thirds of the
opulation.[80] These counties extended from the mouth of the
Cape Fear River to the Virginia border and occupied the west-
rn half of the Granville district, which covered the entire
orthern half of the state. At the termination of the Revolu-
ionary struggle the people of these counties were severely
unished for the stand which they had taken, and their estates

[77] Kemp P. Battle (ed.), "Letters and Documents Relating to the Early
History of the Lower Cape Fear," *James Sprunt Historical Monograph*
Chapel Hill, 1903), No. 4, p. 21.   [78] *Col. Rec. of N. C.*, X, 146.
[79] William Henry Foote, *Sketches of North Carolina, Historical and
iographical* (New York, 1846), p. 142.
[80] R. D. W. Connor, "Race Elements in the White Population of North
arolina," N. C. State Normal and Industrial College, *Historical Publication*
Raleigh, 1920), No. 1, p. 66.

were more generally confiscated than those of any other sec
tion.[81]

The regions bordering on Pamlico Sound and the Chowan
River were also well represented in the groups who lost their
plantations by the laws of confiscation passed by the North
Carolina Legislature. In Bertie County were located the large
holdings of Nathaniel Duckinfield. They varied in size any-
where from one hundred and forty acres to six hundred and
forty acres and were purchased by eighteen individuals. The
purchase price varied from £165 to £5,802.[82]

One method of discovering how widespread was the support
of the King in the Province is to make a study of the record
of the sale of confiscated estates. Such a study reveals the fact
that between June 5, 1784, and November 15, 1787, tracts of
land belonging to Loyalists were sold in twenty-nine counties of
North Carolina: Anson, Beaufort, Bertie, Bladen, Brunswick,
Camden, Carteret, Chatham, Chowan, Craven, Currituck,
Dobbs, Duplin, Edgecombe, Halifax, Hertford, Hyde, Montgomery, Moore, Nash, New Hanover, Orange, Randolph,
Rowan, Sampson, Tyrell, Wake, and Wayne.[83] These counties
extended from Currituck in the east to Rowan in the west, and
from Guilford in the north to Brunswick in the south. The
number of estates sold in each of these counties varied all the
way from one each in Wayne, Currituck, and Camden counties
to fifty-four in Rowan, fifty-eight in Bladen, and ninety in
Orange. This fact would indicate that loyal men of property,
of the planter class, were to be found in practically every section
of the state.

The counties in the east were settled very early, while those
in the west were the last to be settled, and these two sections
contained the greatest number of Loyalists, with the exception
of the Scotch on the Cape Fear. The eastern counties on account
of their trade and commerce felt their interest as allied with

[81] *Audit Office*, Class 12, Vol. 91. R. D. W. Connor had transcripts
made of various English Documents for the North Carolina Historical Commission at Raleigh. All audit office references unless otherwise noted are
to these transcripts: War Office and P. R. O.

[82] *Ibid.*, Vol. 9.   [83] *Audit Office*, Class 12, Vol. 91.

that of the mother country. The western region contained many Regulators and others who had felt no inconvenience from the English trade acts. Many of the Scotch of the Cape Fear section had arrived too recently to feel any loyalty to their new homes. Of the forty officers of the loyal regiment of the North Carolina Volunteers, thirty gave their residence as Scotland, nine as America, and one as Ireland.[84] These men found themselves involved in the Revolutionary struggle before they had the opportunity to settle permanently in any county.

Anson, Bladen, and Cumberland counties, which occupy the south central part of the state and are drained by Rocky River and Drowning Creek, led all the others in the number who fought in both the loyal militia and the regularly enrolled Loyalist regiments. Anson County alone furnished a regiment of Loyalist militia, which participated in the defense of Charleston, South Carolina.[85] The North Carolina Highland Regiment was composed of Highland Scotch from Anson, Bladen, and Cumberland counties in about equal numbers. The names of about five hundred Loyalist soldiers from North Carolina who participated in the defense of Charleston are given in the appendix of this work, but it is impossible to ascertain from what counties many of them came. Some of the soldiers were accompanied by their wives and families who received a stipend from the British officer in charge when Charleston was evacuated.

John Stuart, who had been appointed Indian Agent for the Southern district of the United States, was well aware of the loyalty of the back country at this time. In writing to General Gage in October 3, 1775, he observed that the greater part of the frontier and back inhabitants were attached to and inclined to support the government. For that reason he advised against an indiscriminate Indian attack on the settlement, since it might

[84] War Office 85, Vol. 165, p. 17.
[85] P. R. O. Treasury 50. Bundle 5. No writer of North Carolina history has ever given the names of the individual Loyalists of the state who fought in the militia regiments or in one of the five regularly enrolled regiments. The English Treasury Papers No. 50, Bundle 5, contain the names of about two hundred of the rank and file of some of these companies and the counties from which they came.

do much harm, but, on the contrary, suggested that the Indian should assist their well-disposed neighbors.[86] The freeholder of Currituck County made a statement avowing their loyalty to George III, which was subscribed to by almost every man in the county. A letter from Lieutenant-Governor Frank Eppes to Charles Lee described the counties of Pasquotank and Currituck as being particularly disaffected.[87] In 1776 Griffith Rutherford wrote that the current of Tories was running strong in Anson County.[88] Johnston County reported several obstinate Tories and William Tryon asked for the Light Horse to subdue them. Bladen, Randolph, Rowan, and Surry counties, all contained many supporters of the government. In 1779 there were so many Tories in Burke County that the British officers were able to recruit men there. They became so numerous that they planned to put to death all the patriot officers and people in the country.[89] The people in general supported the more wealthy planters in acting against rebellion in this region.

There must have been many who secretly approved of government and who were afraid to arouse themselves. If a man in North Carolina enlisted in the King's forces, his goods and lands were forfeited; and if caught, he was liable to be tried for treason and shot. On the other hand, if he enlisted in the Continental Army, his property was secured and protected and he received the plaudits of the people. In North Carolina, Loyalism was hit hard when the British Army evacuated Wilmington. The Loyalists who were left behind in the city, as well as those in the near-by country, were abandoned to the mercy of their enemies. In the examination of General Robertson in Parliament in 1779 he declared that after careful observation and inquiry in 1779 in North Carolina he was convinced that no less than two thirds of the people preferred the King's Government to the tyranny of a Congress. Another writer who gave much study to the subject estimated that

[86] Peter Force (ed.), *American Archives* (6 vols.; Washington, D. C 1837-1846), IV, 318.
[87] *Lee Papers, 1754-1776*, pp. 384-385.
[88] *Col. Rec. of N. C.*, X, 727.   [89] *Ibid.*, XIV, 132-133.

one half the people were loyal to the government.[90] That great
numbers were willing to enlist in the King's cause, is shown by
the fact that the Loyalist Samuel Bryant was able on short
notice to raise eight hundred men in the region bordering the
Yadkin River. They were so eager to enlist that one third of
them began to serve without arms.

The number of Loyalists and their leaders who were enrolled in the British provincial companies in North Carolina
and the group to which they belonged are no longer matters
of conjecture. In the Library of Congress are photostatic copies
of the muster rolls which give the names of the officers, and
for some of the states those of the privates also. Unfortunately,
the North Carolina muster gives the names of the officers only.[91]

In addition to these companies it must be remembered that
there were thousands of Loyalists in the state who were fighting
in the militia companies under men like Fanning. Altogether
there were at times more Loyalists in America who were
fighting in the British armies than Washington had in his Continental Army. Governor Martin could well be proud of the
support which was given him by the loyal subjects of a colony
which he had ruled for only a brief period.

[90] Colonel Robert Grey, "Observations on the War in Carolina," *North
Carolina University Magazine*, VIII, 145-160 (Nov., 1858).

[91] North Carolina had the following regiments enlisted in the aid of
Great Britain. The North Carolina Dragoons (they were commanded by
Captain Robert Gillies and Lieutenant Dougald Cockburn), North Carolina
Highlanders (the officers of this regiment were Lieutenants Allen Stewart,
Donald Stewart, and Alexander McDonald, Captain Neil McAlpure, Captain
Angus McDonald, and Lieutenant John McDonald), the North Carolina
Volunteers (their officers were Ensign John Bloxham, Surgeon Thomas
Smith, Surgeon's Mate John Piper, Captain Eli Branson), and Independent
Company (commanded by Captain Hunter and Lieutenant Samuel Jones),
the Royal North Carolina Regiment (this regiment had a large personnel
of officers: Lieutenant Colonel John Hamilton, Major Daniel Manson, Ad-
jutant Roderick McLeod, Reverend John Andrews, Reverend William Duncan,
Quartermasters Daniel Campbell, James Campbell, Alexander Fotheringham,
Donald McAlpine, Christopher McCroe, and John Shaw, Ensigns Charles
Atkinsons, Charles Barters, Donald Campbell, Alexander McCockell, Thomas
McDonald, Malcolm McKay, John McNeil, and John Shaw), and the
North Carolina Independents, a company of cavalry commanded by Captain
Gillies.

CHAPTER III

COMMITTEES OF PUBLIC SAFETY

THE FIRST PROVINCIAL CONGRESS of North Carolina, held at New Bern on August 25, 1774, was the first Revolutionary convention to meet in the state. It was called over the protest of Governor Martin.[1] On December 8 of the previous year, the legislature had appointed a committee of correspondence for the colony, which was the first definite step toward committee government. At this Provincial Congress all the counties were represented with the exception of Edgecombe, Guilford, Hertford, Surry, and Wake. All the eligible towns sent representatives except Hillsboro, Salisbury, Brunswick, and Campleton. Cumberland County was represented by Farquard Campbell and Thomas Rutherford, two men who were later Tories. Governor Martin did everything in his power to prevent this meeting and consulted his council as to the best steps to be taken. On the following day they advised him to issue a proclamation that the meeting was illegal, and to warn all the officers of the King, both civil and military, to take measures to prevent it.[2]

Rowan County had already held a meeting of its freeholders to appoint a committee to keep in touch with the other counties and secure united action against the mother country. This action was followed by several other counties and the town of Halifax. On the day when Congress met, Governor Martin again appealed to his council to inquire if they could recommend any new measures. They declared that nothing could be done.

This Congress remained in session for only three days. One of its most important acts was to pass resolutions that three delegates should be appointed to attend the General Congress to be held in Philadelphia in September. At the same time the members declared their loyalty to the House of Hanover, an

[1] *Col. Rec. of N. C.*, IX, 1041.   [2] Jones, *op. cit.*, p. 127.

avowal which was scarcely in keeping with the series of resolutions adopted.[3] Sympathy was expressed for Massachusetts, and the Boston Port Bill was denounced. After declaring themselves in favor of a Continental Congress, William Hooper, Joseph Hewes, and Richard Caswell were chosen as delegates. Several measures were adopted to prohibit trade with Great Britain. Furthermore, the foundation of a revolutionary government was laid. The counties and the towns having the right to send members to the Assembly were to be represented in future provincial meetings, and in each county a committee of five was to be chosen to take effectual care that these resolves were properly observed, and to correspond occasionally with the provisional and original Committee of Correspondence in their Province.[4] Several of the counties and the town of Halifax, at the same meeting in which they chose representatives to the provincial council, had also formed committees similar in membership and purpose to those provided for by the council. While at this time each group professed their allegiance to the King, they, nevertheless, declared for an association prohibiting trade with the mother country. Governor Martin in a letter to Lord Dartmouth bitterly denounced the action of the council during this convention. He complained that although the council had assured him of its disapproval of the meeting and advised him to discourage it by proclamation, nevertheless, they attended this convention, freely mixed with the delegates, and gave them every encouragement. The only exception was James Hassell, who remained with Governor Martin at the time and faithfully supported him. All this was done despite the fact that Governor Martin had repeatedly invited all members to reside at his home during the critical juncture and had requested them to refrain from attending the convention.

The members of this Congress represented the best talent that was to be found in North Carolina. John Harvey, who was looked upon as a leader of the Whig party, presided.[5] William Hooper, of New Hanover district, was one of the best

[3] *Ibid.*, p. 140.
[4] *Col. Rec. of N. C.*, IX, 1041-1044.   [5] Jones, *op. cit.*, p. 130.

educated men in the state, having graduated from Harvard College at the head of the class of 1760.[6] He was a signer of the Declaration of Independence and one of the first to represent North Carolina in the Continental Congress. Richard Caswell, of Dobbs County, held nearly every office of trust and honor which it was possible for the state to bestow on him. Other prominent members were Thomas Person (Person County and Person Hall of the University of North Carolina were named in his honor), Willie Jones, and Allen Jones.[7]

The first Provincial Congress or Convention of North Carolina adjourned on August 27, 1774, and on September 23 a meeting of the Committee of Safety for Rowan County was held.[8] This was followed on October 4 by a meeting in Pitt County. Both of these counties had organized their committees when they had met to choose delegates to the Provincial Congress of August 25, 1774.

The Rowan County committee at once began to investigate why John and Willis Kelly had sold powder at an advanced price over that charged three months previous. It was resolved that anyone who bought or sold powder at more than five shillings a pound would be deemed an enemy to his country and treated accordingly. Next, it was resolved that John Dunn and Benjamin Booth merited censure and detestation for a false and impertinent advertisement derogatory to the interest of the colony.[9] Both of these men later became famous for their Loyalist activities. Several members of the county committees were later to change their allegiance and remain loyal to England. On November 23, 1774, Robert Hogg was a member of the Wilmington committee, yet in a few months he was persecuted as a Tory.

When the committee of Halifax County met on December 21, 1774, the members had before them a real opportunity

[6] *Ibid.*, p. 121.

[7] Willie and Allen Jones were brothers; the former probably wrote the constitution of North Carolina. For a more detailed account of these famous men see *ibid.*, pp. 137-139.

[8] *Col. Rec. of N. C.*, IX, 1072. A complete record of this meeting has been preserved.   [9] *Ibid.*, IX, 1074.

for discipline. It was reported to the committee that Andrew Miller, a merchant of Halifax Town, had refused to sign the association. Two members were ordered to find him and bring him before the committee. He came before them, but refused to sign for the following reasons:

To wit: that I am largely indebted and have effects in my hands belonging to persons residing in Britain; which debts and effects I cannot remit for by next September; after which time I should be bound by this association not to export any merchandise or commodity whatever to that country without certain laws are repealed, which I think would be unjust as it may be out of the power of my creditors and friends to procure the repeal of any law however willing they may be to exert their influence for that purpose. And as I think it unjust to withhold from any person even at a country at war with this the property which might belong to him in my hands I must therefore object to the signing of that part of the association respecting non-importation to Great Britain and shall continue to do so while I have any property in my hands belonging to people of this country.[10]

The committee then took the following action:

Since therefore there is nothing peculiar or satisfactory in his reasons but on the contrary they indicate an intention to export (if he can) after the first day of September, next, Resolved unanimously (to show our disapprobation of his conduct and encourage such merchants as have signed the Association) that we will not from this day purchase any Goods, Wares, or Merchandise from said Andrew Miller or any person acting for or in partnership with him after paying our just debts and fulfilling the contracts already entered into for commodities of this years' produce. And we shall also recommend it to the people of this country to adopt the same measures.[11]

Signing the association against Great Britain was made the test of patriotism by this safety committee. One of the most active and long lived of the safety committees was that of Wilmington, which from November 23, 1774, through March 7, 1776, held eighty-four meetings. The Wilmington committee illustrated the best type of co-operation between a county and a town committee.[12]

On March 13 the threat made by the Wilmington com-

[10] Ibid., IX, 1101-1102.   [11] Ibid.   [12] Ibid., IX, 1127.

mittee the week previous of publishing the names of those who
refused to sign the association was made good. The names of
John Cruden, Thomas Orr, William McLeod, John Slingsby,
William Whitfield, Thomas Cobham, John Walker, Jr., and
William McMastier were published.[13]

On March 6, 1775, it was resolved that the members of
the committee should visit all housekeepers in town and request
them to sign the association or give their reason for not doing
so, in order that such enemies to their country might be set
forth to public view and treated with the contempt which they
merited.[14] On the following day Dr. Thomas Cobham, John
McDonnel, John Walker, Jr., and William McLeod, John
Slingsby, Thomas Orr, John Cruden, and William McMastier,
merchants, William Whitfield, planter, and Kenneth McKenzie
and Dugald McKnight, tailors, all appeared before the committee and under various pretenses refused to sign the association. The committee then resolved to have no trade or dealings
with those who had refused to sign the association and to hold
them unworthy of the rights of freemen, and advised all others
so to regard them. These resolves were then printed on hand-
bills and distributed throughout the Province. It required a
man of strong convictions to hold out in face of such social
pressure. Before March 13 all of these signed the association
except John McDonnel, Kenneth McKenzie, and Dugald
McKnight. Some idea of the measures used to frighten the
people into signing may be gathered from the resolves of the
committee of Wilmington. They declared that they would be
forced to adopt such measures against the nonsigners as would
be detrimental to them in their occupation, not only for the
present, but also for the future.[15]

That the Tories constantly assailed the actions of the committees is shown by a letter written by Andrew Miller to
Thomas Burke from Halifax, March 11, 1775: "The committees of Nansemond have had their chairman Colonel Riddick
before them as a culprit but could not prove their charge.
Parson Agnew on a refusal to appear is advertised as a violator

[13] *Ibid.*, IX, 1166.   [14] *Ibid.*, IX, 1151.   [15] *Ibid.*, IX, 1164.

as is Mr. Donaldson who has been before them for hiring a Flatt of the Parson's which he was obliged to discharge. The complaint against the parson is that he preached of obedience to the King and the laws of the country and admonished his congregation against riots. Col. Riddick it seems is not very warm to the cause."[16]

Many of the ministers of the Church of England in North Carolina supported the Loyalist cause. This may have been as often a matter of expediency as of conviction. The Continental Congress asked the colonies to observe a day of fasting, humiliation, and prayer, for the purpose of humbling themselves before God. What was more fitting than that the parish minister of New Bern, the Reverend James Reed, should deliver a sermon in the church on that day? Accordingly, he was waited upon a few days in advance but refused the request, giving as an excuse that he was a missionary of the Society for the Propagation of the Gospel in Foreign Parts and would lose his mission if he complied with their request. Since the Safety Committee of New Bern were not impressed by this answer, he was immediately suspended from his ministerial duties in the parish, and the payment of his salary ceased.[17]

Daniel Earl, a clergyman near Edenton, writing to England in August, 1775, described the difficulties under which the ministers labored. He explained that several ministers had been deprived of their salaries by committees and rendered incapable of securing appointments in any of the colonies for their opposition to the general cause of America. As for himself, he declared that he had kept himself clear of censure by speaking only of peace and order and a speedy reconciliation with Great Britain.

The Second North Carolina Provincial Convention met at New Bern on April 3, 1775. A meeting of the Provincial Assembly had been called by Governor Martin at the same place for April 4. This was the last Assembly convened by Governor Martin in North Carolina. Both bodies were made up of practically the same numbers except that the Convention outnumbered the Assembly by about twenty men. On April 2,

Governor Martin issued a proclamation forbidding the meeting of the Convention, but it was without avail. John Harvey was Moderator of the Convention and Speaker of the Assembly. The Assembly became the Convention, or the Convention became the Assembly by the addition or withdrawal of the twenty extra men. One was a legal assembly, the other a revolutionary convention. The Convention at once approved of the association agreement which provided for the nonimportation of goods to England. Representative Thomas McKnight of Currituck County declared that he could not sign on account of particular circumstances in his case.

McKnight was a merchant in debt to merchants in England. If he signed the association it meant that it would be impossible for him to pay his debts to these people. He stated to the members of the Convention that he could not approve of an action collectively that he did not believe in individually. However, he agreed to comply with the nonimportation agreement and to give passive obedience to nonexportation.

The next day the Convention declared that it would accept the substitution of the word *conform to* for *approve*, but when a vote was taken, it was a tie. Next, it was agreed to accept the word *accede*, and a majority voted in McKnight's favor. The minority then announced that unless he would sign exactly as all the others, they would withdraw from the Convention. He then agreed to withdraw to stop dissension and left his colleagues to represent the county. The Convention then voted as follows: "Resolved that if the opinion of this convention that from the disingenious equivocal behavior of the said Thomas McKnight, it is manifest his intentions are inimical to the cause of American Liberty; and we do hold him up as a proper effect of contempt to this continent, and have no future intercourse or dealing with him. Resolved that the above Resolve be published in the Gazettes of this and neighboring colonies."[18]

The other members from Currituck County refused to sign this resolve and were joined in turn by three members from Pasquotank. When they attempted to present their rea-

[18] *Ibid.*, IX, 1184.

sons, the moderator refused to listen, allowed those to sign who were in favor, and closed the journal refusing to allow the dissentients to sign their protest. They withdrew from the Convention and declared that they did not consider themselves or their constituents bound by the proceedings. The members from Currituck County proceeded to condemn the actions of the Convention as extraordinary, rash, and unwarrantable and declared that they felt fully justified in their actions. Here were two instances of merchants driven into Tory ranks on account of their honesty in dealing with their clients and their unwillingness to subscribe to a declaration of which they did not honestly approve.

No act in North Carolina so aroused the people against Great Britain as did the news of the Battle of Lexington. The news reached Chowan County on May 3, 1775, and was immediately forwarded by the committee of that county to Edenton. Thus the news was spread from county to county with scarcely an hour's delay at each stop, until the last rider from the state reached the boundary of South Carolina early in the morning of May 9.[19] It required but six days for the news to travel through ten states from north to south, so well had the committees of safety co-operated with one another. While every effort had been exerted to forward the news southward, the committees were equally urged to disperse copies to all adjoining counties.[20] This news brought home to the people the possibility of conflict in their own colony and the necessity for preparedness. The committees of safety in the various counties began to seize arms and powder within their limits. The Rowan County committee decided that if the owner of powder in their county refused to sell it at a just price, they would seize it, or take the owner into custody to prevent its being sold at a higher price or moved out of the county or sold to the enemy.[21]

William Hewes, Joseph Hewes, and Richard Caswell, who represented North Carolina at the Continental Congress, feeling that their colony was lagging behind the others in measures of

[19] Ibid., IX, 1234.   [20] Ibid., IX, 1237.   [21] Ibid., X, 9.

defense, on June 19, 1775, sent a communication to the various committees of safety in which the committees were censured vigorously for their lack of zeal. They were reminded of all the dangers that confronted them, of the need of military preparation, of the harsh treatment of Boston, and, lastly, of the impending conflict.[22] This appeal to the committees of safety demonstrated how important these committees were considered by the Continental Congress.

The committee of Wilmington was the most active and alert in keeping watch of the movements of suspected persons. On July 3, 1775, they decided to inquire of Allen McDonald, of Cumberland County, in regard to the charge that he intended to raise troops to maintain the ministry against the Americans.[23] Two days later John Thally, of Wilmington, appeared before the committee and disclosed that he had never attempted to alienate any person from his duty in support of the general cause. He was so desirous of being cleared of all suspicion that he requested an advertisement be placed in a public location.[24]

Four days later James Hepburn of Cumberland County, an attorney-at-law, was accused of having attempted to raise a company to act against the American cause. The resolves which were adopted against him illustrated one method of dealing with those who supported the King.

Whereas, this committee hath received information from undoubted sources, that James Hepburn of Cumberland County, Attorney at law, did lately apply to the committee of that county for orders to raise a company under the Militia Law, to preserve the Independence of the subjects, and the dignity of the government, and afterwards disclosed that, had the application met with success the Company intended to fight against the American cause— It is therefore,

Resolved unanimously, the said James Hepburn, is a false, scandalous, and seditious incendiary, who, destitute of property and influence, as he is of principle, basely and traitorously endeavors to make himself conspicuous in favor of tyranny and oppression, in hopes, by violating the primary and fundamental laws of nature and the British Constitution, to raise a fortune up to his family upon the subversion of Liberty, and the destruction of his country.

[22] Ibid., X, 20-23.   [23] Ibid., X, 65.   [24] Ibid., X, 68.

Ordered that this resolve and this preamble upon which it is founded, be published, in order that the Friends of American liberty may avoid all dealings and intercourse with such a wicked and detestable character.[25]

Notices of this kind must have held many true to the patriot cause. A month later Hepburn begged to be restored to the favor of his neighbors. He was required to recant his former sayings and to sign the continental association before being restored.

That the county committees had felt responsible for maintaining order is shown by the action of the committee of Pitt County at this time. Fearful of a Negro uprising, about one hundred men of the county were enrolled in eight companies and given definite parts of the county to watch over; these men were called "Patrolers." They were instructed to shoot one or any number of Negroes who were armed and did not surrender to them, and to shoot any number of Negroes above four who were off their master's plantation and did not submit.[26] Many were caught and scourged daily. Large numbers were sentenced to receive eighty lashes and have their ears cut off. This was carried out in the presence of the committees. The Negroes all confessed to the same thing, namely, that on the night of July 8 they were to kill the family with whom they lived, burn the houses, and retreat to the back country, where they would be received by a large number of people appointed by the British.[27]

The actions of Governor Martin had long since brought him under suspicion, and on learning that he had endeavored to raise the King's Standard, the Committee of Safety of Wilmington on July 10, 1775, resolved that no person should be allowed to communicate with him except by permission of the committee or some other.[28] This action was taken in support of Craven County, which had forbidden all persons to communicate personally or orally with the Governor. The Rowan County committee, suspecting Benjamin Boote of having received letters from Governor Martin inimical to the cause of liberty, de-

[25] *Ibid.*, X, 68.   [26] *Ibid.*, X, 87.
[27] *Ibid.*, X, 95.   [28] *Ibid.*, X, 87.

manded that he come before the committee and produce them. However, when he declined to appear or deliver up the letters, it was decided to guard his house and prevent all food being brought in until he should comply.[29] Thus we see the committee was loath as yet to use violence against an individual even when his guilt seemed most probable.

The Safety Committee of Edenton was on the alert to investigate all strangers, as was shown by their action in regard to two men from New York who left the ship at the entrance of the harbor to proceed to New Bern. The committee wrote to the committee at New Bern to have them secured. The committee at Wilmington was notified to secure them in the event they escaped the vigilance of the committee of New Bern.[30]

The committees were no respecters of persons. The Rowan County committee summoned a Mr. Cook, the Baptist preacher, to appear before them, at which time he recanted most explicitly and in most humiliating terms for having signed a protest against the cause of liberty.[31]

The Safety Committee of Wilmington in July, 1775, learned that Governor Martin intended to raise the people in the back country for the purpose of enforcing the acts of the government. They resolved that as the Governor's going into the back country might be prejudicial to the Province, since he intended to kindle the flames of a civil war, the committees of the different counties should be advised of his intentions and, if possible, should arrest him in his progress.[32] The committees were by this time the most important factors in the Province in watching over and keeping down any opposition against the movement for a redress of their grievances.

James Cotton, a magistrate and a wealthy planter of Anson County, in a statement to Governor Martin on board the sloop *Cruizer* in the Cape Fear River, gave a very accurate account of how the safety committee proceeded in apprehending those unfriendly to the Revolutionary government. In July, 1775,

---

[29] *Ibid.*, X, 93.
[31] *Ibid.*, X, 134.
[30] *Ibid.*, X, 117.
[32] *Ibid.*, X, 124.

about thirty members of the committee of Anson County met at the courthouse and sent for Cotton. Upon his arrival the resolves of the Continental Congress were read to him, and he was given two weeks in which to consider the matter. At the expiration of the two weeks David Love, armed with a rifle, entered Cotton's bedroom early in the morning; he informed Cotton that he had a company waiting outside and that they were determined to take him to the safety committee at Mack's ferry on the Pee Dee. Cotton arose, left his wife in bed, looked out of the window, and recognized many of the company who had come to carry him away. When they had traveled about five miles, the prisoner treated the company to rum and later to plenty of cider.

At this time Cotton escaped from his jailors and returned home. He obtained arms and that night slept in the woods. After sleeping out several nights he found a refuge with Governor Martin aboard the sloop *Cruizer*. A reward was offered for anyone who would capture him and bring him before the committee. Not being able to capture him, the Patriots laid waste his cornfields and informed him that they would burn his house and mill, drive away his Negroes and stock, and not permit him to remain with his family.[33]

Here was a man torn from his family and obliged to seek refuge in the woods and finally to flee to the King's officer for protection, almost a year before independence was declared. Cotton reconsidered and in less than a week asked to be permitted to sign the association. The Committee of Safety of Wilmington thought his case too important for them to decide upon, and he together with Samuel and Jacob Williams, who had also acted against the liberties of America, was taken before the Provincial Congress, which was in session at Hillsboro. All three recanted their former principles and were set at liberty.[34]

Governor Martin recognized the importance of these committees, for on August 2, 1775, the committee at New Bern received a letter from him explaining the charge that he had attempted to bring about a slave insurrection. He denied that

[33] *Ibid.*, X, 127-129.   [34] *Ibid.*, X, 182.

he had ever conceived a thought of that nature, and then added: "I will further add my opinion that nothing could ever justify the design, falsely imputed of me of giving encouragement to the negroes but the actual and declared rebellion of the King's subjects and the failure of all other means to maintain the King's government."[35] This acknowledgment by Governor Martin that a cause might arise which would justify such an act brought forth a stinging rebuke from the committee.

Whenever the county or town committees had cases which they thought important, they left the trial to the Provincial Congress. As a result, several men were confined in the jail at Wilmington. Most of these were offenders against the association. The Provincial Congress voted to send a guard to convey all such offenders to Hillsboro for trial.

The committees in the various states co-operated; for example, Frances Dunn and Benjamin Boote were sent to South Carolina for safekeeping and were confined to the jail in Charleston. North Carolina promised to render a similar service to her sister state and at the same time to reimburse South Carolina for the expense of detaining the prisoners.

As early as the summer of 1775, friendliness for a British colonial official was sufficient to cause one to be suspected of Toryism. Governor Martin, aboard his man-of-war in Wilmington harbor, still considered Farquard Campbell, a member of the Congress at Hillsboro, a friend. His secretary petitioned the Provincial Congress to give safe conduct for the removal of the Governor's horse and coach to the home of Farquard Campbell in Cumberland County. This request of the Governor proved embarrassing to Campbell, since some suspected him of Toryism.[36] Congress, however, absolved him of all suspicion. Yet in a few weeks he was to declare himself for the King. He was one of the many who were unwilling to go to the extremities of war.

The third Provincial Congress was summoned by Samuel Johnston, the leading Patriot of Chowan County, and met at

[35] *Ibid.*, X, 138.   [36] *Ibid.*, X, 191.

Hillsboro on August 20, 1775. All the counties and towns that were eligible to do so sent representatives. A despatch was sent to the Reverend George Micklejohn requesting that he attend and conduct divine service, and he did by reading prayers in the church at Hillsboro. Micklejohn was the same Tory sympathizer who had aided the Regulators. Strange, indeed, must have been his thoughts when called upon to act in this capacity. The first act of Congress was to appoint a committee of forty-one members to inquire into the conduct of one John Coulsen, who had been brought to Hillsboro so that his case might be tried by Congress. The next act was to appoint a committee to win over to the side of the Congress the Regulators who had been engaged in the late insurrection. Maurice Moore, the first member named on the committee, had been one of the justices at the court when they were tried. Richard Caswell had been among the leaders of the forces sent out to subdue them, while the Reverend Mr. Patillo had denounced them in scathing terms from his pulpit. Yet these men were a part of the committee which was supposed to win their loyalty. Doubtless it was intended that the Reverend Mr. Patillo should release them from their oath to the King, which Caswell had rammed down their throats with the bayonet.

On August 24, 1775, the Provincial Congress at Hillsboro appointed a committee

For the purpose of preparing a plan for the regulation of internal peace, order, and safety of this province, and making such an arrangement in the civil policy of this province as may tend to supply in some measure the defect of executive powers of government arising from the absence of His Excellency Governor Martin and that this committee take into consideration the proprietory of appointment of a Committee of Safety, the members to compose it, qualifications of electors and elected, the number of which these shall consist, the power of these committees, also the mode to be observed in calling Provincial Conventions, the time of election, place to be held, qualifications of electors and elected, the number which every town and county are to send as delegated to represent them in such a convention, the powers which this convention are to exercise, and further to report the necessity, if there be any, of forming other committees than before mentioned and every civil power necessary to be formed in order to relieve the province in the present unhappy state to which administration has reduced it.[37]

On September 9 this committee brought in the report to the Provincial Congress. It recommended that a committee of thirteen members be chosen—one to be elected for the Province at large by the Provincial Congress, and two from each of the six military districts. This group was to be styled the provincial council. This provincial council has been called the most important committee ever appointed by popular authority in North Carolina. It possessed supreme executive control during the recess of Congress.

The method devised by the provincial council for controlling the inhabitants by means of committees of safety was a most effective one. Committees of safety for the districts were composed of a president and twelve members who were authorized to sit in the principal towns in each district and receive information which they transmitted to the provincial council. The district committee possessed appellate power over county and town committees of safety which were elected by the freeholders of each county and town. The committee of safety of the district also had power to examine all suspected persons; to arrest, to imprison, and to punish; to prevent persons in debt from absconding; to compel others to pay their debts; and to take special care that the public interest suffered no detriment.[38]

The county committees had grown very powerful in their first year, hence the feeling of the Provincial Congress that their power must be curbed. Their violence and harshness had often angered the better element of the Whigs, who had come to feel that in converting recalcitrant Tories there were other means more effective than tar and feathers. The power which the county committee had exercised of compelling debtors who were suspected of a design to leave the colony to post a bond for their security was limited to debts of £20 and less. The more important cases were to come before the district committees.[39]

[37] *Ibid.*, X, 175-176.   [38] *Ibid.*, X, 208.   [39] *Ibid.*, X, 208.

The town and county committees were left in much the same condition as before the selection of the provincial council except for one important new arrangement. To be a committee-man or to vote for one, it was now necessary to be a freeholder, and the number of committeemen for the county was limited to twenty-one. The towns of Edenton and Wilmington were each allowed a committee of fifteen members; six other towns were allowed seven each.[40] In the autumn of 1775 there were functioning under the authority of the people in North Carolina, a provincial council of thirteen members, six district committees of twenty-one each, three town committees of fifteen each, and six town committees of seven each, making a grand total of nine hundred and thirty-four civil officers.

This move on the part of the committees to restrict suffrage to freeholders was a shrewd one. Under the old qualifications for voting, the Highlanders and Tories had elected officers of doubtful patriotism.[41] By this move were disfranchised many of the poor Highlanders of Cumberland County, who ordinarily would have voted as asked by some wealthy Tory Highlander; thus the Whigs gained control at the elections.[42]

The inhabitants of the counties carved out of Lord Granville's territory were given the franchise if they actually possessed land except by leases, even though they had not been able to acquire legal title of freehold to their land.[43]

The importance of these committees can scarcely be over-estimated. The Continental and Provincial Congresses made resolves, but it was the various committees that enforced them. They administered the oath and enforced the association against trading with Great Britain. It was within their powers to perform the acts and express opinions which made a man a Patriot or a Loyalist. To them, also, it was allowed to determine and to administer punishment. To follow through the activities of these committees in this period is to view the governmental machinery of the colony. So interwoven was their work with

[40] *Ibid.*, X, 212.
[41] Previously a large number of people had voted under the name of inhabitants who were not freeholders.
[42] Jones, *op. cit.*   [43] *Col. Rec. of N. C.*, X, 211.

that of the Provincial Congresses and committees of safety for the state that it is impossible to treat either separately. They had the responsibility, which in some counties was of paramount importance, of carrying out the resolutions of Congress in regard to the Loyalists. They decided who were guilty and innocent, and fixed their punishment. A study of their activities confirms the statement that the Revolution in North Carolina was largely a civil war.

During the latter part of 1775 there was scarcely a meeting of the Committee of Safety of Rowan County when one or more individuals were not brought up for having said or done something derogatory towards the association or the just rights of the Americans. Usually they recanted and signed the association and were allowed to go free.[44]

This was equally true of the Committee of Safety of Wilmington. Early in 1776 Dr. Fallon aroused the ire of this committee by an article put up to public view under the courthouse, in which he cast false and scandalous reflections on its members in an endeavor to inflame the minds of the people. In addition, the article contained an illiberal and groundless charge against one of the high officials of the colony. Upon his refusal to give security for his good behavior to the sum of £500 proclamation money, he was removed to jail.[45] There was some disadvantage to the public in having a prominent doctor in jail; consequently, on January 18, John Ashe, the foremost Patriot, asked that the doctor be allowed to attend his family.

When the provincial council met at New Bern in February 1776, they at once considered the charge against William Bourk of that city who had admitted that he hoped the Americans would be subdued and who added further that he wished it

[44] *Ibid.*, X, 253, 262, 280.
[45] "Resolved that Dr. Fallon be continued under guard for the present time, and that Colonel Moore be requested to refuse admittance to any person but such as he or the officers on guard may think proper; and that Dr Fallon be not precluded from the use of pen and ink and paper, but that when the officer of the guard may think he has any letters to send out and requests admittance for any particular person, that person be admitted for so long a time as the officer may think proper" (*ibid.*, X, 412).

would happen that instant. He was at once jailed at Halifax.[46] John Stronge, who informed on Bourk, was ordered two days later under a bond of £500 to depart from the colony with his sloop *King Fisher*. The charge against him was that he had imported goods contrary to the association.

As the feelings of the colony became more bitter, more stringent efforts were used to secure the conviction of the disloyal. When Farguard Campbell was brought before the provincial council in March, 1776, and nothing could be proved against him, he was released but not discharged. He was required to appear before the council, at which time Captain Robert Roman was empowered to enforce the attendance of such witnesses as he might think had evidence against Campbell. This council resolved that all persons should be disarmed by the town and county committees, and other suspected persons who had not taken up arms should take an oath not to aid the enemies of America or else be imprisoned.[47]

The next provincial council in April had the opportunity of dealing with many of the prisoners taken at the Battle of Moore's Creek. On April 5, 1776, General McDonald, who was in jail at Halifax, was admitted to parole under the following conditions.

That he does not go without the limits of the town of Halifax. That he does not directly or indirectly while a prisoner correspond with any person or persons who are or may be in opposition to American measures, or by any manner of means convey to them intelligence of any sort. That he take no draft nor procure them to be taken by anyone else of any place or places in which they might be, while upon his parole, that shall now or may hereafter give information to our enemies which can be injurious to us, or the common cause of America; but that without equivocation, mental evasion, or secret reservation, he pay the most exact and careful attention to the intent and meaning of these conditions, according to the rules and regulation of war; and that he every day appear between the hours of ten and twelve o'clock to the officer of the guard.[48]

This standard form of parole for captured Tory officers was also administered to Colonel Allen McDonald on April 11.

[46] *Ibid.*, X, 471.   [47] *Ibid.*, X, 476.   [48] *Ibid.*, X, 548-549.

Having won the Battle of Moore's Creek and feeling that the Tories had been conquered, the Provincial Congress, which was in session in April, 1776, believed that it could adopt more generous measures towards them. Accordingly, on April 29, a declaration was set forth which justified the past harsh measures which had been taken but announced a more lenient policy for the future. The prisoners had been sent into other colonies where their influence would be of less importance in harming the cause of liberty. They were blamed for their disloyalty to the colony which had poured riches into their laps and treated them liberally. Now even though subdued, they were declared to be unrepentant and only waiting for the assistance of the enemy to drench the Province in blood again. The action of Congress was justified in the following proclamation:

These have been our motives for exercising a severity with regard to the common safety, and that the first principle of nature, self-preservation prompted. Justice demanded it in our hands, and in the anguish of our hearts we lament the sad necessity which the frailities of our beings have alloted to our share; still we wish the reformation of those who in this unhappy state are severed from us, and from those endearing ties which nature and social connection have formed for them, and who still remain amongst them. To them we administer this consolation, that they rest assured that no wanton acts of cruelties, no severity shall be exercised towards the prisoners; nor restraints imposed on them, but what shall be necessary to prevent them from using their liberty to the injury of the friends of America.[49]

The resolution continued to wish for the redemption of the erring. Those left behind were then assured of good treatment, but warned that their conduct would largely determine the treatment which would be meted out to those in confinement. Had previous promises been kept, much suffering might have been prevented on both sides.

Before adjournment, the Provincial Congress of April 4, 1776, named a committee to inquire into the conduct of the insurgents and other suspected persons. This committee met April 20, 1776, to inquire into the charges against the prisoners

[49] *Ibid.*, X, 548.

in Halifax and from their observations divided them into four different denominations: (1) prisoners who had served in Congress, (2) prisoners who had signed tests or associations, (3) prisoners who had been under arms without such circumstances, and (4) prisoners under suspicious circumstances.[50]

The Council of Safety for the whole state of North Carolina met at Wilmington, June 5, 1776. This council was established by the Provincial Congress in May, 1776, and was to perform the work formerly done by the provincial council and the committees of safety.[51] On the second day it was voted that all the people in Bladen County who had participated in the late insurrection and who were hiding out for fear of capture should be permitted to return home, provided they would take an oath to submit to such regulations as should establish the government

[50] Under the first category came Farquard Campbell, Thomas Rutherford, Alexander McKay, and James Hepburn. The first two had served in the Congress which had appointed the committee.

Under the second came Alexander Legate, who had not only signed the test but also acted as a member on the committee for Bladen County; in spite of this he took up arms and fought at Cross Creek; and also in this group was Mathia Sapenfield.

Under the third came Alexander McDonald, Alexander Morrison, Alexander McDonald son of Kingsborough, James McDonald, Alexander McLeod, Murdock McAskell, Alexander McLeod, Jacob Pope, Angus McDonald, Neill McArthur, Francis Frazier, Samuel Snead, Lewis Lowery, James Mews, John McLeod, Thomas Wier, John McLinzie, John Milkson, Morris Nowland, Nathaniel Stead, William John Smith, William Garner, Kenneth McDonald, Aaron Verdie Murdock McLeod, D'Arcy Fowler, Donald McLeod, Norman McLeod, John McLeod, Archibald McEchern, Roy McKinnen, Donald McLeod, Loughlin McKinnen, Thomas Bradford, James Munroe, Donald Morrison, John McLeod, Donald Stuart, Seymore York, William Draper, Matthias Sappingfield, Samuel Diviney, Stephen Lisney, William Shannon, Frederick Craft, William Field, Jeremiah Field, Robert Field, Joseph Field, Robert Turner, William Armfield, Stephen Parker, Allen McDonald, John Bethune, John Piles, Jr., William Parker, Thomas Bradford, David Jackson, Enoch Bradley, John Downing, Duncan Sinclair, Robinson Yorke, Daniel McDaniel, Alexander McRaw, John Simmons, Kenneth Stuart, Colin McIver, John Dowak, Joseph Dobson, Michael Holt, James Low, Robert Adams, Alexander McLaine, Thomas Collins, George Mylue, Angus Campbell, Alexander Stuart, William Austin, James Thomas, Hugh McDonald, John McDonald, Daniel Cumerson, Daniel McLeon.

Under the fourth came George Mylue, Conner Dowd, Petter Hay, Robert Gillies, and Malcolm McNeill. The above-named men were all prisoners in the Halifax jail (*ibid.*, X, 594, 603).

[51] Bessie Lewis Whitaker, "The Provincial Council and Committtee of Safety in North Carolina," *James Sprunt Historical Monograph* (Chapel Hill, 1908), No. 8, p. 19.

of the colony and would promise to take up arms for the defense of the colony and the cause of independence.

Much of the time of the council was consumed in maintaining order within the state and taking care of accused persons. On June 15, William Maxwell, Colin Campbell, and Donald Campbell were placed in jail at New Bern for having corresponded with the enemy; others were placed in jail at Halifax, while Andrew Wilson and Thomas Erskine were placed on parole not to leave the limits of the town.[52] Sometimes the charges against a person were general, as in the case of James Emory, who was accused of using practices which tended to inflame the minds of the people of Craven County and to prevent the militia from turning out in defense of the Province. He was compelled to move from his residence in New Bern to Dobbs County and to remain there two months. After that time he was allowed to return on giving bond for his good behavior.[53]

The safety committees of the various counties worked in harmony with each other. The committee of Tryon County sent one of their disaffected to the committee of Rowan County for safekeeping, and he was lodged in the Salisbury jail. The members of these committees who were given the task of apprehending those who might differ with them in political belief were sometimes men of little education, as was shown by the paper which accompanied the prisoners at the time. This paper signed by John Walker, James McEntire, George Black, and James Cook was written in the following manner:

Gentlemen of the Community of Rowan County,

With these we send under guard Ambrous Mills one of the greatest Enemys of our pese in Tryon County a companion of Robinson, and been lying out in the mountens since before the South Carolina Campaign; has held a Coraspondence with Camron, has acknowledged himself to have been in the Indian Nations, he Seems Simple but is Subtile and Insinuating to and has had influence enough to pradgudise not only his neighbors but many at a great distance against the cause of American liberty. In Short his character is so netorious that we expact that every gentleman in Rowan is ac-

[52] *Col. Rec. of N. C.*, X, 631.   [53] *Ibid.*, X, 672.

quainted with it and we hope that he will be confined till he has had a Fare Tryell in every article above mentioned, and a great deal more can be proved against him when required. For further particulars Inquire of Captain Cook, Commander of this guard for fear of a Risque we will not inform you of our own circumstances but hope that Mr. Cook will think to inform you.[54]

From August 25, 1774, to November 12, 1776, North Carolina was governed by provincial councils and committees of public safety. It was indeed revolutionary government, for North Carolina had no constitution. The men who were prominent in the provincial councils and the councils of safety also made up the Constitutional Convention which gave North Carolina a legal government. The training which they received during this period was a valuable asset to them in the administration of the new government.

[54] *Ibid.,* X, 609-610.

CHAPTER IV

MILITARY ACTIVITIES OF THE LOYALISTS IN THE EARLY PART OF THE REVOLUTION

In Governor Martin, the Tories of North Carolina possessed a leader whose efforts for his King were not exceeded by those of any other colonial governor in America. Although compelled to take refuge on the sloop-of-war *Cruizer* in the harbor of Wilmington in July, 1775, from this safe refuge he was able to guide the activities of his loyal subjects on shore during the early part of the Revolution.

Martin's position at this time was not an enviable one. He, without an army or guns, had sent his wife and family to New York City for their safety. The ship on which he took refuge became a veritable prison. His fiery proclamations were ignored, and his messages to the interior were intercepted. Congresses, conventions, and committees daily usurped his power, while he remained powerless to act.

The sentiment of the public, however, was divided. He found ardent supporters among the recently arrived Scotch immigrants. These late arrivals were influenced by those of their countrymen who had come over earlier and who were people of rank and property.[1]

A year before the Declaration of Independence, these Scotch leaders and others visited Governor Martin on board his ship and planned the defense of the colony. One of the most active of these men was Colonel James Cotton, surveyor for the county of Anson, and one of the most intelligent citizens of the county. With his wealth and fine manners, he had great influence in winning the people over to the support of the Royal Government, and large numbers in Anson County at this time signed a protest against the proceedings of the Continental Congress.

[1] Caruthers, *Interesting Revolutionary Incidents: and Sketches of Character, Chiefly in the Old North State*, p. 51.

Colonel Cotton was highly approved by Governor Martin, who gave him every encouragement.[2] At the same time Colonel Spencer of the Anson County Militia was urging the people of the county to sign the association. Later he was named captain general by the safety committee. This action of Colonel Spencer's was as heartily denounced by Governor Martin as the action of Cotton had been commended. The Loyalists were further encouraged by news that the rebellion in New England had been put down.

That the Patriots were not unaware of the activities of James Cotton and other Tories may be seen from the depositions of those people who were forced to seek refuge with Governor Martin aboard H.M.S. *Cruizer* in the Cape Fear River.[3] In the first of the depositions Samuel Williams, who had brought a petition to Governor Martin early in July, declared that on his return he spent only one night at home and then proceeded to Kingsborough to deliver a message to McDonald. He brought word from Governor Martin of the success of the British at Boston, which so angered the Patriots that they decided to kill him. At Kingsborough he received a message from his wife that about thirty men with guns and other weapons had entered his house in search of him. Meetings were held at the homes of the famous Tories, and while Williams was attending a meeting at the house of McCaskets, about two hundred armed men came to capture him, the greater part of whom came from South Carolina. He concealed himself near the road and saw them carry away Wilson Williams, whom they afterwards compelled to swear allegiance to the colony.

At this time Governor Martin felt that he had the support of a large number of counties in the interior. In March, 1775, a group of four counties, Surry, Rowan, Anson, and Guilford, extending from Virginia on the north to South Carolina on the south, had assured him of their loyalty. Samuel Bryan and one hundred and ninety-four Loyalists had sent him a statement of

<hr>

[2] Force (ed.), *American Archives*, pp. 75, 111.
[3] These depositions taken from B.P.R.O. American and West Indies, North Carolina No. 222, are to be found in *Col. Rec. of N. C.*, X, 125-129.

loyalty in behalf of themselves and many others of Guilford and Anson counties. The inhabitants of Guilford felt that they were especially under suspicion because of the late Regulator insurrection in their county and took this opportunity to declare their support of the Royal Government.[4]

The Tories of Anson County had declared not only their loyalty to the King but also their detestation of those who were opposing him both in North Carolina and in other colonies. They especially singled out Massachusetts as an object of their detestation. If Governor Martin was misled by these promises to believe that he had the support of a larger group than was true, we should blame the people who failed in their promises rather than him who trusted them.[5]

At the time of receiving these assurances of loyalty Governor Martin had written to the Earl of Dartmouth that the people in some parts of the colony were beginning to open their eyes to the artifices and delusions which had misled'them.[6] The Earl was so pleased when he received the news of the loyalty of these counties that he thought this sentiment ought to be encouraged. He ordered Governor Martin to inform these people that His Majesty was greatly pleased at their testimony of loyalty and that a proclamation of general pardon would be extended to all the insurgents who had participated in the War of the Regulation, Herman Husband alone excepted.[7] If actual fighting should come, Governor Martin was instructed to grant to the leading gentlemen commissions suitable to their rank, and every other encouragement which was generally offered to soldiers.

In October a letter was received from the Earl of Dartmouth with a promise that, if possible, ten thousand stands of arms

[4] Ibid., X, 1161.

[5] It was the general opinion in England in the autumn of 1775 that a respectable naval and military force sent to North Carolina would not only enable Governor Martin to recover his own colony but would also be the means of regaining control of the whole South.

[6] Col. Rec. of N. C., IX, 1166-1168.

[7] Francis L. Hawks, David L. Swain, and William A. Graham, A Revolutionary History of North Carolina, in Three Lectures, comp. William D. Cooke (Raleigh, 1853), pp. 111 f.; Col. Rec. of N. C., X, 1241.

and a large number of light field pieces would be sent to North Carolina, and a complete battalion under an able and intelligent officer would be sent to Cape Fear. In reply to this letter, Governor Martin promised his full support, but added that seven months had elapsed since his first appeal for aid, and he had not received the shadow of support; while, on the other hand, the spirit of disaffection had been very busy.[8]

Later in the month information came that seven regiments of troops would embark from Cork about December 1. These troops were to be commanded by one of General Howe's officers, but Governor Martin was assured that he would be placed in command of any provincial corps that might be formed at this time. Governor Martin was to receive the pay of a British colonel, but was not to be entitled to rank in the army or a claim to half pay,[9] since he had sold his commission in the British Army some years before, and to restore it to him would be an injustice to the other officers.

Having decided to send an army to North Carolina, the British discovered that the entrance to the Cape Fear River was too shallow to allow the ships of war to give the landing troops sufficient protection. Hence, the Earl of Dartmouth desired assurance from Governor Martin that their landing would be immediately supported by such a number of loyal inhabitants as would assure them of success.[10] The Governor was again reminded that only upon his recommendation and that of the other Southern governors was this attempt being made. He was further instructed that in view of all that had been said, if he was still of the opinion that success could be obtained, he should "Lose no time in sending emissaries amongst the Inhabitants of the well-disposed Counties with Authority and Commissions to the principal persons of trust and confidence for raising and embodying as many men as could be procured, and informing of His Majesty's intention of supplying them with Arms and giving them the same pay as the Regular troops, as soon as they come down which they should

[8] *Col. Rec. of N. C.*, X, 267.
[9] *Ibid.*, X, 299.   [10] *Ibid.*, X, 307.

be encouraged to do as soon as they hear of the arrival of the troops upon the coast, bringing down with them horses and wagons for the use of the army, for which they will be very liberally paid and rewarded."

These men were to be assured that they would not be obliged to serve out of the Province without their consent or beyond the time of the present trouble. As a further inducement it was suggested that all arrears of quit rents be cancelled, that grants of land be made to each according to his rank and merit, and that all quit rents be exempted for twenty years from the date of the grant.[11] In a communication to General Howe which informed him of the plans for the Southern colonies, it was noted that, even if the expedition failed, it would be in no wise weakening to the operation in the north, as the army could be posted in the Southern Provinces with security, and when the time arrived for them to join the forces in the north, this junction could be made in a shorter time than from England.[12]

Scottish emigrants, who were readily won over to the royal cause by the Governor, continued to arrive from their native land during these troublesome times. They asked for permission to settle on the vacant lands of the Crown. Governor Martin was the more willing to grant their request because he could not prevent them if he would, and by making the grant he won them more firmly to the side of the government. One hundred and thirty-six came over, all but five of whom were laborers. During October and November, 1775, over three hundred came. They declared their loyalty and attachment to the King, and promised, if need be, to lay down their lives in defense of His Majesty's Government.[13] The Scotch Highlanders, in general, were at this time thought to be loyal, and together with the other well-affected were believed by Governor Martin greatly to outnumber the rebels in all the populous western counties.

On January 9, 1776, Maurice Moore wrote to Governor

---

[11] *Ibid.*, X, 308. [12] *Ibid.*, X, 314.
[13] P.R.O. Treasury, Class 47, Bundle 12.

Martin and suggested that he call an assembly and give the people of North Carolina a chance to submit to government and enjoy the political condition that had existed in 1763.[14] On the next day Governor Martin issued a proclamation in which he summoned all loyal subjects to repair to the Royal Standard. They were promised forgiveness for all past offenses, even for having taken up arms.[15] Governor Martin's action showed how ignorant he was of the real feelings of the people and the progress of the Revolution. Three days later he wrote the Earl of Dartmouth that he had received late information from interior parts of the Province that the Regulators to the number of between two and three thousand men would join the King's Standard whenever called upon. Encouraged by this report and by the loyalty of the people of Brunswick County and other back counties, together with the activity of the King's supporters in the upper parts of South Carolina, Governor Martin determined to make use of this strength to put down the "unnatural" rebellion. This uprising was now timed to coincide with the arrival of the officers and troops which were promised by the Earl of Dartmouth, and which would make victory all the more certain.[16]

Great was Governor Martin's amazement when he learned that the troops had been delayed a month in leaving England. He had given orders for the raising of the Royal Standard, and so difficult was communication with the interior that he could not change the orders, even though the troops would not arrive on schedule. He feared that the rebels, having intercepted some of his messengers, were in possession of the names of the Tories who had been given commissions, and that they would be seized by the committees and the movement crushed in its inception.[17] Encouraged by the report from his agent MacLean that two or three thousand men, half of them well-armed, were ready to advance, he decided that it was best to proceed. While his emissaries hastened into the back country to contact the leaders in the movement, Governor Martin made

[14] *Col. Rec. of N. C.*, X, 396.   [15] *Ibid.*, X, 397.
[16] *Ibid.*, X, 407.   [17] *Ibid.*, X, 489.

ready for their reception at Wilmington. He was again heart
ened by a messenger from MacLean, who reported that th
Loyalists, in high spirits, were fast collecting, would be si
thousand strong, were well furnished with wagons and horses
and at the latest would be in possession of Wilmington b
February 25, 1776.

Meantime, Governor Martin sent commissions by his emis
saries to his leaders in the back country.[18] These men wer
authorized to raise the King's Standard and to muster an arm
and to array in arms the loyal subjects in their several counties
In addition, they were permitted to issue commissions to an
whom they thought deserving. Governor Martin must hav
been in error in regard to the sentiments of some of the mer
whom he chose for officers, for Barringer and the two Hawkins
later were Whigs and did not accept the commissions.[19] Hol
and Hunter deserted the Loyalist cause and took the oath o
allegiance to the colonies. In making up his list of officer
Governor Martin chose many who had been prominent a
Regulators, however, and the loyalty of such men as the Field
brothers proved that his confidence was not misplaced.

Donald McDonald held the highest office, that of brigadie
general. Alexander McLeod was second in command with th
rank of colonel. The highest commission which it was in th
power of the Governor to grant was issued to Allan McDonal
of Kingsborough, who was made a major. He had come t
America in 1775 and settled in Kingsborough with his cele
brated wife, Flora, and one son.[20] Their son, John McDonald

[18] Allen McDonald, Donald McDonald, Alexander McLeod, Allen Stew
art, William Campbell, Alexander McDonald and Neal McArthur, esquire
of the counties of Cumberland and Anson; John Pile, esquire of the count
of Chatham; William Fields, James Hunter, Robert Fields, Jeremiah Field
and Saymore, esquires of the county of Orange; Paul Barringer of th
county of Mecklenburg; William Spurian, William Bryan, Samuel Bryar
and Matthias Sappingfield, esquires of the county of Rowan; Gideon Wrigh
and James Glyn, esquires of the county of Surry, and Philomen Hawkin
senior, and Philomen Hawkins, junior, esquires of the county of Bu
(Force, ed., *American Archives*, IV, 981).

[19] Ashe, *op. cit.*, I, 497; John H. Wheeler, *Historical Sketches of Nort
Carolina from 1584 to 1851* (2 vols.; Philadelphia, 1851), I, 67, 426.

[20] Hawks, Swain, and Graham, *op. cit.*, p. 116.

was made captain; Caruthers in his *Old North State* observes
that Captain Alexander McLeod was probably the son-in-law
of Allan and Flora. McDonald and McLeod had come down
from New England to Edenton in July, 1775, where their
mission was suspected. The Committee of Safety at Edenton
at that time warned the committee at New Bern of their
approach.[21] The *Gentlemen's Magazine* for June, 1776, announced that toward the close of 1775 two Scotch officers,
McDonald and McLeod, passed through New Bern: "They
were suspected of some sinister designs and questioned by the
provincials concerning their business. They pretended they were
officers who were wounded at Bunker Hill and left the army
with a desire to settle among their friends."

The influence of these officers, who were much respected by
the common people, doubtless turned many to the side of the
King.[22] When these two men received their commissions, the
Patriots knew they had been correct in their suspicions, that the
two men had been sent from Boston under the orders of General Gage to raise Highlanders to aid the English.[23] It was,
perhaps, to counteract the influence of these men that the Provincial Congress in session at Hillsboro on August 23, 1775,
resolved to send McLaine, McAllister, Farquard Campbell,
Rowan, Thomas Wade, Alex McKay, John Ashe, Spencer,
Gibson, Kinnon, and Hepburn as a committee to the newly
arrived Highlanders to explain to them the nature of the conflict with Great Britain, and to urge them to unite with the other
inhabitants of America in defense of their rights.

A manifesto issued by Donald McDonald was intended to
secure recruits for the government and at the same time to
assure the population in general that it was in no danger. This
document read as follows:

Whereas the powers and authority have been invested in me to
array in arms His Majesty's loyal subjects in this province. I hereby
command all His Majesty's loyal people to repair to the royal banner
agreeable to the Governor's Royal Proclamation of date the 10th

[21] *Col. Rec. of N. C.*, X, 116.
[22] Caruthers, *The Old North State in 1776, First Series*, p. 58.
[23] *Col. Rec. of N. C.*, X, 325.

day of January last, I do hereby declare it my intention, that no violation whatever shall be suffered to women, children or private property, to sully the arms of Britons or free men employed in the glorious and righteous duty of rescuing and delivering this country from the usurpation of rebellion, and that no cruelty whatever be offered against the laws of humanity, but what resistance shall make necessary; and that whatever provisions and other necessaries be taken for the troops shall be paid for immediately; and in case, any persons or person shall offer the least violence to the families of such as will join the royal standard, such persons or person may depend that retaliation will be made; the horrors of such proceedings, it is hoped will be avoided by all true Christians.[24]

This manifesto was dated February 5, 1776, and already the men were beginning to gather.

When the Committee of Safety for the District of New Bern met on February 10, it was informed that a number of men from the counties of Cumberland, Anson, Bladen, and Guilford under the command of Fields and Herman had begun hostilities against the Patriots, and on February 5 had begun their march to Cross Creek, from which place they planned to march to Wilmington. These counties comprised a compact unit of about twice their present area and extended from Virginia through the center of the state nearly to Wilmington.[25] It was also reported to the committee that the Governor's proclamation authorized this body of troops to force the Sons of Liberty to join them or have them executed as rebels.[26] This news so aroused the committee that it was resolved that in order to frustrate this plan of the King's supporters, Colonel Richard Caswell should march immediately with his forces to join those who might come from other parts of the Province.[27] Each side was attempting to intimidate the other, and many were afraid to join the Tories and were equally afraid not to.

Thomas Rutherford, colonel of the Cumberland County

[24] *Ibid.*, X, 443.

[25] This region, bordered by the Cape Fear and Haw rivers on the east and the Yadkin on the west, was populated mainly by Regulators and Highlanders and remained loyal to the King.   [26] *Col. Rec. of N. C.*, X, 444.

[27] Dobbs, Johnston, Craven, and Pitt counties were especially urged to raise as many of the militia as might be necessary to join the minute men under Caswell's command.

Militia and a prominent Loyalist, called a muster of the county at Cross Creek on February 12. So many failed to appear, and those who did come showed such fear, that the next day he issued a manifesto declaring that if His Majesty's faithful subjects of Cumberland County did not repair to the King's Standard at Cross Creek on or before February 16 prepared to join the King's army, they must expect to suffer the consequences of rebellion and the just resentment of their King.

Meanwhile, the Patriots were busy in all parts of the Province. In the west they collected at Charlotte, Salisbury, and Hillsboro. Colonel Ashe of New Hanover County was reported at the same time en route to Cross Creek with two thousand men to fight the Regulars. In Dobbs County he was joined by the colonel from Craven County with his thousand minute men and militia. A like number under Colonel Ashe set out from New Hanover County. New Hanover and Craven counties were east from Bladen County and on the coast. While these two counties contained some Loyalists, they were predominantly patriotic. Surry and Guilford counties furnished men for both sides. In the former the Patriots were able to prevent the Loyalists from marching. In Guilford County a skirmish ensued between the two groups, in which Captain Dent, the leader of the Patriots, was killed. He was perhaps the first North Carolinian killed in the contest.[28]

Messages were exchanged by General McDonald and Colonel Moore in which each set forth to the other the terms of surrender and the justness of his cause. General Moore, to gain time, promised a more particular answer to follow his first reply. In his second communication General Moore pointed out the impossibility of Tory success and reminded McDonald of the oath which he and some of his officers had taken at New Bern on their entry into the country, an oath which, he thought, they would find difficult to reconcile to their present conduct.[29]

General McDonald found himself in command of a group of men, many of whom were lacking in discipline. Stedman, a

[28] *Col. Rec. of N. C.*, X, 560, 599.
[29] Hawks, Swain, and Graham, *op. cit.*, Appendix.

British author, attributes the failure of the Tories at this time to the lack of co-operation among their leaders. The older militia officers were jealous of the Scotch newcomers. Some became so dissatisfied that they left and joined the Whigs. Others deserted the Loyalists on account of the deception of their leaders. In answer to the royal summons they had come from Anson, Chatham, Guilford, Rowan, Bladen, and Orange counties. Their number was estimated at between thirty-five hundred and five thousand. They had been told that Governor Martin with one thousand Regulars was already at Cross Creek. This town, located on the Cape Fear River in southeastern Cumberland County, had been chosen as the meeting place for the Loyalists. When they found that Governor Martin was not there, they lost confidence in their leaders and many returned to their homes.[30]

On February 18 the Loyalists started out from Cross Creek toward Wilmington. The army marched four miles the first day and encamped for the night. The next day it was promised that they would attack General Moore's provincial army at Rockfish only four miles distant. At this news, two companies of Colonel Cotton's corps under the leadership of Captain Sneed deserted the cause. No engagements took place, but on the nineteenth news reached General McDonald that Moore was about to be joined by a force of six hundred men under Colonel Caswell. Upon receiving this intelligence McDonald decided to move at once in order to prevent this juncture of the enemy. He was unable to overtake Caswell and slowly continued his march toward Wilmington. On February 26 the Loyalists had traveled forty-one miles and reached Moore's Creek Bridge on the Cape Fear. Here they found their path blocked by Caswell and Lillington, who had thrown up entrenchments surmounted by cannons. A council of war was held to determine the course of action. The older and more experienced officers decided that to attack such a strong position without artillery and with untrained men was foolhardy. The younger element were for attack, and by accusing the others of

[30] Ashe, op. cit., I, 501; Col. Rec. of N. C., X, 491.

cowardice they gained their way, and an attack was planned for the next morning.[31]

Since General McDonald was ill, the command fell upon Colonel McLeod. The Whigs were led by Colonel Caswell and Colonel Lillington, and it is a moot question among North Carolina historians as to who was actually in command.[32] The battle was short and decisive. In the early morning of February 27, 1776, Colonel McLeod and Captain John Campbell attempted to lead an advance of soldiers across a bridge consisting only of round pine logs, since the planks had been removed. Many of the Loyalists fell from the bridge into the water. Those who succeeded in getting across were mowed down by the murderous fire of the Patriots. McLeod and Campbell fell leading their men. The latter received in his body more than twenty balls. Other Patriots forded the stream and attacked the Loyalists from the rear. With the loss of their leaders the Loyalists fled in every direction. About eight hundred and fifty were captured, among whom were many officers including the commander, General McDonald.[33] The war materials and money taken were a great aid to the American cause. These included three hundred and fifty guns and shot bags, one hundred and fifty swords and dirks, £15,000 sterling, and thirteen wagons with complete teams of horses.[34] General Moore, who commanded the Patriots, estimated the loss of the Tories to have been about fifty killed and wounded, while his own losses were only two wounded, one of whom died.[35]

The great disparity in numbers in the losses suffered by the two combatants is due to the fact that the Patriots fought from behind breastworks, while the Loyalists attacked from the open.

[31] Caruthers, *The Old North State*, pp. 86 f.
[32] The whole campaign was planned by James Moore of Brunswick, colonel of the First North Carolina Regiment in the Continental Army. The success of Lillington and Caswell was due to his foresight and planning of the battle. The weight of evidence gives the command to Lillington, for Caswell did not arrive until the former was on the field and had thrown up entrenchments awaiting the Loyalists (M. C. S. Noble, "The Battle of Moore's Creek Bridge," *North Carolina Booklet*, Raleigh, 1904, Vol. III, No. 11).
[33] *Col. Rec. of N. C.*, X, 482.   [34] *Ibid.*, X, 478, 480.
[35] Hawks, Swain, and Graham, *op. cit.*, p. 219.

This method of attack, however, was contrary to the judgment of the trained soldier, McLeod, on whom the leadership fell because of the illness of General McDonald.

The number engaged on the Patriot side, according to the report of Colonel Richard Caswell, was about one thousand. General McDonald claimed his army contained fifteen or sixteen hundred Tories.[36] Governor Martin, on the contrary, maintained that only about seven hundred men were engaged on the side of the King, six hundred Regulators and Scots and about one hundred of the country people.[37]

The results of the battle were out of all proportion to the numbers who were engaged or lost. The provincial militia under their own officers had met and defeated a superior force under British leaders. It gave the Americans confidence, and equally discouraged the Tories. The Patriots, in fact, became overconfident and, as it proved, held the Tories in too great contempt. This mistaken idea of the ability of the Tories later cost the Patriots the loss of many engagements. The captured Tories were sent to various prisons, while the leaders, who had been called upon to raise the King's Standard, in addition suffered the loss of their property.[38] Had the Loyalists been successful, all those who had deserted would have rejoined the Highlanders, and there might have been ten thousand by the time they reached Wilmington. This would have so strengthened Clinton and Cornwallis that North Carolina could easily have been conquered for the British in 1776. Instead, these British generals were met by the Patriots, who were able to turn out nearly ten thousand men, enough to crush insurrection and to protect themselves from invasion.[39] This victory, no doubt, persuaded the Provincial Congress, which met at Halifax in April, 1776, to empower its delegates to concur with the delegates of the other colonies in the Continental Congress and to declare for independence. Thus the people of North Caro-

---

[36] *Col. Rec. of N. C.*, X, 482.   [37] *Ibid.*, X, 491.

[38] *Annual Register* (London, 1776), p. 158.

[39] George Bancroft, *History of the United States of America, from the Discovery of the Continent* (New York, 1882-1884), IV, 391.

MILITARY ACTIVITIES OF THE LOYALISTS   97

lina were the first in America to vote explicitly for independence. Virginia took similar action the following month.[40]

The Provincial Congress at Halifax had to decide what was to be done with the prisoners taken at and after the Battle of Moore's Creek. Two men who were speedily apprehended are worthy of special mention. They were Farquard Campbell and Thomas Rutherford. Both were men of wealth and distinction from Cumberland County. They had represented their county in both the Assembly and the Provincial Congress.[41] They were suspected and accused of Toryism, but could not be convicted. They were members of the Second Provincial Congress, which met at Halifax on April 4, 1776, and voted for the resolution instructing the North Carolina delegates in the Continental Congress to vote for independence. As colonel of the Cumberland Militia, Rutherford had on February 13, 1776, issued a manifesto asking the people to join the King's Standard at Cross Creek.[42] He was reported to have fought at Moore's Creek and to have run hastily from the battlefield.[43] In view of these facts, it is difficult to explain how he was allowed to sit in the Provincial Congress in the following April. Tradition says that Campbell, just previous to the battle, was equally loyal to both sides. As a Tory he conferred with General McDonald and as a Patriot with Caswell and Lillington. On the day of the battle he was present with Caswell and Lillington, apparently a Whig.[44] The committee appointed to investigate the conduct of the insurgents and suspected persons reported as follows in regard to the two men:

Your committee are of the opinion that Farquard Campbell, disregarding the sacred obligations he had voluntarily entered into to support the liberty of America against all usurpation, has traitoriously and insidiously endeavored to excite the inhabitants of this Colony to take arms and levy war in order to assist the avowed enemies thereof. That when a prisoner on his parole of honor he gave intelligence of the force and the intention of the American army

[40] Ashe, op. cit., I, 517.
[41] Col. Rec. of N. C., IX, 1188; X, 172, 500.
[42] Ibid., X, 452.   [43] Ibid., XI, 290.
[44] Caruthers, The Old North State in 1776, First Series, p. 104.

under Colonel Caswell to the enemy and advised them in what manner they might elude them and that he is a Freeholder and lives in Cumberland county.

That Thomas Rutherford regardless of the said obligations did actually take up arms and lead forth to war as Colonel of a regiment, a Division of men for the avowed purpose of assisting the enemies of America and that he is a Freeholder and lives in Cumberland county.[45]

One week later Congress resolved that these two men should be removed from the state, and that Rutherford should be permitted to take with him his horse and Negro man, and Campbell his horse.[46]

Congress felt called upon to justify its action in ordering the removal of these two prisoners from their friends and families to other states. Their excuse was that if these people were allowed to remain, they would exert their influence to the prejudice of the country and delude the wicked, the ignorant, and the unwary. Congress further declared that it would forgive them and receive them with open arms when they should reform, and that their families whom they left behind should be well treated.[47] The council in June, 1776, voted that the malcontents of Bladen County, who were hiding and wished to return to their homes, could do so if they would submit themselves to the regulations of the colony and agree to take up arms in defense of the colony when called upon.

To Colonel Ebenezer Folsom fell the task of keeping the Tories in order in Cumberland County and the adjacent counties, in the period immediately following the victory at Cross Creek. In May, 1776, he was placed at the head of one hundred light cavalry and two hundred infantry, with headquarters at Cross Creek.[48] On June 15 he was given the pleasant task of capturing the escaped Regulators: James Munroe, William Garner, John Piles, John Piles, Junior, David Jackson, and William Catlett.[49] He conducted his search through Chatham, Moore, and Cumberland counties, and ultimately captured John

[45] *Col. Rec. of N. C.*, X, 595.
[46] *Ibid.*, X, 543.
[47] *Ibid.*, X, 547-549.
[48] *Ibid.*, X, 567.
[49] *Ibid.*, X, 631.

Piles and his son at the home of Farquard Campbell. Because of the prevalence of Tories in the county, the regular county committee did not function, and Folsom's word was law. By his high-handed acts he soon became so odious to Tory and Patriot alike that the people of the county petitioned for his removal.[50] During the next year he was tried for the common crime of usurpation and abuse of power.[51]

Great hardships were suffered by the wives and families of some of the Tory leaders. The Council of Safety of North Carolina, meeting at Wilmington in June, 1776, resolved that Mrs. Jean Dubois and Mrs. McNeill and their families must remove from the town of Wilmington within eight days to some town up the river.[52] This removal of families from one place to another caused great, and perhaps unnecessary, suffering. They were charged excessive rents and were always liable to insults and persecutions from their new neighbors. Once in jail it was not easy to get out, even though the prisoner was willing to support the Revolution. William Maxwell, incarcerated at New Bern, repeatedly importuned the council and Governor Harnett for his release. He declared that his condition was disagreeable beyond description and that death was preferable.[53]

The disaffected without resorting to arms were able to do much harm to the cause of liberty by persuading the people not to enlist in the militia, and by using obstructive tactics wherever possible. When caught and convicted they were either jailed or paroled to some neighboring county.[54] Another method of obstruction was to depreciate the colonial currency. This was accomplished by offering larger sums of the bills of credit issued by the Congress at Hillsboro when they purchased goods or by demanding larger sums of money for their merchandise when it was sold, than they demanded in proclamation money, or in gold and silver. Anyone who was caught doing so was compelled on oath to render an inventory of all his real and personal estate.[55]

[50] *Ibid.*, X, 630.
[52] *Col. Rec. of N. C.*, X, 631.
[54] *Ibid.*, X, 622.
[51] Jones, *op. cit.*, p. 267.
[53] *Ibid.*, X, 672 f.
[55] *Ibid.* X, 644.

Being a minister of the Gospel was no excuse for refusing to join actively the Patriot cause. James Childs, of Anson County, was accused of practices injurious to the cause of liberty. His excuse was that he was a preacher of the New Light Baptist persuasion and that one of the rules of his church prohibited members from bearing arms. He refused to take an oath of allegiance to the state and was paroled to the town of Edenton.[56]

The difficulties of a person who resided in North Carolina and owned property in England are illustrated by the case of Dugall Campbell. He set forth his predicament to Cornelius Harnett:

When last at Wilmington my business there was to wait on you and let you know the disagreeable situation I was in with regard to mustering in this county, which still continues, and only last week a party under arms came to this house to demand and levy fines off me. Tho' I have been bad of a fever since ever you saw me when at Wilmington, I endeavored to make you sensible how unconvenient it was for me to muster or take up arms you saw by a factory I left with my friends at home that all the property I have is in Great Britain and that holding of the Crown. You know and are sensible there are many of my country people here that would be glad of an opportunity to inform against me were they to know that I took up arms for this country—then my property would be immediately confiscated to the King. The consequence must be my ruin—my own people are more inveterate against me than others, for no reason than that, I did not nor would not join in the last insurrection, not only that but I advised   against it, which was taken so much amiss among them that I was obliged to fly here for protection. Now, sir, I should be very happy and at the same time infinitely obliged to you if you would put me on a plan of preserving my property—for little as three or four thousand sterling, it is my all and I think as well in my hands as the King's—I will only ask you or any Gentleman of sense and property in America what would they do in my situation—I suppose them at present in Britain and their property here—I want no particular favor shown me, I want only to be done as you or any one of the council would choose to be dealt with was their case mine—By and by (as I have no place of residence of my own) I go to some other country to tarry a while there and then I am in the same dilemma—what then am I to do,

God bless you do tell me—I, as a stranger beg your advice and assistance in this affair—as I do and did look upon you as a friend I hope you won't neglect me—I hope you will forgive the trouble I have given you but necessity has no law—please offer my very respectful compliments to Messers Ashe, Sharp, and Warner. Your answer by Major Clinton I expect which will be always esteemed as a very singular favor. . . .[57]

Through unable to collect in large numbers, the Loyalists throughout the summer of 1776 continued to harass the Patriots. In July, Ransom Sutherland wrote to the Committee of Safety of Wilmington complaining of the acts of a David Jackson, who had escaped from his guards while being conducted northward to jail after the defeat at Moore's Creek. He reported that Jackson and Jacob Kragle were suspected of having killed one man and of having badly wounded another. These two Tories were declared to be hiding out in the woods, and he recommended that Colonel Folsom be sent into this settlement of the Tories, and that these two men be shot on sight, and the country laid waste if the inhabitants refused to deliver them up.[58]

Anson and Cumberland counties found it necessary to be on the alert throughout the summer, as was shown by a request to the committee of safety that a company of light horse be held ready on call, since the Tories were collecting along the waters of Drowning Creek.[59]

Governor Caswell was constantly in receipt of letters warning him of Tory uprisings. In July, 1776, Lieutenant Colonel Irwin wrote to him that there were many evil persons at Tarboro and in the neighboring counties who were joined in a most wicked conspiracy, and that he hoped to frustrate them. He succeeded in defeating thirty of them who attacked the town; then he compelled them to take the oath.[60] Perhaps this was the conspiracy which was reported a week later by Colonel John Williams, for he asserted that over one thousand men had gathered in Orange and Chatham counties. Being questioned, they maintained that they were going to Cross Creek for salt.

[57] *Ibid.*, X, 722 f.
[59] *Ibid.*

[58] *Ibid.*, X, 669.
[60] *S.R.N.C.*, XI, 521.

This commodity was scarce and most difficult for the colonists to obtain. Williams suspected their purpose was to get lead, and decided to arrive ahead of them with sufficient men to prevent it.[61]

Conditions were no better thoughout the summer. Colonel Folsom reported to the provincial council in August that in the counties which he was watching over, the Tories needed only an opportunity and they would all immediately hasten to join the Indians, whom they openly espoused. At this time the Indians had promised to remain neutral, but John Stuart, the British Indian agent, had hopes of winning them to the side of the British. Colonel Folsom was hampered by the fact that he had only seventy-five men now under his command and possessed a very limited supply of ammunition.[62] Guilford County was compelled to raise a company of light horse to apprehend the disaffected and to enforce the resolves of the Provincial Congress. The committees experienced much difficulty in raising the company and seemed in doubt as to its authority. The committee took this action only because it seemed certain that the Tories would take the initiative.[63]

In November, 1776, drastic action was taken by the committee of the Provincial Congress which had been commissioned to consider the best means of capturing David Jackson and his accomplices, who had been committing depredations in Chatham County. The trouble began when Joseph Moore had his horse shot down at the plow, as he suspected, by Hugh Patton, a follower of Jackson. Next, Patton came to Moore's house and demanded £5 of hard money, which, he declared, Moore had offered for his arrest. Moore was then compelled to kneel down and thank him for what he had done. Two months later Patton, Jesse Beverly, John Beverly, and Morgan Morgan came back and demanded guns and ammunition, which were given them. Moore was then whipped, robbed of his money, and left helpless. They meted out similar punishment to a Mr. Lyons, who had joined the light horse in search of them. A party of

[61] *Ibid.*, XI, 527.
[62] *Col. Rec. of N. C.*, X, 732.   [63] *Ibid.*, X, 761 f.

from twenty to thirty similarly robbed George Henry, and although they were partly disguised, he was able to recognize them. Complaints came from various parts of Chatham and Guilford counties.[64]

Since the Tories were in the majority, it was impossible for the two counties to cope with the situation. They decided to raise a company of light horse and to empower the captain to take David Jackson and the other culprits wherever found, and in case of resistance or flight, to kill them. He was further empowered to seize the estates of any persons harboring them and to send them to jail.[65] The disturbances in Guilford County finally became so great that the provincial council decided to raise five hundred men, to reinforce General Rutherford in that action.[66]

In the summer of 1777 it was estimated that two thirds of the people of Bladen County were Tories and were contemplating leaving the state. At this time an oath of allegiance to the state was required of every citizen, and those refusing to take it were required to leave the state within sixty days. The Scotch were much exasperated by the oath, and almost all of them refused to take it. The numbers of the Tories made them so sure of their strength that they were insolent, and it was feared that they would become troublesome. Colonel David Smith urged that a company of fifty light horse be sent there at once.[67] Richard Caswell, who found himself in power as the first governor of the sovereign state of North Carolina on the adjournment of the Provincial Congress in December, 1776, needed the consent of the council to comply with this request. At the last meeting there had not been a quorum

[64] *Ibid.*, X, 993-995. [65] *Ibid.*, X, 940.
[66] S.R.N.C., XI, 335. Records relating to the Colonial period of the state regard that period as extending to the adoption of the state constitution in December, 1776, and Vol. X of *The Colonial Records* ends with the close of the year 1776. Walter Clark, who edited *The Records of North Carolina* beginning with January, 1777, thought the dividing line between *Colonial* and *State Records* ought to be July 4, 1776. His volume for 1777 is the first to be designated *State Records* and is Vol. XI of *The Records of North Carolina*. In this volume are a number of papers bearing on the Colonial period which are not to be found in the volumes edited by Saunders.
[67] S.R.N.C., XI, 534.

present, and hence no business had been transacted.[68] The weakness of the executive at this period was a serious handicap to the effective conduct of military operations.

On his visit to Wilmington the latter part of July, 1777, General Ashe thought that the Tories were a real menace. He found there several Scotch Tories and other disaffected persons from Cross Creek and Bladen County and learned that under the pretext of coming down for salt they intended seizing the powder magazine by surprise. To prevent this, he ordered out all the militia of the county, but secured only three hundred men. It seemed that the attempted march of the previous year might be repeated. Colonel Robertson of Bladen County was ordered to be in readiness to attack and harass the Tories should they leave Cross Creek. In fact, all the colonels of the district were warned to be prepared.[69] Certainly at this period the danger from the foes within the country was a real one. In Edgecombe and the neighboring counties a plot was formed whereby the leading Tories in each county would rise simultaneously and kill all who would not join them. William Brumage and his father-in-law, Black John Stewart, two of the leaders, were placed in the Edenton jail. Allen Jones thought that hanging a dozen of them would have a good effect on the state, and that they were designed by Providence for such an end.[70]

Throughout the state large numbers remained steadfast in their loyalty to the King. They interfered with the recruiting and were a menace to the peace of the communities in which they lived. They threatened to seize magazines in the different parts and exerted a bad influence on their neighbors.[71]

Sometimes efforts were made to prove people Tories because they happened to oppose the ruling faction, or because they criticized the harsh measures which were being meted out to them. This was true in Cumberland County when William Rand and Philip Alston were in control. Rand was unknown until he became wealthy from plundering the Scotch after their

[68] Ibid.
[70] Ibid., XI, 561 f.
[69] Ibid., XI, 540.
[71] Ashe, op. cit., I, 579.

defeat at Moore's Creek. He and Alston finally accused Robert Rowan of being disloyal, in spite of the fact that he had been one of the first to put down the threatened insurrection of the Scotch and Regulators.[72]

The enemy appeared active in Craven County. In September, 1777, Captain John Nelson was ordered to raise a company of militia to ambuscade, harass, distress, and destroy the enemy in every way possible, and at all times to observe their motions and to report them to Governor Caswell.[73]

Throughout the remainder of 1777 and a part of 1778, there was comparative quiet in the state so far as actual fighting was concerned. Perhaps patriotism was also at a low ebb at this time. Since there seemed no danger of an immediate attack by the British, the people became indifferent. Judge Ashe at the June meeting of the Wilmington District Court upbraided the people for their lack of patriotism and urged them to enlist.[74] The Tories were not inclined to begin the strife so long as they were left unmolested.

In the autumn of 1778 it became evident that the long threatened campaign against the South was about to materialize. South Carolina called on her sister state for help, and recruiting in North Carolina became active. Likewise, when Colonel John Hamilton of North Carolina, early in 1779, was organizing a Loyalist regiment in Florida, his adherents at home were active. Colonel Boyd of the Lower Yadkin River in Anson County, near the South Carolina border, collected a force of Loyalists and started to join him. In South Carolina they were joined by others, and lived off the land as they pursued their march. Before reaching Augusta, they were defeated near Kettle Creek, South Carolina, by Colonel Pickens. Forty of their number were killed, and the remainder dispersed or were captured. At this time the Loyalists were also being aroused to activity by British agents. One of these, George Carey, a British naval officer, who entered the Cape Fear under a flag of truce, was seized and thrown into jail.[75]

---

[72] S.R.N.C., XI, 627-631.
[74] Ibid., XIII, 443.
[73] Ibid., XI, 775.
[75] Ibid., XIII, 296-297.

When the Assembly noticed the activity among the friends of the British, they directed Governor Caswell to raise two hundred and fifty infantry and to disarm all persons in Cumberland, Anson, Guilford, and other counties, who might give trouble. Such swift action was taken that Colonel John Moore, who had raised three hundred Loyalists, was forced to flee the country, and the rest of the inhabitants were overawed. Moore succeeded in reaching Colonel Hamilton in Georgia and later assisted him in the defense of the city of Savannah. Of the many soldiers who successfully defended Savannah in 1779 against 6,000 French and Americans, 90 were Loyalists from North Carolina.[76] The whole defending force, including regulars, militia, volunteers, and sailors, was about 2,350 men.

In midsummer of 1779 a fresh outbreak of Toryism occurred in Edgecombe, Nash, and Johnston counties. These counties occupied the region between the headwaters of the Pamlico and Neuse rivers and were an eastern extension of the Tory stronghold in the center of the state. This outbreak seems to have come about more by chance than by design. A number of the Continental troops had deserted and, in addition, had formed associations to prevent others from being drafted. The Tories attempted to give these deserters protection and thus aroused the ire of the Patriots. When Governor Caswell sent a small military force among them, order was quickly restored.[77] About this time General Rutherford reported that the Tories of Burke County were robbing the friends of America and in some cases murdering them.[78] Burke County was located in the far western part of the state. This incident shows how widely dispersed were the Tory activities.

The Tory uprisings in the state from 1776 to 1780 were sporadic in character and generally lacking in efficient leadership except for the attempt to march on Wilmington, which resulted in defeat at Moore's Creek. The efficiency of the organization of the Patriots constantly increased; as a result,

[76] Franklin B. Hough (ed.), *The Siege of Savannah* . . . (Albany, 1866), p. 39.
[77] *S.R.N.C.*, XIII, 321.   [78] *Ibid.*, XIII, 129, 137.

they were able to act quickly whenever disaffection showed itself. With the arrival of the British fleet in the Cape Fear River in May, 1776, the hopes of the Tories were aroused only to be disappointed when it departed the same month without having accomplished anything. Many came forward and declared their allegiance to the state. With no British force in the state, the Tories knew that it was hopeless to wage open warfare; hence, obstructive tactics were resorted to, especially in regard to the draft. Disturbances were reported from nearly every county in the central part of the state, extending from Edgecombe County in the east to Burke County in the west. A show of force on the part of the Patriots was generally sufficient to restore order with little or no bloodshed. The danger from the foe within, however, was always sufficient to prevent the state from using its entire force against the British. Sufficient troops had to be maintained within the state at all times to put down any potential uprising.

The chief contribution of the Tories of North Carolina to the British cause during the first four years of the war was not so much in what they accomplished as in what they prevented the Patriots from accomplishing. Many of those who were more desirous for active service managed to leave the state and join Colonel Hamilton in Georgia, while others left with the British fleet in May, 1776, for New York. That the Tories of the state to become active needed only the support of British troops was soon to be proved. The invasion of the state in 1780 initiated a conflict which became a veritable civil war.

CHAPTER V

SUFFERINGS OF THE LOYALISTS

GREAT AS WAS THE suffering of the Patriots of North Carolina, still greater was that of the Loyalists or Tories who supported the established government. Rather than turn against their sovereign they suffered imprisonment, banishment, loss of their homes, and execution. Two of the first to suffer at the hands of the Revolutionary committees were Benjamin Boote and John Dunn. They were denounced by the Rowan County Committee of Safety for having posted in September, 1774, an advertisement which protested against the actions of committees of safety. It was resolved by the committee that the notice was false, scandalous, wicked, and impertinent, and that the authors merited the censure and detestation of their country. A copy of the resolutions against Boote and Dunn was nailed on the gallows and whipping post, to show the contempt in which the committee held them.[1]

In July, 1775, Dunn, a lawyer and acting attorney for the Crown in the Rowan County Court, was seized at his home in Salisbury. Boote, who had been denounced with him the previous year, was seized at the same time. In spite of protests from members of the Salisbury Committee of Safety, they were led off into the woods as felons. They were then conducted to Mecklenburg Courthouse, where they were promised a trial. Instead of being tried, they were sent under guard of horsemen to the Camden jail, South Carolina, and from there to Charleston. These men were hurried away without change of clothing, money, or necessities of any kind. They had never been examined, tried, or convicted of any offense, yet were confined in jail in circumstances which were contrary to the rules of the General Congress. Their wives and families, in the meantime, suffered great distress and hardships in North Caro-

[1] *Col. Rec. of N. C.*, IX, 1074-1075.

lina. The two men were given permission to return home if they would release and indemnify the men who had brought them there from all actions or causes of actions, which might accrue to Dunn and Boote on account of their sufferings. They were held a year, and Boote was compelled to pay the physician who had attended him while he was ill in the prison.[2] This punishment was meted out to these men without trial or conviction.

Another early sufferer was James Cotton, who held various offices in the colony. He was early apprehended and made to suffer for his steadfastness to the government.[3] In May, 1775, he was summoned before the committee of Anson County and asked to sign the association. Upon his refusing he was arrested and started on a thirty-five mile journey to be tried. While his captors were refreshing themselves at a public house, he escaped. His freedom proved to be of short duration, for he was again captured and tried by the Bladen County committee. During his confinement he was knocked down and robbed by the sentinel. Being a man of much importance, he was sent to Wilmington to be tried by the Grand Committee. Here his guilt was confirmed, and he was ordered to be closely confined and sent a distance of two hundred miles to Hillsboro for trial before the Provincial Congress. On his arrival at Hillsboro, the officer of the day, Colonel Francis Nash, ordered him confined in a dungeon, and the next day he was told by Colonel Samuel Spencer, a member of Congress, that if he did not make a recantation of his principles he would be hung before twelve o'clock. Under this threat, at ten o'clock he made a recantation and was set free. He was given a large number of pamphlets to distribute among his former companions and thus turn them from the King's cause. He burned the pamphlets and, hiding in the woods, evaded his enemies until he was sum-

[2] *Ibid.*, X, 673-676.

[3] The accounts of many of these sufferers are to be found in the claims filed with the British Government for compensations and pensions for losses. Transcripts of the petitions of the North Carolina claimants have been made for the North Carolina Historical Commission at Raleigh. These are the transcripts that have been used, and as all claims are arranged alphabetically, citation will be made only to *Loyalist Transcripts*.

moned by Governor Martin at the Battle of Cross Creek. He raised over five hundred men for Martin and narrowly escaped capture after the battle.

For some time he then lived in a cave only fifteen miles from his home, where he was fed by Loyalist neighbors. Anxious for his capture, the colonial officials offered £500 for his capture dead or alive, but this sum was not sufficient to induce his friends to betray him. Since they had failed to capture him, his movable property was plundered and confiscated by the Patriots. A detachment of the army encamped on his farm and burned the dwelling house, barns, mills, and fences, leaving only waste fields. Meantime his wife died, and the children were given to whoever would take them. After a three weeks' seclusion in the cave and the destruction of his property, he traveled by foot at night through the wilderness seven hundred miles to join His Majesty's forces at St. Augustine, where he equipped himself and later joined the army under General Clinton at Charleston. Misfortune possessed him, and twice more he lost all his possessions through capture by the enemy. To add to his misery, his former Loyalist friends now blamed him for the loss of their property, since he had been foremost in encouraging them to fight for the King.[4] A study of the claims presented by the Loyalists to the British Government discloses a surprising number of similar cases.

The men taken prisoners at Moore's Creek were confined in common jails, and complained bitterly of their sufferings. Joseph Hughes sought to be moved from Charlotte, Mecklenburg County, to Salisbury, since he could find no home for his family in the former town. His request was granted.[5] James Hepburn petitioned the council from the same town that he could secure no home for his family, although he had offered £40 a year for a house not fit for a stable. He wished to be moved to Salisbury, where he might make better provision for his family.[6]

Sometimes action against the Tories took the form of compelling them to move from one part of the country to another.

---

[4] *Loyalist Transcripts.*   [5] *Col. Rec. of N. C.*, X, 550.   [6] *Ibid.*, X, 758.

Perhaps the greatest hardships fell upon the families of those who were left behind after the Battle of Moore's Creek. With the husband or father in jail or a captive, there was no one left to protect his family and property from the vengeance of the aroused Whigs.

Typical sufferers were Norman McLeod and his family. He was taken prisoner at Moore's Creek and confined in jail in Pennsylvania for a period of four years and ten months. This was an unusually long time; most of the prisoners were either exchanged or paroled before that time. McLeod's home and plantation in Anson County were repeatedly robbed and pillaged by the Whigs, until at last his wife was compelled to flee for her life to Charleston, leaving the children behind. At Charleston she secured a flag of truce and made her way, as best she could, through the country to her home in North Carolina, a distance of three hundred miles, to obtain her children that she might bring them to Charleston and provide them with the necessities of life. On this journey, in spite of her flag of truce, she was detained a prisoner by the enemy for the space of seven weeks at a great expense to her husband. Robbed of all their possessions, the family finally reached Charleston. They were not too generously treated by Parliament, and received only £202 for what they had lost in America. McLeod also received a pension of £20 a year, which was to cease if he went to Nova Scotia.[7]

Many of the officers who escaped capture at Moore's Creek sought safety in the South, while others went to Philadelphia. Among the latter were Duncan McNabb of the North Carolina Highlanders. For several weeks he concealed himself in the forests, expecting daily the arrival of the British. Disappointed in this, he left his wife and family behind and set out overland on foot to join the British in Philadelphia. He finally reached his destination after great fatigue and danger of being captured by the Whigs. After the evacuation of Philadelphia, he marched to New York and later sailed to Georgia and participated in the siege of Savannah. From Georgia he returned to North Caro-

[7] *Loyalist Transcripts.*

lina and raised a detachment of troops for Governor Martin until ordered to Charleston. Meantime, his wife in North Carolina had been robbed of everything belonging to her, even her clothes, and ordered out of the Province to Charleston. She was compelled to leave her child behind to the mercy of the enemy. Her misfortunes were not unlike Mrs. McLeod's. At Charleston she received a flag of truce to return into the country three hundred miles for her child, but was seized and held a prisoner for several weeks. For the expense her husband was compelled to pay. Soon after her return to Charleston the city was evacuated, and the distressed family set out for East Florida. Finding that province in the hands of the Spanish, they sought a haven in Halifax, Nova Scotia. Unable to find support for themselves there, in the midst of winter, December 23, 1783, they sailed for London and threw themselves on the mercy of the English Government, as did many of their fellow sufferers.[8]

Of all the prisoners taken at Moore's Creek Bridge, perhaps none suffered greater hardships than Captain Alexander Mc-Donald and his family. He was confined in a filthy jail for one year and subjected to the most shocking insults before he was released on parole. After a year and a half on parole he was exchanged and sent to New York, where he found himself considered only an officer on half pay, although he had been promised by Governor Martin the same pay as was received by His Majesty's regular troops.

Captain McDonald next embarked with Colonel Campbell for the attack on Savannah. He was captured en route, and on being exchanged a second time, he aided Sir Henry Clinton in the capture of Charleston. After this successful venture he joined Lord Cornwallis and aided him in his campaigns in the two Carolinas and was prevented only by the difficulty of communication with the back country from raising a full company of Highlanders. Meantime his family, which consisted of a wife and five children, suffered cruelties which exceed description. Their home was robbed repeatedly, and they were finally

[8] *Ibid.*

urned out into the woods, where they must surely have died
ad not a kind-hearted Patriot officer conducted them within
he British lines.[9]

Even women were not always exempt from persecution. On
June 15, 1776, the committee at Wilmington decreed that
within eight days Mrs. Jean DuBois and Mrs. McNeill and
heir families should move the place of their residence from the
own of Wilmington to some place at least twenty miles distant
up the river. In such troubled times, this was no small punishment. Having left Wilmington under compulsion, they were
 certain to be suspected and mistrusted by their new neighbors.[10]

We have the example of the Reverend Mr. Micklejohn as
o what happened to people who failed to move within the
pecified time. When he failed to move himself to the part of
Perquimans County to which he had been ordered within fifteen
days, it was resolved that he should be removed at his own
xpense. The commanding officer of the Second Regiment of
he County of Orange was ordered to see that this resolve was
arried into effect.[11] Another example was that of the Reverend
Mr. Reed, of New Bern, who was dismissed from his charge in
August for his refusal to preach for the Revolutionists on the
general fast day. All attempts at persuasion proved in vain,
ince he preferred the loss of his living to a violation of his
oath. The Reverend Mr. Earle, of Edenton, in writing to the
Secretary of the Society for the Propagation of the Gospel, well
described the position of the clergy in the colonies:

The situation of the clergy in this part of the world is at present
truly critical, on account of the difficulty comporting themselves in
such a manner as to give no offense to the inhabitants. Some of them
have been suspended, deprived of their salaries, and in the American
manner proscribed by the Committees, and thereby, rendered incapable of getting any settlement in any part of the united Colonies and
all of this, on account of charges against them, of opposing the
general cause of America, and how far they are to blame I am not
able to determine, but verily believe that if the most learned and
eloquent Divine in England was to endeavor to dissuade the Amer-

[9] *Ibid.*
[10] *Col. Rec. of N. C.*, X, 631-632.   [11] *Ibid.*, X, 646.

icans from their present Resolutions he could make no impression on them, but contrarywise, rather inflame them, so tenacious are they of the manner they have adopted. As for my own part, I have as yet kept clear of any censure of my parishioners, and I never introduce any topic into the pulpit except exhortations and prayers for peace, order, and a speedy reconciliation with Great Britain.[12]

Even the members of the Continental Congress were moved by the sufferings of their former friends and neighbors whom they saw daily languishing in jail. In the autumn of 1776 William Hooper, one of the delegates, wrote to the Convention at Halifax, North Carolina, describing the plight of the prisoners and adding that their sufferings would increase during the winter for want of clothing. He expressed regrets at the sufferings of their families and requested that these prisoners be returned to their families as soon as possible with safety to North Carolina.

So bitter did Ranson Sutherland, of Wilmington, feel toward the Tories who inhabited the region of his country home, that he asked the committees of safety to send four hundred men into the region and put these people to death on sight and lay waste the country wherever the inhabitants refused to yield to the authorities.[13] As early in the war as November, 1776, the Assembly of North Carolina at Halifax offered sums ranging from £50 to £100 for the arrest of certain Tories. In case of resistance or attempted flight the officer was authorized to kill or destroy them, and was granted immunity from impeachment for the deed.[14] One reason for this action was the fact that armed forces were unable to capture them, while some had been taken in consequence of a reward. No one, once he declared himself in favor of the mother country, was safe from the Whigs. Thomas McKnight, who was held in great esteem, was chosen unanimously by his county to represent it in the second convention in North Carolina. When a resolution was passed that the members of the convention should sign the nonexportation agreement of the General Congress and declare their full approbation of a measure that was calculated to prevent his

[12] *Ibid.*, X, 237.   [13] *Ibid.*, X, 663.   [14] *Ibid.*, X, 939.

doing the common justice of paying his debts owed to Great Britain, McKnight protested. He still remained loyal to his King, in spite of the tempting offers of the Revolutionary leaders and the entreaties of his friends. This action so exasperated the Patriots that they persecuted and menaced him with every species of terror and finally threatened him hourly with assassination. He was compelled to flee to Lord Dunmore, Governor of Virginia, for protection and to leave behind property valued at £30,000.

The members of the medical profession were usually left free to carry on their practice regardless of their sentiments. They were less likely than the preachers to be called before a committee on account of their utterances. Dr. James Fallon, of Wilmington, was one of the few doctors in the colony to be cast into prison. He wrote a paper addressed to "Those who have a true sense of distributive justice and trammeled residents of the borough of Wilmington," and signed "A Lawyer." This was copied and circulated by William Green, and when Dr. Fallon was found to be the author, he was ordered to be kept in close custody until he should give security for his good behavior for six months, in the sum of £500 proclamation money. Dr. Fallon refused to give such security, and was ordered to be confined to the guardhouse. He was allowed visitors only for a brief period, and all the letters sent off by him were first censored by the commanding officers. Later he was removed to the common jail, and it was resolved to keep him there until he should make full confession for his offense to the public and ask pardon of the committee for the repeated insults he had in person offered them. It was also resolved that "The Sheriff and jailer give strict orders that no person be admitted to Dr. Fallon except in case of sickness, but a servant to carry him necessities, and keep his apartment clean; and that the said Fallon shall not be suffered to send any letters or writings but such that may be approved by this committee, or the commanding officer of the forces, and that the prison door be kept locked."[15]

The county committees possessed a great deal of power and

[15] *Ibid.*, X, 420.

operated more or less independently of each other. In July 1777, Duncan Archibald, of Cumberland County, was called upon to take an oath of fealty to the state, and upon his refusal was required to give bond and security to depart from the state within sixty days. In the meantime, he went to Mecklenburg County, where he was arrested and required to appear in October. Should he fail to appear at that time he would forfeit the security which he had given in Cumberland County in July.[16] Others found themselves in equally perplexing dilemmas.

The Continental Congress often enacted laws which proved a great inconvenience to the Loyalists who wished to leave the country. James Green, who was compelled to leave North Carolina, sold his property and purchased a vessel and cargo of corn and hoped to sail for Europe. Meantime, Congress, on November 5, 1775, passed a resolution prohibiting the exportation of any produce of the Province except from one port to another unless by persons engaged to bring returns in warlike stores. In this predicament Green learned that Governor Martin wanted a vessel to carry some stock and baggage to him, since he was confined on a vessel at Cape Fear. Green obtained permission to execute the errand. Before departing, he signed a bond of £250 for security that the stock and baggage of corn would be delivered only at Cape Fear. On his arrival at Cape Fear he delivered Governor Martin's goods and decided to forfeit his bond, to carry his corn to the British West Indies, and to bring back to Cape Fear, rum and other necessities for His Majesty's fleet, which was expected daily. Governor Martin and Captain Parry gave him passes and clearance for the islands and he set sail for Antigua. When the Provincial Congress of North Carolina heard of this, Green's bond was forfeited and his other property seized.

During his voyage he received information that several vessels had been condemned to forfeiture at Antigua, under a recent Act of Parliament forbidding all trade and intercourse with the colonies. Feeling secure with his passes or certificates, he went on to the West Indies, where his ship and cargo were seized.

[16] *Ibid.*, X, 419-420.

The Court of Admiralty decided that the seizure was legal, and the ship and cargo to the value of £1,400 sterling were lost. In his petition to Parliament for compensation Green stated:

Your memorialist cannot help thinking it hard that at a time when he had abandoned his home and establishment rather than he would abandon his allegiance, when he was flying with such effects as he hoped to save with his person from the fires of American rebellion, he should be doomed to lose the fruits of his labor by the operation or at least the construction of the British Acts of Parliament made to punish the American Rebels upon the whole, therefore your memorialist is a sufferer by the continued prosecution of ill fortune from different quarters, he has been pillaged by rebels of seven hundred and ninety three pounds sterling as being a loyal subject and departed of nearly fourteen hundred pounds sterling by his Majesty's subjects as if he were a rebel.[17]

His only hope of compensation was to make application as a Loyalist sufferer. He was granted £279. Such treatment was enough to try the endurance and loyalty of His Majesty's most loyal supporters.

Even tavernkeepers needed to be mindful to whom they extended their hospitality. Owen Griffin, tavernkeeper of Ocracoke, came under suspicion because he allowed the officers of His Majesty's Navy to reside at his tavern. When he refused to sign the association, an armed body of what he termed rebels surrounded the house, entered it, and burned and destroyed the greater part of his furniture. Search was made everywhere for treasonable papers, but none were found. They then boarded his schooner and robbed it of gunpowder and guns and did much damage to it. When he applied to the Safety Committee at New Bern for redress, he was imprisoned and released only upon the condition that he come to New Bern to live. By February, 1776, fearing for his life, as many had threatened his destruction, he got together as many of his belongings as possible and sailed for the British West Indies, where his ship met the same fate as that of Green's.[18]

The sufferings of George Lyon, a planter of Bladen County, are representative of that of a very large number. On account

[17] *Loyalist Transcripts.*   [18] *Ibid.*

of his zealous attachment to the King's cause he became obnoxious to the leaders of the Revolution and was so harassed
and cruelly treated that to preserve his life he was compelled
to abandon his house and friends. After enduring innumerable
hardships and wandering about from place to place, he enlisted
in Governor Martin's provincials and served for a period of
three years. His estates, houses, lands, household goods, Negroes, and effects of all kinds were seized. His house was
burned and destroyed. His land, goods, and chattels were confiscated and sold for the use of the state of North Carolina.

So bitter was the feeling of neighbor against neighbor that
Mathew Colvel, who resided near Elizabethtown, North Carolina, was murdered in his bed in cold blood because he attempted to persuade his neighbors to join the British cause. His
lands, slaves, and goods were seized and lost to his family.
When his sister, who was residing in England, sent her two sons
to America, in 1789, to sue and recover his property in the court
as provided for in the Treaty of Peace, they were not only
unsuccessful but they narrowly escaped with their lives.[19]

Isabella McDonald, widow of Captain James McDonald,
remained on her plantation throughout the war, only to have it
plundered several times. The signing of the Treaty of Peace
brought no respite of her abuses but on the contrary augmented
them. Her neighbors feared that by the terms of the treaty
she would be restored to her property and at once hastened to
rob her of the remainder of her possessions, even to her furniture and wearing apparel.

Tories who raised companies of men to assist in the King's
cause were often held responsible for any damage that might
occur to the Patriot's property in the regular course of action.
James Monro, who fought at Moore's Creek and who spent four
years and two months in jail while his family was plundered and
turned out of doors, was one who found himself thus treated.
In his petition for aid from Parliament on November 27, 1788,
Monro declared that his brother sent to America to look after
his property found that it had all been sold or taken possession

[19] *Ibid.*

of by different persons. Each claimed it for damages that he declared had been done by the British Army. Monro's wife and children were likewise stripped of all their remaining possessions when the Treaty of Peace was signed.[20]

Tories were being murdered by the Whig militia almost a year before the Declaration of Independence, and this without fear of punishment by the civil or military authorities. Daniel Maxwell early aroused the suspicion of his neighbors and was obliged to seek safety in flight to the woods, from which point he watched his neighbors plunder his house and destroy his property. Returning to his sawmill one day, he was met by a body of militia under Major Gordon and commanded to surrender. An arrangement was agreed upon whereby he was to be tried by a committee, when Major Bonnar, another militia officer, rode up and shot him dead on the spot. No punishment was inflicted upon Bonnar, while the property of the murdered man was abandoned to the depredations of the multitude.[21]

The Williams family of Anson County were one of the first in that part of North Carolina to declare themselves for the King. The father raised a company of Loyalists and his four sons joined him. One of the sons lost a leg, while another was killed at Fort Cornwallis. A third, Major Henry Williams, was shot through the shoulder the day after he surrendered in Georgia. His wife and seven children, to escape persecution at the hands of the Patriots, walked a distance of two hundred miles to join him in Georgia. Much of this journey was through a wilderness and a hostile country. Bedding and food were carried on the backs of two horses, while all slept in the open at night.[22] Historians of the Revolutionary War have entirely ignored the hardships which were willingly endured by this large group.

Throughout the latter part of the war the district courts were most active in indicting the Tories for treason, and an indictment usually resulted in conviction. At the court held in Salisbury, September 20, 1779, Iredell reported: "Upwards of eighty persons were indicted, and mostly for capital crimes, the

[20] *Ibid.* [21] *Ibid.* [22] *Ibid.*

greatest number for treason (Toryism)." The court found time to try only ten, all of whom were convicted. Several of those condemned were young men, four of whom the jury recommended for mercy.[23]

Major John Eliot is mentioned by Caruthers as being one of the better class of Tories. His humaneness, however, profited him but little. On a visit to Wilmington, accompanied by two other Tories, Samuel Still and Michael Robbins, he found Colonel Dugan, a Whig prisoner, about to be hanged on the prison ship. Major Eliot felt a great compassion for his old friend and interceded so well in his behalf that he secured his freedom and permission to return home. When the Tories Eliot, Still, and Robbins were returning home, they met two men who had been paroled and now contrary to the terms of the parole were fully armed. Eliot began to chastise one of the men, Henry Johnson, for carrying a gun and broke his sword over Johnson's head. Eliot's companion, Still, then put a rifle ball into the head of the injured man. The Whigs of the neighborhood, under the leadership of the same Colonel Dugan whom Eliot had saved from death at Wilmington, now set out to capture them. They were seized, tied to trees, and shot, and in accordance with the heartless custom of the times left in the position in which they had been killed. The reader naturally asks the question: Why did not Colonel Dugan intercede to save his friends who had saved him but a short time previous? One account is that Dugan did attempt to save the life of Eliot but was outvoted by his followers; another, that Dugan felt that Eliot ought to die for the murder of Johnson.[24]

The revenge taken by the Whigs for the five or six of their number who were killed on Piney Bottom, a branch of Rock Fish Creek, in Cumberland County, was perhaps the most savage of any during the war. Colonel McDougal, the leader of the Tories, threatened Ferguson with instant death if he harmed

[23] Griffith J. McRee, *Life and Correspondence of James Iredell* . . . (New York, 1857-1858), p. 434.
[24] Caruthers, *Interesting Revolutionary Incidents: and Sketches of Character, Chiefly in the "Old North State,"* First Series, p. 355.

a certain boy, but in spite of this Ferguson split the boy's head open so that half fell on either shoulder. Colonel Wade and Captain Culp decided to wreak vengeance on the Tories and soon had collected one hundred dragoons for the purpose. They began by beating an aged piper, Daniel Patterson, who was in sympathy with the Tories, until he revealed the names of all those who had participated in the slaughter of their men. Early the next day Wade and Culp first captured Alexander McLeod and his younger brother John, and a little later John Clarke, Daniel McMillan, Duncan Currie, Allan McSweene, and a British deserter. That night Captain Bryan, who was now in charge, ordered that all the men should be killed by having their heads split open with a sword. Alexander McLeod was the first victim. The men, rising in their stirrups, struck him several blows which he, though unarmed, so successfully parried with his bare hands that they had to put three musket balls into him. The others, sensing their fate, preferred to be shot down in flight rather than murdered with swords. The young lad, John McLeod, was the only one spared because one of the soldiers, a little more humane than the others, interceded for him after having cocked his gun at him.

Particularly ghastly and revolting was the killing of Daniel McMillan: "Daniel McMillan came into the house begging for his life, with the blood streaming from his side, his hunting shirt on fire, where he had been shot in the shoulder, his wrist cut and broken by a sword, his arm shattered and torn by a musket ball, two or three musket balls having passed through his body; but revenge was not yet satisfied, and another ball through his breast near the left shoulder, soon put an end to his suffering."[25] Mrs. McSweene and her young child, who were occupants of the house, witnessed the horrible scene. Her husband, Allan, with his arms pinioned behind and his hands tied in front, ran through the house only to be shot down; then his head was split open to the nose. Amidst this horror Mrs. McSweene was jerked prostrate to the floor. All the

[25] Ibid., pp. 388-389.

prisoners except young McLeod were killed, although only two of them, Duncan Currie and David McMillan, were alleged to have participated in the attack on the Whigs.

The Patriots then proceeded through the country destroying the property of the Loyalists and killing the men whom they found at home. To be doubly sure of making the destruction complete, chests of china were broken and books cut down the back and destroyed. Two daughters of Flora McDonald, who happened to be visiting their friends, fell into the hands of the Whigs. Gold rings were pulled from their fingers, and silk handkerchiefs from their necks. As a further humiliation the soldiers put their swords into their bosoms, split down their dresses, and stripped them of their outer clothing.[26] The raid was continued, and the Tories were put to death wherever found. Archibald McBride, a staunch Whig, who happened to be found at the home of Peter Blue, a Tory, was murdered before any inquiry was made whether he was friend or foe. It was enough that he was found in company with a Tory. His death was greatly lamented. The Tories who escaped vengeance this time were still liable for trial in the civil courts after the war ended. John McNeill was thus brought to trial by General Wade and escaped conviction only because Colonel Folsom testified under oath that McNeill was at his house at or about the time, sundown, the evening before the so-called massacre.[27]

The conflicts between neighbors resembled somewhat the bloody feuds of more recent times. John Cornelison, attacked by a band of Tories, retreated to his home, where he was hit with clubs and guns as he sought the shelter of the mantle piece. Here he was shot down, and fell into the fire, from which he was pulled by his wife. A relative of Cornelison, named Spiney, learned the identity of the man who had committed the act, and determined to murder him. He followed the man into Tennessee and, pushing the muzzle of his gun through the cracks in the logs, shot him down. Having satisfied his vengeance, he returned home to North Carolina.

After the capture of Wilmington by Major Craig, the feel-

[26] *Ibid.*, p. 391.   [27] *Ibid.*, p. 395.

ngs of the Whigs and Tories against each other became more
ntense. Loyalists who attempted to join Lord Cornwallis were
often summarily hanged when captured.[28]

A good example of this hate is shown by the action of Margaret Balfour after her brother Andrew, a Patriot, had been
killed by David Fanning. One of the men who accompanied
Fanning was Frederick Smith, who was afterwards captured
and taken to Hillsboro for trial. Although he had not actively
participated in Balfour's killing, it was enough for her to know
that he was one of Fanning's men. In a letter to her sister-in-law Eliza she gave the following description of her action:

I heard that one of Fanning's men was in Hillsborough jail,
and, as the court commenced the first of April, I went to Hillsborough, and witnessed against him. The crime was proved so
plainly, that not one lawyer spoke a word in his favor, though he
had two or three of them employed. My story was so affecting that
the court was willing to give me every satisfaction in their power;
and in order to do this they broke a little through the usual course,
for they had the villain tried, condemned, and hung, all in the space
of the court. While the judge was giving the jury their charge,
I heard several gentlemen of my brother's acquaintance wishing to
God the jury would not bring him in guilty that they might have
the pleasure of putting the rascal to death with their own hands;
and if the jury had not brought him in guilty, I am sure they would
have killed the wretch before he could have got out of the house.[29]

This trial took place in April, 1783; and since at this time the
war had come to an end, one might question the need of this
severity.

After the evacuation of Wilmington by Craig in November,
1781, the Tories were proceeded against in the courts by the
civil authorities. All of the disaffected were thought of as law-breakers and subject to trial, and some of those convicted of
high treason and sentenced to death were later exchanged for
Patriots in the hands of the British.[30] Their sufferings indeed
did not end with the Treaty of Peace, for many were yet to lose
their property and to be scourged out of the land, and not a few
were executed. Only time could bring about a complete forgetting of the deep hatreds that civil strife had engendered.

[28] McRee, op. cit., p. 517.
[29] Caruthers, op. cit., p. 326.   [30] S.R.N.C., XVI, 216, 220.

CHAPTER VI

FINAL STRUGGLE BETWEEN PATRIOTS AND LOYALISTS

ON MAY 12, 1780, when Charleston surrendered to the British, a feeling of dismay prevailed among the Patriots of North Carolina. The Loyalists were on the contrary jubilant; the opportunity for which they had been awaiting for four long years seemed to have arrived. Included in the surrender were over a thousand of the North Carolina Militia, besides sixty-three officers and eight hundred and fourteen of the Continentals.[1] With little resistance Cornwallis proceeded to occupy Ninety Six, Camden, and Cheraw, the three strongholds which dominated the entrance to North Carolina. In possession of these he felt that the conquest of the state would be easy. British emissaries who were sent among the disaffected inhabitants to arouse them to action caused the Patriot leaders much concern.

Although the war had been in progress for four years, North Carolina had thus far been free from invasion by British troops except for the foray made on shore by Cornwallis in 1776. North Carolina had been generous in sending her Continentals to the aid of Virginia, South Carolina, Georgia, and even to the Northern States. She was now to be called upon to use every effort to protect herself.

The Assembly immediately ordered the light horse to disarm all persons in Cumberland, Anson, Guilford, Tryon, and other counties from whom injury might be apprehended. Many in North Carolina were doubtless influenced to join the King's forces by the actions of the leading men in South Carolina. Charles Pinckney, who had been recently president of the South Carolina Senate, declared that he had been misled by the hurry and confusion of the times, and voiced his loyalty to the King.[2]

---

[1] *S.R.N.C.*, XIV, 816.   [2] *Ibid.*, XIV, iv.

Rawlins Lowndes, who had lately been president of the state of South Carolina, made a similar decision. Henry Middleton, president of the first American Congress, promised to do nothing to keep up the spirit of independence and to declare himself as a faithful subject.[3]

The Loyalists of North Carolina looked upon Cornwallis as a deliverer, but could not refrain from disobeying his orders and rising before the appointed time. It was his desire that they should stay at home until the wheat crop could be harvested and thrashed in order that there might be enough food for the soldiers. Colonel John Moore, who lived in the vicinity of Ramsaur's Mill in Lincoln County, had joined the British. John Hamilton, who had been made lieutenant colonel of Hamilton's Tory regiment, was sent into the region to arouse the people. They were told that the loyal would be rewarded and protected but that the rebellious would be severely punished.[4]

Ramsaur's Mill was one of the points at which the people had been assembled after the Battle of Alamance and had been required to take an oath of allegiance to the King. They were now living up to that obligation, while the men who had forced it upon them, were in revolution.

Colonel Moore called a meeting of the Tories, June 10, 1780, at his father's residence on Indian Creek, near Ramsaur's Mill. Here he was met by forty men, to whom he revealed Cornwallis's plan of campaign. Before the meeting adjourned, it was revealed that Major McDowell with a company of Patriot militia of Burke County was only eight miles distant and in search of some of their number.[5] They determined to make a surprise attack upon McDowell, who learned of their action and escaped. Moore directed the men to meet him on the thirteenth at Ramsaur's Mill, and the readiness with which the Tories responded may be judged from the fact that over two hundred appeared at that time and on the next day many others, among

[3] Bancroft, op. cit., V, 394.
[4] William Alexander Graham, "The Battle of Ramsaur's Mill, June 20, 1780," North Carolina Booklet (Raleigh, 1904), Vol. IV, No. 2, p. 6.
[5] William Alexander Graham, General Joseph Graham and His Papers on the North Carolina Revolutionary History (Raleigh, 1904), p. 219.

whom was Major Nicholas Walsh of Colonel Hamilton's regiment. By the twentieth the number had grown to thirteen hundred, about one fourth of whom were without arms. They were encamped on a hill about three hundred yards from Ramsaur's Mill and a half mile north of the present village of Lincolnton.[6]

Here they were attacked by McDowell and Locke with about four hundred men. The Tories were defeated, but the loss in dead and wounded on each side was about equal. Neighbor fought against neighbor, kindred against kindred. Old personal and political enemies sometimes met, and then the fighting was doubly ferocious. In order to identify themselves, the Whigs at first wore white paper in their hats and the Tories a sprig of green, but since these identification marks attracted the fire of the enemy, they were soon abandoned. The Whigs despaired of victory as Captain Warlick rallied his men to the bloody charge again and again. William Shays, noting this, set about to kill him in real Indian fashion. Stealthily he made his approach from tree to tree and was at last close enough to pick off the brave and gallant Warlick. With his loss the whole Loyalist line slowly gave way.[7]

Officers and men on each side to the number of twenty were killed, while over two hundred were wounded. Captain Kimik, a Whig, was captured by a Tory captain, Abram Kiener, his personal friend. He would probably have been killed had Kiener not made him a prisoner and graciously spared his life.[8] Moore with thirty followers escaped to the British Army at Camden, where he was threatened with court-martial for having led the Loyalists into action before the time appointed by the Commander-in-Chief.

This defeat of the Tories was of the greatest importance. Had Moore awaited the advance of Ferguson he might have had two thousand men ready to aid him. Colonel Bryan, who

[6] *Ibid.*

[7] General Rufus Barringer, "Battle of Ramsaur's Mill," *Davidson College Historical Association Magazine* (Davidson, N. C., 1898), Vol. I, No. 1, p. 54.

[8] Graham, "The Battle of Ramsaur's Mill, June 20, 1780," p. 18.

was raising a force of Tories, meanwhile retreated from the Yadkin. When Cornwallis arrived, the people, having been defeated once, were loath to rise to his aid, and he lost more by desertion than he gained by recruits.[9] Of the Tories captured, all were paroled except a few who had committed serious depredations, and these were placed in the Salisbury jail. Those who were paroled were as honest now in keeping their new pact as they had been before in keeping their former one to the King.

So loyal were the people of the Upper Yadkin section that Colonel Bryan soon raised a large force. Fearing to meet General Rutherford after the Battle of Ramsaur's Mill, he proceeded down the Yadkin, where the disaffected constantly joined him. By rapid marches he outwitted General Rutherford and Colonel Davidson and was able to join Major McArthur. A party of about three hundred who encamped near Colson's Mills were not so fortunate. They were surprised in an attack by Colonel Davidson, and lost ten prisoners, four or five wounded, and three killed.

The militia which made up this fighting force of the Patriots was difficult to discipline. Though enlisted for regular periods, the men went home when things became dull, and returned again when called. They could not endure the dull routine of camp duty or the privations of army life. Each brought his own camp equipment or utensils and was responsible for the same. Officers seldom called the roll and could tell who were present only when they saw them in camp.[10]

The militia of North Carolina was organized according to a law passed by the first assembly held under the new constitution in 1777. This law was never greatly altered. The unit of organization was the county. Companies were organized of not less than fifty men, who were required to meet once a month. The companies of each county were organized into battalions, which held two musters a year. All the officers were elected by the assembly, and the governor was commander-in-chief. Since

[9] *Ibid.*, p. 21.
[10] Graham, *General Joseph Graham and His Papers on the North Carolina Revolutionary History*, p. 235.

no accurate muster rolls were kept, there is no complete record of their service. When well led, the militia often performed valiant service, as is shown by the victory of the Virginia and Carolina militia at King's Mountain.[11]

Constant action was necessary to hold the Patriot militia together. At the Battle of Hanging Rock, about eight hundred militia attacked five hundred British regulars and Tories under Lord Ramdon. Of the latter, one hundred and sixty were members of Tarleton's infantry. Sumter and Davie made the mistake of attacking Colonel Bryan's Tories instead of the British. Nevertheless, the attack was successful until the commissary stores were captured and the men became intoxicated and loaded with plunder.[12] Thus were Sumter and Davie deprived of a victory within their grasp and one to which their zeal entitled them.[13] In this battle the contest was largely one of North Carolinians against North Carolinians, a fact which rendered the contest all the more bitter.

Any joy derived from the outcome of the Battle of Hanging Rock was soon dissipated by Gates's ignominious defeat at Camden. Here North Carolina lost in prisoners five hundred men including Brigadier General Rutherford and many other officers, with numerous transports and supplies of war.[14]

Many Tories near Waxhaw Creek who had been held in restraint by Colonel Davie's cavalry now joined forces with Cornwallis. The only force left in North Carolina to oppose the British was two small companies of riflemen under Major George Davidson.

The defenseless condition of North Carolina at this time was due to the generous aid she had given to other states. Her two Continental regiments, which when full comprised fifteen hundred men each, had been captured in the fall of Charleston, May 12, 1780, after serving on the Hudson and in New Jersey and Pennsylvania. At Charleston one thousand men of the

---

[11] Connor, *North Carolina*, I, 438.   [12] Wheeler, *op. cit.*, II, 193.

[13] Henry Lee, *Memoirs of the War in the Southern Department of the United States* (London, 1869), p. 178.

[14] Graham, *General Joseph Graham and His Papers on the North Carolina Revolutionary History*, p. 248.

North Carolina Militia were also made prisoners of war. At the defeat of Gates, North Carolina had present a full division of militia under Major General Caswell and lost in prisoners five hundred men. Appeals of South Carolina for aid had never been in vain.

On September 8 Cornwallis set out from Camden to accomplish the conquest of North Carolina before Congress could bring another army into the field to oppose him. His plan was to spend the winter restoring the royal authority, laying up supplies and providing horses for the next campaign, and filling in his ranks with Tories. His march was disputed by Colonel Davie, who with a small force fell upon a small detachment at Wahabs Plantation and carried off ninety-six horses and one hundred and twenty stands of arms.[15] Cornwallis continued his march towards Charlotte the following day, constantly threatened by Colonel Davie, whose force of one hundred and fifty men had been augmented by the arrival of one thousand militia under Sumner and Davidson. Although, after a stout resistance, the British occupied Charlotte, their stay was brief. Food was obtained from the surrounding country with difficulty, and everywhere their foraging parties were disastrously attacked by the militia. In these encounters each side lost heavily in officers and men.[16]

In order to stimulate Loyalist recruits Governor Martin, who had accompanied Cornwallis to Charlotte, in a proclamation to the inhabitants on October 3, appealed to them as follows:

I do hereby exhort and invite all the young men and able bodied men to testify the reality of their loyalty and spirit, by enlisting in the Provincial Corps, which are forthwith to be raised and put under my command, as his Majesty's Governor of the Province, hereby informing and assuring them, that they are and will be required to serve only during the rebellion, and within the Provinces of North and South Carolina and Virginia, under officers of their own recommendation, that each man will receive the bounty of three guineas at the time of enlistment and all the pay, clothing, appointments, and allowances and encouragements of soldiers of his Majesty's

---

[15] Lee, *op. cit.*, pp. 195-196.   [16] *Ibid.*, p. 192.

army, and will be entitled at the end of the Rebellion when they are to be discharged to free grants of land.[17]

Several Tories were at once sent off to distribute the proclamation throughout the country. The Board of War for the state, which had been recently set up by the Assembly, commenting on this proclamation, asserted that it was the same method that had been used in South Carolina, but they doubted that it would have any effect on their state.[18]

While Cornwallis was advancing on Charlotte, he sent Colonel Ferguson over Broad River with one hundred and fifty regulars and a like number of Tories with spare arms and ammunition to arouse, arm, and equip the Loyalists in that region, who were only awaiting an opportunity to join their friends.[19] There they flocked to him in great numbers, whom he rapidly armed and organized into companies until his force amounted to thirteen hundred men, all of whom were well armed and equipped. Many of the weaker Loyalists at this time were kept true to the King through the acts of their still more loyal neighbors. It was declared that whoever should act a treacherous part by abandoning the royal cause, deserting his battalion, or disobeying the order of his commanding officers, was a worse enemy to the King and country than were the rebels themselves.[20] Sometimes it was difficult to distinguish the honest Tory from him who might support the British merely to save his property. When it was feared that Ferguson might pass through Burke County, Colonel McDowell called the leading men together and suggested that they should take the British protection at Gilbert Town, thus saving the Whig stock so necessary for the support of the country. Several of the leading men refused to engage in such a dishonest deal, but Captain John Carson, Benjamin and William Davidson, and others professed allegiance to the King and saved many valuable herds of cattle.[21]

[17] Graham, *General Joseph Graham and His Papers on the North Carolina Revolutionary History*, p. 235.   [18] *S.R.N.C.*, XIV, 771.
[19] Graham, *General Joseph Graham and His Papers on the North Carolina Revolutionary History*, pp. 274-275.
[20] Draper, *op. cit.*, p. 140.   [21] *Ibid.*, p. 150.

Ferguson permitted his Tory followers to visit their homes on brief furloughs. This good strategy tended to keep up their morale and to induce others to join him. When Ferguson received the news that the "Over the Mountain Men," led by such men as Shelby and Sevier, were about to attack him, he became worried. He needed recruits and sent out the following appeal to the inhabitants of North Carolina:

> DENARD'S FORD, BROAD RIVER
> LYON COUNTY, OCTOBER 1, 1780
>
> GENTLEMEN: Unless you wish to be lost in an inundation of barbarians who have begun by murdering an unarmed son before the aged father, and afterwards lopped off his arms, and who by their shocking cruelties and irregularities, give the best proof of their cowardice and want of discipline: I say if you wish to be pinioned, robbed, murdered, and see your wives and daughters in four days abused by the dregs of mankind, in short if you wish or deserve to live, and have the name of men, grasp your arms in a moment and run to camp.
>
> The Back Water men have crossed the mountains; McDowell, Hamilton, Shelby, and Cleveland are at their head, so that you know what you have to depend on. If you chose to be degraded forever and ever by a set of mongrels, say so at once and let your women turn their backs on you, and look out for real men to protect them.
>
> PAT FERGUSON, Major 71st Regiment

Five days later he sent an appeal to Cornwallis for three or four hundred soldiers, part dragoons. It was only because he was greatly outnumbered that Ferguson felt this need for aid.[23] His army at this time consisted of about one hundred rangers, who were provincial troops raised in New York and New Jersey and about one thousand Tories from North and South Carolina.[24] Raper, in his account of the Battle of King's Mountain, observes that these Tories seem to have been a class of men quite as unobjectionable as the temptation and unrestrained recklessness of war ordinarily could permit the military to be,

[22] *Virginia Gazette*, Nov. 11, 1780; Wheeler, *op. cit.*, p. 103; James G. M. Ramsey, *The Annals of Tennessee to the End of the Eighteenth Century* . . . (Charleston, 1853), p. 203; Draper, *op. cit.*, p. 204.
[23] Sir Banastre Tarleton, *A History of the Campaigns of 1780 and 1781 in the Southern Provinces of North America* (London, 1904-1909), p. 193
[24] *Ibid.*, p. 156.

and that they were by many accounts as brave and reliable as any British troops in America.

The battle resulted in the defeat of Ferguson and his Tory soldiers. The action of the Patriots towards the defeated was perhaps the most brutal and unforgivable of that in any encounter during the entire war. Even after the soldiers surrendered and exhibited white flags, they continued to be shot down. This was largely in retaliation for the treatment Colonel Bedford's men had received from Colonel Tarleton the preceding May. One author writes that even after submission the slaughter continued until the Americans were weary of killing. Colonel Campbell had at last stopped the needless murder, when the Americans were fired upon by a band of Loyal Militia returning from foraging and unacquainted with the surrender. At any rate, Colonel Campbell ordered his men to fire upon the now disarmed and surrendered men, and several hundred were reported killed.[25] This was doubtless an exaggeration. Of the eleven hundred rangers and Tories present, over six hundred were captured and nearly all the rest killed or wounded. There was one instance of brother killing brother in this battle, and a family, the Logans, had two sons fighting on each side.[26]

When the victors reached Gilbert Town a week after the battle, they held a court-martial, tried thirty-six men, and found them guilty of breaking open houses, killing the men, turning the women and children out of doors, and burning the houses. Some of them seem to have been convicted on one-sided and prejudiced evidence.[27] Nine of the condemned men were executed in the evening of the day on which they had been tried. Their names were Colonel Ambrose Mills, Captain James Chitwood, Captain Wilson, Captain Grimes, Lieutenant Lafferty, John McFall, John Bibby, Captain Gilkey, and Augustine Hobbs. They were swung off three at a time and left suspended at the place of execution. Contemporary writers spoke very highly of the way in which these men went to their death:

[25] Draper, *op. cit.*, p. 285.
[26] *Ibid.*, p. 315.　　　　[27] *Ibid.*, p. 332.

"They died like soldiers, like martyrs, in their own and in their friends estimation. These brave but unfortunate Loyalists with their latest breath expressed their unutterable detestation of the Rebels and of their bad and infamous proceedings; and as they were being turned off, extolled their King and the British Government. Mills, Wilson, Chitwood, Lafferty, Bibby, McFall, and Gilkey were from North Carolina."[28]

That the rest of the condemned men were pardoned may have been due to the fact that one of them had already escaped through the aid of his younger brother, who had cut the cords that bound him. According to some writers, fear of retribution that might be visited on them by Tarleton, should he succeed in capturing them, brought an end to the execution. This motive would appear to be contradicted by Allaire's newspaper narrative, which gave the following account:

On the morning of the fifteenth Colonel Campbell had Intelligence that Colonel Tarleton was approaching them, when he gave orders to his men, that should Tarleton come up to them, they were to immediately fire upon Captain De Peyster and his officers who were in the front, and their second volley on the men. During this day's march the men were compelled to give thirty-five continental dollars for a single ear of Indian corn, and forty for a drink of water, they not being allowed to drink when fording a river; in short the whole of the Rebels conduct from the surrender of the party into their hands is incredible to state. Several of the militia were worn out with fatigue, not being able to keep up they were cut down and trodden to death in the mire.[29]

During the long march many of the prisoners escaped, but if unfortunate enough to be taken, were executed. The trial of the prisoners continued, and Captain Green and Lieutenant William Langman in the absence of Colonel Campbell were tried before Colonel Cleveland and sentenced to be executed. Green by accepting a British commission and fighting at King's Mountain was charged with having violated the oath he had taken as an officer, to support the government of the state of North Carolina and of the United States. That night they escaped from their captors and long survived the war.

[28] Ibid., p. 340.   [29] Ibid., p. 346.

This defeat was a death blow to the Loyalists of the Carolinas, from which they never recovered.[30] Bancroft declared that the victory of King's Mountain changed the aspects of the war in that it encouraged the spirit of resistance, not only in the Carolinas, but also in the other colonies from Virginia to New York.[31]

The Tories were so closely watched that they found it difficult to join Cornwallis. When they passed through the country, they plundered, paroled, and disarmed the inhabitants who supported revolution until they were defeated by the Virginia and Carolina militia.[32] On news of Ferguson's defeat, Cornwallis immediately retreated from Charlotte and established his camp at Winnsboro, South Carolina, between Camden and Ninety Six, in order to be able to protect these two important posts. This was the more necessary since the Tories in the vicinity of Ninety Six had informed Cornwallis that they were ready to submit as soon as the rebels arrived.[33]

In the meantime the Battle of Cowpens in South Carolina was fought between Morgan and Tarleton. In the conflict, which lasted for less than an hour, Tarleton lost one hundred killed, two hundred and twenty-nine wounded, and six hundred prisoners, altogether about 85 per cent of his command. Morgan's loss was only twelve killed and sixty wounded.[34] Realizing that he was not strong enough to meet the main army of Cornwallis, Morgan retreated northward with Cornwallis in pursuit. When General Greene, on the Pee Dee River, learned of Morgan's victory and retreat, he hastened to join him on the east bank of the Catawba River. In close pursuit of Morgan, Cornwallis reached the river only to find it impassable on account of recent rains. At Ramsaur's Mill, when only twenty miles behind Morgan, Cornwallis burned all tents, baggage, and extra supplies in order that his army might travel faster and overtake the fleeing Morgan.

[30] Benson J. Lossing, *The Pictorial Field-Book of the American Revolution* (2 vols.; New York, 1860), II, 428-429. [31] Bancroft, *op cit.*, X, 340. [32] *S.R.N.C.*, XIV, 698-699. [33] *Ibid.*, XV, 288.
[34] Francis Vinton Greene, *The Revolutionary War and the Military Policy of the United States* (New York, 1911), p. 231.

Now began the famous retreat of Morgan to the banks of the Dan River in Virginia, with Cornwallis in hot pursuit. This retreat, called one of the most memorable in the annals of war, exhibited great military skill on the part of Greene.[35]

After crossing the Catawba, Greene lingered with the militia to dispute the crossing of Cornwallis and Tarleton. He was almost captured by the British scouting parties before he rode forward and joined his main army. He joined his men under Morgan, who had reached the Yadkin and crossed over in boats. When Cornwallis arrived, he was again forced to seek a crossing at a more shallow ford thirty-five miles upstream. He did not think this a disadavantage, since it would enable him to reach the fords of the Upper Dan ahead of Greene and thus force him to fight; he did not think the latter could cross the Lower Dan.

Greene had now assembled his entire force, but was not strong enough to risk battle without the aid of the militia. These refused to rise to his aid, and he continued his retreat to the Dan and crossed over in the boats which he had collected.

Cornwallis was now in a dilemma. Greene had escaped from him and was in a position to continue his retreat farther into Virginia and to join with Steuben, whose combined forces would be too strong to be attacked. Already two hundred and thirty miles from his base of supplies, Cornwallis decided to retrace his steps back across North Carolina and raise the Royal Standard at Hillsboro in an attempt to raise the Loyalist Militia in that region. Greene now moved in pursuit of Cornwallis, and the pursuer became the pursued.

At the news of the approach of Cornwallis to Hillsboro, David Fanning had been able to raise three hundred Loyalists, who were eager to join his standard.[36] These men under Colonel Pyle were disastrously defeated by Lieutenant Colonel Lee, over ninety being killed, while Lee did not lose a man. Lee accomplished this one-sided massacre by disguising his men as Britishers and friends of the Loyalists. Suddenly his men

[35] Tarleton, *op. cit.*, p. 229.
[36] Narrative of David Fanning, *S.R.N.C.*, XXII, 121.

fell upon the unsuspecting Loyalists, who were stunned by the action and asked them to stop firing as they were their best friends. Stedman, in describing the encounter, writes: "Humanity shudders at the recital of so foul a massacre; but cold and unfeeling as it was, it proved most effective for intimidating the friends of the Royal Government."[37] At the close of the engagement some Catawba Indians arrived under Captain Oldham and with their spears were allowed to kill seven or eight of the wounded men.[38] Such atrocities usually led to retaliation on the other side. The cautiousness of the Tories after this encounter led to their undoing. A few days later a group of seventy or eighty Loyalists from the Deep River section and the eastern part of Rowan County attempted to join Tarleton. They were marching at night and, being hailed by a group of dragoons, were fired upon before they cautiously made reply. Four were killed and twenty or thirty badly wounded; most of the others escaped and went home. This mistake, coming soon after the massacre of Pyle's men, did much to discourage the Loyalists in this section.[39] Although the Loyalists hesitated to join the British forces, they still proved such a menace to the Patriots that the latter when their time of service expired were compelled to travel to their homes in squads under the leadership of an officer, since they made their way through the Tory settlements east of the Yadkin.[40]

Greene delayed meeting Cornwallis until all of his re-enforcements had arrived and he could be on equal terms. The meeting took place at Guilford, where Cornwallis suffered the greater loss in killed and wounded, although Greene was forced to retreat.

Cornwallis's victory was not of a nature to attract any number of Tories to the King's Standard. He later stated, in speaking of this defeat in North Carolina, that his failure was not due to his inability to protect the rising of the Loyalists

---

[37] Lee, *op. cit.*, p. 257.
[38] Graham, *General Joseph Graham and His Papers on the North Carolina Revolutionary History*, p. 320.
[39] *Ibid.*, p. 339.   [40] *Ibid.*, p. 341.

but to their timidity and unwillingness to take an active and useful part. After the success at Guilford Courthouse he declared: "Many of the inhabitants rode into camp, shook me by the hand, said they were glad to see us and that we had beat Greene and then rode home again."[41] Cornwallis now moved to Cross Creek, where he claimed that he received no material part of the promised assistance and supplies and so was obliged to continue his march to Wilmington. Lee, in his *Memoirs*, writes, on the contrary, that while Cornwallis was at Cross Creek the friendly Highland settlement zealously contributed from its small stock everything necessary for his army which the district afforded.

Clinton blamed Cornwallis entirely for the failure of the Loyalists to rally to his support. In his controversy with Cornwallis he stated that they rose after the victory of Camden, but afterwards when Ferguson was defeated they were left entirely without support, to be massacred by the rebels. After the victory at Guilford, Cornwallis did not have seven hundred men to support the Tories. His provisions were sufficient for only ten days, and he was actually in retreat when he called upon the Tories to support him.[42]

Cornwallis found Wilmington a haven of refuge. After taking care of the sick and wounded he decided to march northward to Virginia, since his army was insufficient for offensive operations against Greene.[43] With no army in North Carolina to oppose him, his march was a leisurely one. The Whigs in his path fled to the woods and swamps, while the friends of government rose in great numbers to wreak vengeance on their neighbors in retaliation for what they had suffered. So far as possible Cornwallis kept his soldiers from committing any outrages, for he hoped by this method to secure the co-operation of all the Loyalists in North Carolina. Lieutenant Colonel Hamilton, well known and universally esteemed and respected by the Loyalists of North Carolina, accompanied Cornwallis.[44]

[41] Benjamin Franklin Stevens (ed.), *The Campaign in Virginia, 1781* . . . (London, 1888), I, Introduction, p. xl. [42] *Ibid.*, I, 80.
[43] *S.R.N.C.*, XVII, 1017. [44] Lee, *op. cit.*, p. 412.

To him was due in a great measure the fine discipline maintained by the troops. Upon the arrival of the troops in Halifax County some outrages were committed upon the inhabitants in spite of the efforts of the officers. A sergeant and a private dragoon accused of rape and robbery were condemned to death, and the sentence was immediately put into effect.[45] Thus did Cornwallis carry out the best traditions of the British Army.

The inhabitants suffered much, however, from outrages committed by a train of loyal refugees who trailed the army and under its protection enriched themselves by plundering the inhabitants. Many of the Loyalist inhabitants were now so encouraged by the apparent success of the British that they began to assemble and to hold councils and to attack their neighbors, taking many prisoners.[46]

These conditions were augmented by the presence of Major James H. Craig, who with four hundred and fifty British Regulars had captured Wilmington in January, 1781. He, an active officer, at once set about capturing the most famous Whigs in the community and bringing them to Wilmington. One of the first to be taken was Cornelius Harnett, a Patriot, who lived just outside Wilmington. He attempted to flee, but was captured in Anson County, where he had been compelled to rest on account of a severe attack of gout. He was confined and, notwithstanding his condition, hurried to Wilmington on horseback.[47] On account of illness he was paroled after three days, and lived only a short time. General John Ashe suffered a similar fate. For a time he concealed himself in a swamp and visited his family only by stealth. His confidential servant betrayed him to Major Craig, who sent a body of dragoons to capture him. In attempting to escape he was shot in the legs and carried to Wilmington. He was tried and courteously treated by Major Craig, but contracted smallpox, was paroled, and soon afterwards died.

Craig and his men were mounted on the best horses of the Cape Fear region, and the swiftness of his excursions into the

[45] *Ibid.*
[46] James Owen Carr (ed.), *The Dickson Letters* (Raleigh, 1901), pp. 16-17.
[47] Katharine De Rosset Means, *Annals of the De Rosset Family*, p. 50.

country perhaps rivaled even those of Tarleton. Dubois, Slingsby, and other Tories awaited his signal for plunder and carnage.[48] The Patriots became so discouraged that large numbers gave themselves up to the Tories. John Ramsey, writing to Governor Burke from Deep River on April 13, 1781, was pessimistic. He wrote that the success of the Tories at Rock Fish Bridge seemed to be the finishing stroke and that the Whigs were so distressed that they were obliged to stay away from home constantly and to hide in the woods.

The fighting in North Carolina between the Whigs and the Tories now became a true civil war and was waged with fierceness rarely surpassed in border contests.[49] Secure in the protection of Craig, the inhabitants declared their Toryism in ever-increasing numbers. In an attempt to raise Whig troops in Duplin County in the spring of 1781, over half of them refused to enlist and openly declared for the King.[50] A little later Colonel Joseph Hawkins reported that of the people at the head of the Black River, all were Tories with the exception of one family.[51] Colonel Hawkins could secure provisions only by force, for the inhabitants had taken all their supplies to Wilmington and sold them to the British.

Major Craig invited the inhabitants to proclaim their allegiance before August 1 on pain of being treated as rebels. Many of the Scotch in the back country declared their loyalty to him and received commissions.[52] At this time the cause of the Patriots seemed almost hopeless in contrast. Men refused to enlist, and supplies could only be obtained by confiscation.[53] Governor Burke painted a dismal picture, indeed, when he wrote: "I perceive the country everywhere unprepared for defence; without arms, without discipline, without arrangements, even the habits of civil order and obedience to laws changed to licentious contempt of authority and a disorderly indulgence of private propensities."[54]

---

[48] William Alexander Graham, "British Invasion of North Carolina in 1780, and 1781," *North Carolina University Magazine*, Vol. I, p. 531.
[49] *Ibid.*, II, 366-389.   [50] *S.R.N.C.*, XV, 465.
[51] *Ibid.*, XV, 487.   [52] *Ibid.*, XV, 511.
[53] *Ibid.*, XV, 521.   [54] *Ibid.*, XVII, 910.

Cries for assistance against the Tories came from Bladen and Cumberland counties and the whole Upper Cape Fear region. The new Tory officers in Bladen County were most successful in raising volunteers. Some of the Patriots, afraid to stay in their homes at night, looked forward with apprehension to August 1, when they might all be destroyed.[55] This fear, however, did not deter them from wreaking vengeance on Colonel Brown, one of the newly appointed Tory officers: they broke into his house, murdered him, and plundered the premises of everything that could be found. At this time the Tories actually under arms in Bladen County outnumbered the Patriots five to one. Conditions in Cumberland County were even worse. The people were so frightened by Craig that when a muster was ordered only eight officers and men appeared.[56]

On August 1 Craig set out from Wilmington in the direction of New Bern to punish those who had not come and declared their allegiance. His force was composed of two hundred and fifty regulars and eighty Tories, which in Duplin County was augmented by three hundred more Tories. On the nineteenth of August, he reached New Bern, having destroyed every Whig plantation en route.[57] After robbing the inhabitants and destroying much property in the city, Craig returned to Wilmington by a more northern route in order to lay waste the plantations of his opponents. The Patriots followed in his wake and pillaged and put to death those Tories who had aided him.

One of the chief leaders of the Loyalists in this section was David Fanning, a North Carolinian, who had espoused the King's cause almost from the beginning. Probably no friend of the government during the entire war accomplished more for the British, and certainly none received less credit, either during the conflict or after its close. A. W. Savary in his introduction to *Colonel Fanning's Narrative of His Exploits* writes that he was one of the most remarkable characters developed by the American Revolution. He has been so often accused of cold-

[55] *Ibid.*, XXII, 543-548.
[56] *Ibid.*, XV, 569.   [57] *Ibid.*, XXII, 564, 566.

blooded murder by historians that his name has long been a synonym for all that was cruel and bloodthirsty. As a matter of fact, his killings were in retaliation for like offenses of the Whigs. In his writings, he usually told whose murder was being avenged at each killing. Savary defends him: "I conclude that Fanning had been grievously maligned by American writers who have been unable to view his career with other than the jaundiced eyes of the partisan. If he had done just what he had done in the American cause instead of the Loyal cause, he would have been acclaimed as one of the bravest and best of their leaders."

Caruthers has done much to blacken Fanning's name.[58] He speaks of the deeds of robbery, devastation, and wanton barbarity. Caruthers's statement that Fanning made it a point to kill every active and resolute Whig that he could get in his power, is so thoroughly disproved by the hundreds of prisoners paroled by Fanning that only a thoroughly prejudiced mind could have made it.

Fanning left a manuscript of about fifty pages in which he set forth his exploits in the Revolution. It is the best contemporary account of the Loyalists for the latter period of the war.

Fanning's decision to be loyal was arrived at early in the struggle. In May, 1775, the men of the company of which he was sergeant were given a chance to sign in favor of the King or in favor of the rebellion. The two groups at once began to oppose each other. One of the first of the Loyalists to be punished was Thomas Brown, who afterwards became colonel of the regiment of the East Florida Rangers, at Augusta. He had his feet burned, his hair cut, and was tarred and feathered.[59] Fanning had a number of exciting experiences. In January, 1776, he was made a prisoner by Captain John Burns, urged to take the oath of allegiance, stripped of everything, and four days later released on parole.[60] On June 25 he was again

---

[58] Caruthers, *Interesting Revolutionary Incidents: and Sketches of Character, Chiefly in the "Old North State,"* p. 54.

[59] David Fanning, *Colonel Fanning's Narrative of His Exploits* (Toronto, 1906), p. 9.   [60] *Ibid.*, p. 10.

confined, having been betrayed by a supposed friend, but he managed to escape and after a few months was again home. He was again captured but escaped before reaching the jail at Ninety Six and, after being aided by some Quakers and Loyalists, joined a party of King's men. Soon he found himself in the hands of the enemy and was tried for treason for raising arms against the United States of America, but was acquitted. Nevertheless, he was compelled to pay £300 for fees and expenses of his confinement. Not discouraged, he joined a party of the Loyal Militia in March, 1778, to march to East Florida. At the Savannah River the force turned back, and he and a companion subsisted for six weeks without bread or salt on what they killed in the wilderness. His captures and escapes continued regularly until he finally procured a commission from Major Craig.[61]

Fanning labored under difficulties for a while, since he lacked a regular commission from the King's Government. In July, 1781, in response to a general demand from the Loyalists he visited Major Craig at Wilmington, who commissioned him colonel in the Loyal Militia in Randolph and Chatham counties. The commission read as follows:

By James Henry Craig, Esq.; Major in his Majesty's Regiment commanding a detachment of the King's Troops in North Carolina, To David Fanning Esquire,

These are to appoint you to be Colonel of the Loyal Militia in Randolph and Chatham Counties, who are ordered to obey you as such, in all lawful commands whatever, and you are authorized to grant commissions to the necessary persons of known attachment to his Majesty's person and Government, to act as Captains and Subalterns to the different companies of militia aforesaid. As Colonel you are hereby fully empowered to assemble the militia, and lead them against any parties of rebels or others the King's enemies, as often and as necessary to compel all persons whatever, to join you, to seize and disarm and when necessary to detain in confinement, all rebels or others, acting against his Majesty's Government; and to do all other acts becoming a King's officer and good subject.

Given at Wilmington this 5th day of July, 1781.

J. H. CRAIG.[62]

[61] Ibid., p. 12.   [62] Ibid.

A week later he ordered a general muster and appointed a number of officers for each of the two counties. With his commission in hand and with his power to commission officers and enlist men, Fanning at once became the outstanding Tory leader in the state. He found it easier to raise men than to equip them, for of the four hundred and fifty men who flocked to him at this time at Deep River he had to return all but fifty-three for want of arms.

His first accomplishment was to attack the court at Petersboro, which was to hold a court-martial for the trial of several Loyalists who had refused to bear arms in opposition to government. The court was not in session when the town was attacked. Among his fifty-three prisoners were a colonel, a major, a Continental captain with three delegates of the General Assembly, and all the militia officers of the county except two who were absent. All were paroled except the fourteen who had been most violent against the government. Those not paroled were delivered to Major Craig at Wilmington.[63]

En route to Wilmington, George H. Ramsay and some of the prisoners signed a letter to Governor Burke in which they stated that most of Fanning's party consisted of men who had suffered great cruelties at the hands of the Whigs, having been unlawfully drafted, whipped, and ill-treated, without trial, their houses burned and plundered, and their neighbors barbarously treated. The fact that the Patriot leader, Philip Alston, was accused of having put a man to death had greatly incensed the Highlanders. In spite of all this the captured rebels stated that they had received nothing but respect and politeness at the hands of Fanning.[64]

Now for the first time rules and regulations were drawn up by Colonel Fanning and confirmed by Major Craig for the governing of the Loyal Militia of the state. Article X provided that quitting camp without permission, disobedience of orders, shirking of duty, plundering, and all irregularities and disorders

[63] *Ibid.*, p. 19.
[64] Caruthers, *Interesting Revolutionary Incidents: and Sketches, Chiefly in the Old North State*, pp. 165-166.

were to be punished at the discretion of a court-martial constituted as above mentioned, and by the approbation of the colonel or commanding officer, who had power to pardon or remit any part of a punishment, but not to increase or alter it.

Court-martial for the trial of an officer consisted of all the officers of the regiment he belonged to, except the colonel or commanding officer, and for the trial of a noncommissioned officer or private, of two captains, two subalterns, and three privates, the latter to belong to the same company as the person to be tried. The eldest captain presided, and the sentence of the court was to be determined by a plurality of votes and to be approved by the commanding officer.[65]

Colonel Fanning now proceeded through the country making war on the enemy wherever found. One of his first encounters was with Philip Alston, who was then on Deep River with twenty-five men. On Fanning's approach, Alston with his followers took refuge in a large house but was compelled to surrender. Fanning had determined to put them to death for having shot one of his pilots, when Colonel Alston's wife begged him to spare them. He generously did.[66]

In the summer of 1781 Fanning marched through the country with little opposition. He decided to march to Wilmington to secure a supply of ammunition, and on August 11 at Cross Creek on the Cape Fear River he was joined by Major Samuel Andrews and others. As they marched along the river, they captured prisoners, arms, and horses, and burned the plantations of the two Patriots, Captain and Colonel Robertson, who were brothers. All of the prisoners were paroled with the exception of twenty, who were delivered to Captain Leggett at Wilmington. Having delivered his prisoners, he remained but two days and immediately set out for the upcountry.[67]

When he reached Elizabethtown, he found Colonel Slingsby, who now commanded the Loyalists, in charge of the town with many Whig prisoners. The inhabitants of the neighborhood had suffered so much from the depredations of the Tories that

[65] Fanning, op. cit., p. 20.
[66] Ibid., p. 21.   [67] Ibid., p. 20.

an attack had been decided upon, although they were outnumbered almost three to one.[68] The attack was made in the early morning, and the Tories were completely surprised and routed. Slingsby, their leader, was mortally wounded, and eighteen of his command were killed, wounded, or captured. Large quantities of stores and ammunition were captured. This was one of the most disastrous defeats suffered by the Tories during the entire struggle.

Colonel Fanning persevered and continued to win many victories by rapid marches and by appearing on the scene when he was supposed to be elsewhere. If a Tory officer was in danger of capture, Fanning sent him aid as quickly as possible. When Colonel McGill with only seventy men was in danger of capture at Drowning Creek, Fanning marched all night and appeared in the morning with one hundred and fifty-five men to assist him. Undaunted by the fact that his opponent, Colonel Wade, had an army outnumbering his ten to one, he immediately ordered an attack.

So skilfully did he handle his men that in a little more than an hour Wade was defeated with a loss of nearly one hundred killed, wounded, and prisoners. Fanning's loss was five men wounded, one of whom died. After the battle Fanning's surgeons cared for the wounded—Whigs as well as Tories. Fanning also captured two hundred and fifty horses, most of which were laden with loot from the friends of the government.[69] In a comparison of the accounts Fanning's description is the more modest. Caruthers writes that had Colonel McGill carried out Fanning's orders, all of Wade's men would have been captured. He also gives Fanning the highest praise for his conduct during the battle. Caruthers is the only writer of North Carolina history who has spoken even once in Fanning's favor. After describing the battle Caruthers remarks of Fanning:

This was the first time he had been engaged, at least when invested with authority, and considered merely as a commanding officer he certainly acquitted himself with honor. Cool and self-possessed every-

[68] *S.R.N.C.*, XXII, 205.   [69] Fanning, *op. cit.*, p. 20.

where, judicious in his arrangements, ready to expose himself when really necessary, vigilant and quick to perceive where an advantage might be gained, and prompt and energetic to avail himself of every circumstance that could be considered auxillary to success, he showed that, with proper intellectual training and moral culture when his character was forming, he might have been made a commanding officer of higher grade and of much distinction, in a better cause too, and a more extended theatre.[70]

Colonel Fanning, on his way to Coxe's Mill, felt powerful enough to print the following notice and to circulate it throughout the country:

This is to let all persons know, that do not make ready and repair immediately to camp, they should be sent to Wilmington as prisoners, and there remaining, as such in the provost; and be considered as rebels, also, if any rebel is willing to surrender and come in he shall reap the benefits of a subject.

DAVID FANNING

Camp Coxe's Mill, 6th September, 13 H, Col's Com'g Loyal Militia.[71]

This appeal was not without its effect; four hundred and thirty-five men came almost at once and joined Fanning. This number was soon augmented by enough volunteers to make a total of nine hundred and fifty men. Colonel McDugald came forward with two hundred men from Cumberland County and Colonel Hector McNeil with seventy from Bladen. These numbers so encouraged Fanning that he determined it an opportune time to put into execution his cherished scheme of capturing the rebel Governor Burke of North Carolina. Acting with his accustomed promptness, Fanning marched his troops all day and the following night, and arrived at Hillsboro on the morning of September 12. In the skirmish that followed he suffered the loss of one wounded man, while he killed fifteen Patriots, wounded twenty, and took over two hundred prisoners, among whom were the Governor, the council, some Continental colonels, several captains and subalterns, and seventy-one Continental soldiers.[72]

[70] Caruthers, *Interesting Revolutionary Incidents* . . . , pp. 173-175.
[71] Fanning, *op. cit.*, p. 23.   [72] *Ibid.*, p. 24.

This was without doubt the most brilliant exploit of any group of Loyalists in any state throughout the Revolution. After releasing all the Loyalists and British soldiers, one of whom was to have been hanged that day, he left Hillsboro at noon with his prisoners for Wilmington. At Lindley's Mill on Cane Creek he was attacked by four hundred Continentals under command of Colonel Maybin and General Butler. Colonel McNeil had failed to take the necessary precautions for safety, and except for the masterful way in which the command was handled by Fanning, the prisoners might have been rescued. In the encounter the Loyalists lost eight men, including Colonel McNeil. After the retreat, in order to secure the prisoners, Fanning renewed the attack and in four hours put the rebels to flight. In this encounter he lost twenty-seven killed, and ninety wounded, sixty so badly hurt that they could not be moved. Among the casualties was Colonel Fanning himself, who received a shot in the left arm that broke the bone in several places. He was so weak from loss of blood that he remained behind in the woods and left the command to Lieutenant Colonel Archibald McDugald, Major John Ranes, and Lieutenant Colonel Archibald McKay. These men proved worthy of the trust their commander had placed in them and successfully eluded their pursuers until they met Colonel Craig, who had set forth from Wilmington to meet them.

Governor Burke was confined in the common jail in Wilmington for about two weeks and then removed to a fort on Sullivan's Island. In November he was paroled to James Island, where his life was endangered by North Carolina Loyalists who had fled there for protection. He broke his parole and escaped January 16, 1782; the military officers of his own state never quite condoned this action and lost their respect for him. In a long letter to General Greene he sought to justify his action, but Greene was not convinced.[73] Many of the other American officers also condemned Governor Burke's action in breaking his parole. Within two years after the expiration of his term as governor he died from dissipation.[74]

[73] S.R.N.C., XVI, 184-185.   [74] Connor, North Carolina, I, 493.

In twenty-four days Fanning had partially recovered and was joined by one hundred and forty new recruits. With these men he captured a large quantity of leather intended for General Greene at Camden. The amount was sufficient to outfit his entire company with a surplus left over for destruction. He was not to be let alone and was at once attacked by one hundred and seventy men and, while at first successful, was compelled to retreat. He then separated his men into small parties to await the arrival of ammunition from Wilmington. The ammunition was received with information that Major Craig had abandoned the city.

The Patriots who had been active, upon hearing this news, now separated into small parties and started for home. This made them easy prey for Fanning, who was especially anxious to capture those who were carrying away the goods and furniture of the Loyalists. One of his captives, Captain Kennedy, who had been taken with eleven men, now gave Fanning news of Captain Lopp, who with sixty followers was on his way up-country. Colonel Fanning with his thirteen followers attacked three times and compelled Lopp's men to disperse through the woods. During the attack Captain Kennedy took no part in the conflict, though guarded by only two men. For acting so honorably Fanning returned to him one of his horses, a saddle and bridle, and all of his men.[75]

At this time the Patriots were so worried at the activities of Fanning that Colonel Isaacs came down from the mountains with three hundred men to capture him and made his camp at Cox's Mill. Captain Cox issued a proclamation, signed by Governor Alexander Martin, in which pardon was promised to all Tories who would come and enlist in the Continental battalion for one month. This pardon was not to include anyone who had been found guilty of murder, robbery, or housebreaking.[76] The Loyalists suffered severely at the hands of Colonel Isaacs at this time. Their homes were burned and destroyed. One Loyalist, David Jackson, was caught and hanged without ceremony. Many of them laid down their arms when they were told by

[75] Fanning, *op. cit.*, pp. 26-27.   [76] *Ibid.*, pp. 26-27.

Colonel Isaacs that, if they would surrender, he would give them protection. Instead, they were made prisoners of war and lodged in the Salisbury jail.

At this time Colonel Fanning was powerless to aid his friends but he was gradually collecting a small band. With these, he immediately set out to have revenge on those who had been killing and plundering his supporters. The houses of Captain Cox and his father were burned, and an attempt was made to capture Captain Golson, who had been especially active in distressing the Loyalists. Captain Golson was not apprehended, but one of his chief assistants was captured and killed.[77] That Colonel Fanning could be merciful as well as severe was proved by the fact that another man was promised safety if he would desist from attempting the murder of Fanning's men. He forfeited his life when after his capture he attempted to escape.

Colonel Fanning, who was very fond of horses, was willing to take any risk to recover one when it had been taken from him. At this time a rebel named Thompson, having captured a horse which belonged to him, returned it to Fanning on account of fear and informed Fanning that the rebels would give him limited bounds if he would come to peace with them. Fanning also desired peace and sent his generous terms by a prisoner to Lawyer Williams and Captain Ramsay to be forwarded to Governor Burke. He asked only that neither he nor his followers should be called upon to say or do anything detrimental to His Majesty's cause for the remainder of the war. In case his terms were not accepted he threatened to continue warfare against the Patriots.[78] Williams and Ramsay, writing to Fanning as soon as they received his communications, promised to do everything in their power to bring about a settlement of the conflict. Both thanked Fanning for his fine treatment of them when they were prisoners in his hands and assured him that they would do everything possible to establish peace between him and Governor Burke. On January 15 Colonel Fanning received word from Captain Ramsay that his request for parole had been com-

[77] *Ibid.*, p. 28.   [78] *Ibid.*, p. 28.

plied with. His parole ground was to have its center at Hammond-Coxe's Mill and to extend thirty miles east and west and fifteen miles north and south. Within this area he and his followers would be free from attack. However, those of his party who had been guilty of wilful murder or plundering were not to be given immunity.

Colonel Fanning doubted the sincerity of these promises, for one of his followers, Captain Linley, was cut to pieces at this time. Fortunately, Colonel Fanning apprehended two or three who were responsible for the crime and in retaliation hanged them on the same limb. Negotiations continued, and on December 17, 1781, he and his officers with Captain Hinds and Captain Golson arranged terms of peace until he could write to their superior officers. Again Fanning expressed his determination to continue the struggle if his terms were not accepted.

The terms were not acceptable to General Butler, and on March 5, 1782, he wrote Colonel Fanning of his objections, but promised to send them to Governor Burke. Meanwhile, he exhorted Fanning to postpone the desperate measures which he had in contemplation.

Many of the Loyalist officers were now anxious for a truce, but until it could be arranged, the skirmishing continued with but little quarter being given by either side. Captain Walker and Captain Currie of the Loyalist Militia fell in with a body of the enemy and after an indecisive skirmish agreed to stop fighting, while their colonels arranged an armistice. When the proposition was made to Colonel Balfour, he replied, "There is no resting place for a Tory's foot upon the earth."

This delay in arranging terms led to the killing of a number of men, among whom was Colonel Balfour himself. In less than a week after his boastful reply, Colonel Fanning sacked his plantation and killed him and, as he himself said, "Put an end to his committing any more ill deeds." Fanning and his followers now ranged through the country, making prisoners of the enemy and burning their houses. Among the officers who had their property destroyed was Colonel Collier of Randolph County, who escaped with three bullets through his shirt. Not so fortunate was Captain John Bryan, who refused to come out of his house and accept parole. When his house was set on fire, Bryan promised to surrender if Fanning would spare the house on account of his wife and child. When he came out, he had his gun cocked and his sword ready for action, but was immediately killed.[79] So powerful was Fanning at this time that the men who were to meet at the Randolph Courthouse to appoint assemblymen, hastily scattered at news of his approach.

Major Dugin's house and plantation and all the other rebel officers' property in the neighborhood for a distance of forty miles were next destroyed. Colonel John Collier, much worried by the strength of the Loyalists, asked Governor Burke for aid. He declared that Fanning and his followers were well armed, mounted on the best horses, and able to rob and murder with impunity. This work was made easier by the fact that the inhabitants of the region aided and secreted them.[80] In March, 1782, William O'Neal and Major Roger Griffith both wrote to General Butler concerning Fanning. Major Griffith accused him of barbarously murdering women.[81]

Governor Burke now sent a message to Colonel Fanning that he was ready to accept terms as presented and that he would do everything in his power to have the council and Assembly agree to them. Meanwhile, the Governor ordered the captains of the light horse to depart to their various stations until they received further orders from the Governor and the council. Major Roger Griffith, Captain Joseph Rosur, William Calston, Thomas Duggan, and Edward Guin, all wrote to Colonel Fanning and expressed satisfaction with the terms which had been agreed upon. The Assembly refused to accept all the terms, and Colonel Fanning refused to withdraw any of the articles. Activities were resumed, and a William Doudy was killed as he attempted to escape after he had been made a prisoner.

Colonel Fanning was at this time desirous of peace and heartily weary of fighting. He desired to marry and to live a quieter life, and two of his officers, Captain William Hooker and Captain William Carr, agreed to be married at the same time. The day before their wedding they were attacked, and Captain Hooker was killed. Fanning and Carr were married,

[79] *Ibid.*, p. 32. [80] *S.R.N.C.*, XVI, 203-204. [81] *Ibid.*, XVI, 210-213.

and their wives were concealed in the woods, while news was given out that Fanning had gone to Charleston.[82] Finally, a truce having been arranged, Colonel Fanning, on May 7, went to Major Rainey's truce land on the Pee Dee in South Carolina and remained there until June, when he took refuge in Charleston. There he was joined by Mrs. Fanning. Upon the evacuation of Charleston they along with many others took passage to East Florida. When this colony was ceded to Spain, they sought refuge the next year in September, 1784, in Halifax, Nova Scotia. In his memorial to the British Commissioners in which he sought compensation, he declared that he commanded from one to nine hundred and fifty men, with whom he was engaged in thirty-six skirmishes in North Carolina and four in South Carolina. For all these services he received but £60 from the British Claims Commission.

The departure of Fanning from the state ended the civil war in North Carolina. Had Governor Martin offered more generous terms of pardon in January, 1782, the partisan warfare might have ended at that time instead of four months later. When Fanning saw his followers being tried in civil courts, convicted of treason, and hanged, he decided to keep up the struggle as long as possible. In retaliation, Fanning put to death such prisoners as he had captured.

The accomplishments of the Loyalists of North Carolina exceeded those of any other state both in the number of their engagements and successes. Beginning with the Battle at Moore's Creek Bridge in February, 1776, unaided by the British, they engaged in intermittent and often successful warfare against the organized militia of the state until 1780. The British depended upon them for support in practically every engagement in the state during 1780 and 1781. Although the last British soldier left North Carolina on November 18, 1781, when Major Craig evacuated Wilmington, Colonel Fanning with his faithful followers continued the struggle until May, 1782. Then Colonel Fanning left the state. No other group of Loyalists could boast of having captured the governor and the entire legislature of their state.

[82] *Ibid.*, XXII, 225.

CHAPTER VII

ANTI-LOYALIST LEGISLATION

ANTI-LOYALIST legislation in North Carolina, broadly speaking, may be thought to consist of the acts and resolves of the various committees of safety and of the various provincial and state congresses. These acts and resolves may be classified as follows: confiscation, disqualification, and banishment. The legislation began as early as 1774 and did not cease until the ratification of the Federal Constitution. One of the first, if not the first, resolve of any committee against a disaffected person was that taken by the Safety Committee of Halifax County in December, 1774, against Andrew Miller. They resolved that after the payment of their just debts and the fulfillment of their contracts they would have no further dealings with him.[1] Since the resolves and the work of the committees were for the most part considered in the chapter on committees of safety, they will not be discussed here.

After the Battle of Moore's Creek Bridge in February, 1776, it was inevitable that some action should be taken by the Colonial Congress against the late insurgents and their supporters. The Provincial Congress which was in session at Halifax on April 27, 1776, published a declaration which explained the necessity the Congress had been under to remove the prisoners to the other provinces for the safety of North Carolina. At the same time the Provincial Congress passed a resolution authorizing the Committee of War, Secrecy and Intelligence to remove not more than forty of the Tories with their families to such places as the committee should find most safe and convenient. The feeling against the Tories at this time was not very bitter, since the resolves also provided that they should be allowed to make such disposals of their estates and property as they saw fit.[2] The preceding Congress, while in session in

---

[1] *Col. Rec. of N. C.*, IX, 1102.   [2] *Ibid.*, X, 545-546.

March at New Bern, had passed resolutions that all persons who should be disarmed by the town and county committees, and that all other suspected persons who had not taken up arms against the colony should be required to take the following oath of allegiance:

I do solemnly and sincerely swear on the holy Evangelists of Almighty God that during the present unhappy contest between Great Britain and America, I will not under any pretense whatever oppose or take up arms to oppose the Continental or Provincial Congresses or any troops raised by acting under the authority of these nor will I directly or indirectly, either personally or by letters, consult, or advise, or give intelligence to any of his Majesty's Governors, general officers, soldiers or others employed by land or sea to carry into execution and enforce obedience to the several Acts of British Legislature, deemed oppressive to these colonies: I will not by example, opinion, advice or persuasion endeavor to prejudice the people or any of them in favor of Parliamentary measures or against those recommended by the General and Provincial Congresses until it shall please God to restore peace and good understanding to the contending powers.[3]

In May, 1776, the Provincial Congress resolved that any inhabitants of the colony who should be convicted of taking arms against America or giving aid to the enemy should forfeit all his goods, chattels, lands, and tenements to the colony to be disposed of by Congress.[4] Independence from Great Britain had not been declared, but laws against the Tories were already in effect.

The first important act to affect the Tories was passed by the General Assembly of the state of North Carolina in April, 1777, and was entitled "An act declaring what crimes and practices against the State shall be Treason and what shall be Misprison and Treason, and providing punishments adequate to Crimes of both classes, and preventing the dangers which may arise from the persons disaffected to the State." The act declared, first of all, that people then residing in the state owed allegiance to it. People guilty of certain acts against the state were also guilty of treason, the punishment of which was death,

[3] *Ibid.*, X, 476.   [4] *Ibid.*, X, 545.

with the confiscation of the estate of the person convicted. The judge was permitted to appropriate as much of the estate as was necessary for the support of the family. Those who had not directly aided the enemy, but who had given them intelligence and spoken against independence, when convicted, were to be judged guilty of "misprison of treason" and to suffer imprisonment during the war and to forfeit to the state one half of their lands, goods, tenants, and chattels. Any creditable person could bring the accusation and exact surety for his appearance at the next meeting of the superior court of the district, or lacking such surety remove him to jail.

Another section of the act was intended to take care of all those people in the state who still considered themselves subjects of Great Britain or were in any way friendly towards the mother country. It provided that all former officers of the King of Great Britain and all subjects of the state (Quakers excepted) who were now living within the state or should come to live within the state and had traded immediately with Great Britain or Ireland within the last year either in their own right or acted as factors, storekeepers, or agents there or in any part of the United States of America or Ireland, should take the following oath of abjuration or allegiance or depart from the state:

I will bear faithful and true allegiance to the State of North Carolina, and will truly endeavor to support, maintain and defend the independent Government thereof, against George the Third of Great Britain, and his successors, and the attempts of any other Person, Prince, Power or State or Potentate, who by secret acts, Treasons, Compromises, or by open Force shall attempt to subvert the same, and will in every Respect conduct myself as a fearful orderly subject: and that I will disclose and make known to the Governor, some member of the Council, or State, or some Justice of the Superior Courts, or of the Peace, all treasons, conspiracies, or attempts committed or intended against the State which shall come to my knowledge.[5]

The Quakers, Moravians, Mennonites, and Dunkards took a similar oath except that it did not obligate them to defend the

[5] *S.R.N.C.*, XXIV, 11.

government. The county courts and the justices of the peace had full authority to bring people to court and to force them to take the oath. Failure to take the oath carried with it the sentence of banishment from the state within thirty days with the necessity of posting bond for compliance. At the end of sixty days the court was authorized to send the person out of the country, either to Europe or to the West Indies, at the expense of the offender. In case the offending person returned to the state after being sent away, he was to be adjudged guilty of treason and to be proceeded against accordingly.[6]

In a few months the feeling against the Tories became more bitter, and a new and more stringent act was passed. This act of December, 1777, required an oath of allegiance of all males over sixteen years of age. Those refusing to take the oath were to be proceeded against as in the previously mentioned cases, or at the discretion of the court might be permitted to remain within the state. Those who were permitted to remain were deprived of the right to vote or to hold office, bring suit at law, acquire land by purchase or inheritance, keep arms or guns within their house, or leave the state after the expiration of sixty days without consent of the governor and the council.[7] The passage of this confiscation act was by no means unanimous. The vote was twelve for and nine against it. Those voting favorably were Elisha Battle, Benjamin Exum, Robert Summer, Ralph Gorrell, James Coor, James Sanders, Robert Salter, David Lourie, John Spicer, John Gray, A. MacLaine, and Luke Sumner. The opposition consisted of Memucian Hunt, Ambrose Ramsey, John Carter, Charles McLaine, Griffith Rutherford, Benjamin Seawell, James Kenon, Charles McDowell, and Michael Rogers.[8] Many opponents of the bill had friends among the Tories whose estates they were anxious to save.

The following year, 1778, it was found necessary to pass another act to alter and to carry out more fully the provisions of the foregoing one. The lawmakers were inexperienced in this kind of legislation and could use only the trial and error method. This act seemed necessary, since large numbers had

---

[6] *Ibid.*, XXIV, 12.　　　[7] *Ibid.*, XXIV, 84-89.　　　[8] *Ibid.*, XII, 252.

failed to take the oath and their property was liable to confiscation. In order that the commissioners of confiscated property might have a record of all Tory property, they were authorized to ask the constables in the counties to require the Tories to come and to declare all their property. The commissioners of each county were required to keep a record of all lands forfeited by this act which came into their possession, together with the names of the former owners. The forfeited land was not permitted to be rented in tracts larger than six hundred and forty acres nor for longer periods than one year. Provision was made that the Negroes and other personal property forfeited by the act should be sold at public auction at such times and places as the court should think proper. A further clause provided that the wife or children of such absentee Tories, now in or under the protection of the state, should be allowed as much of the estate of the absentee as they might have enjoyed had he died intestate in any state in the United States. This section removed much of the harshness of the former law. In addition, this act empowered the commissioners to collect for the state any money due to a person whose property had been forfeited, and to sell the real estate as well as the personal property of a Tory to satisfy judgments against a Tory estate. Finally, the law provided that the commissioners should receive and give discharge for all debts which the inhabitants should voluntarily offer to pay the Tories who had left the state. The indigent parents of these absent Tories were allowed to receive as much of the estate as they had heretofore received and as much more as would be necessary for their subsistence.[9]

This act at once brought forth a blast of criticism from both the friends and the foes of the Tories. Mecklenburg County sent a remonstrance to the Assembly in session at Halifax in October, 1779, complaining that the act was so partial to the Tories that it was repugnant to the nature and intention of confiscation, and that the public was not sufficiently indemnified for the injuries that it had sustained. The opponents of the law also complained because they thought the absentees through

[9] *Ibid.*, XXIV, 209-210.

their friends would enjoy the proceeds of their estates. It wa
contended that the land ought to be sold outright instead o:
being rented for one year, for sale would make it impossible
for the former owners to recover it by intrigue. The greatest
objection arose from the fact that there was no time limit within
which the heirs were required to claim their property; they
would eventually be able to claim all estates now declared to be
forfeited.[10]

As the war continued, the feelings against the Tories became
more bitter; in November, 1779, a bill was introduced into the
Assembly to carry out the confiscation act in a more severe
manner than had been done under the former law which had
been passed for the same purpose. This latter act doubtless was
satisfactory to the people of Mecklenburg County; but the
friends of the Loyalists in the Assembly, led by James Howard,
entered bitter protests. This act gave a long list of names of people whose property was declared confiscated because they were
absent from the state on July 4, 1776, or had since withdrawn
from the state and had not returned.[11] The men whose names
are in this list represented many of the most prominent Loyalists of North Carolina. Many of their names will appear later
among those who sought compensation from England. The
liberal provision of the former act in regard to widows and
children was changed to read that a widow should receive only
one third of her former rights with an additional allowance for
the subsistence of herself and minor children.[12]

Since this act was much more severe in its treatment of the
Tories than were any of the former, the more conservative
members of the Assembly, led by James Howard, presented a
protest to that body and set forth their objections. First, they
declared that the present act confiscated the property of a large
number of people who departed the state under compulsive
authority of the treason bill, although the bill specifically stated
that such persons should not come under the said confiscation
bill. The present act also condemned the property which was

[10] *Ibid.*, XIV, 345-347.
[11] *Ibid.*, XXIV, 263-264.   [12] *Ibid.*, XXIV, 268.

possessed of July 4, 1776, even though they had disposed of it legally according to the treason bill, and condemned it for the reason that the persons named had not returned and admitted themselves to the General Assembly for the purpose of receiving citizenship and regaining their property, while according to the treason act if they had appeared they would have suffered death. Another inconsistency set forth was in the fourteenth section of the present act which declared that bona fide sales made agreeable to the treason act should not be void.[13] A protest was then entered against that part which dealt less generously with the innocent wives, children, and parents. Lastly, the critics of the measure sarcastically remarked that they were signing their names to this protest in order that no merit be imputed to them as members of the House of Commons for the bright display of wisdom, virtue, and humanity which had been exhibited by that body.

In spite of this protest the law was passed by a convincing majority in October, 1779. When the bill had been voted on previously, in January of the same year, it had been defeated by a vote of thirty-two to sixteen. This indicates how sentiment against the Tories had increased throughout the year.[14] Threatened invasion of the state by the British, renewed activity on the part of the Tories, and need for the money which could be obtained by the confiscation and sale of Loyalist property were all factors in bringing about this changed sentiment.

Seizure and sale of the land began at once.[15] When Henry McCulloch, one of the largest losers of confiscated property in America, heard of the loss of his property, he began a lengthy correspondence with his friends in America in an endeavor to recover it. On March 3 he wrote from London to his friend Mr. Brimmage in North Carolina that the property already confiscated in 1778 was worth over £40,000. At the same time he said he could have saved it by the sacrifice of his allegiance and principles, a price which he would never pay. In August, 1778, McCulloch arrived in New York and anticipated an early journey to North Carolina. He wrote to a relative, James Ire-

[13] *Ibid.*, XIII, 992.   [14] *Ibid.*, XIII, 771.   [15] *Ibid.*, XIII, 992.

dell, to petition the Assembly on his behalf in an endeavor to save his property.[16] Iredell and his brother-in-law, Samuel Johnston, were frequently called upon by wealthy and prominent Tories to defend them or to present their petitions. A petition in favor of McCulloch was presented by Iredell in 1779, but was rejected by the Assembly. Although this petition cited the long years of service to the colony which McCulloch had performed as its agent in England, it was all in vain.[17]

By the summer of 1780 the jails of the state were overflowing with prisoners accused of treason. The state was in danger of invasion by the British and it became highly desirable that these prisoners should be disposed of. Accordingly, in September, 1780, an act was passed which provided that the accused could be tried by the magistrate of any county in which he happened to be held and that he would not be allowed counsel. If the prisoner was convicted, the magistrate was permitted to order immediate execution, while the sheriff was empowered to confiscate all the condemned man's property, both personal and real estate.[18]

Seizing the property of the Tories became so profitable that at last the Assembly found it necessary to regulate this seizure by law. Household utensils, wearing apparel, slaves, and anything else that could be carried off were taken in the name of patriotism. The innocent suffered with the guilty. The act provided that none except the commissioners of the confiscated estates in each county, or for want of commissioners the sheriff or coroner, should have authority to take charge of the confiscated property. Another section was provided to prevent the plundering of the inhabitants of South Carolina from the depredation of the people of the North. The sheriff was given authority to seize all property brought into the state from South Carolina, and, if the owner proved himself a faithful citizen of the United States, his property was to be returned to him. Persons convicted of stealing were to receive thirty-nine lashes

[16] McRee, *op. cit.*, I, 412.
[17] *Ibid.*, I, 438-442.
[18] *S.R.N.C.*, XXIV, 349.

upon the bare back for their first offense, while the second offense was punishable by death.[19]

Because of the presence of the British troops in the state throughout 1781 and 1782, the authorities hesitated to be too drastic in punishing the Tories. The laws passed always contained some defective clauses and had constantly to be amended. Their titles often became cumbersome to the extreme. A law passed early in 1781 was entitled "An Additional Act to an Act, entitled an Act for securing the quiet and inoffensive inhabitants of this state from being injured, for preventing such property as both, may be confiscated and from being wasted or destroyed, and for other purposes; and for continuing an Act, entitled an Act for suspending the operation of an Act, for carrying into effect an Act Commonly called the Confiscation Act."[20]

Provision was made for the seizure of all property described in the foregoing acts, and the commander of the militia in the county was compelled to aid in its seizure or to be subject to a fine of twenty thousand pounds. In order that the people might be encouraged to return to the allegiance of the state one clause read: "Provided nevertheless, that the estates of all such persons as have been heretofore in arms against and are now in service in defense of their State, and who shall continue therein so long as to complete the term of eighteen months actual service from the time of their entering respectively, and also the estates of all such persons who having joined the enemy, may return and serve in the army of this State, agreeable to a resolve of this General Assembly, shall be suffered to be and remain in the favorable possession of the respective families of all such persons, anything in this or any other law to the contrary not withstanding."[21] Many persons had sold their property or otherwise disposed of it to avoid confiscation, and all such transactions were declared null and void. Likewise, punishment was provided for all those who had made entries upon the land which was subject to confiscation. To restrain the many men in the state who had attached themselves to the enemy since June

[19] *Ibid.*, XXIV, 350-351.
[20] *Ibid.*, XXIV, 376.   [21] *Ibid.*, XXIV, 376.

of that year from voting at the next annual election for members in the General Assembly, it was decided that all of them should be ineligible to participate in the election.

Loyalists continued to fill the jails, and in 1781 an act was passed which, it was hoped, would provide for the trial of a large number. The Governor was empowered to call a court in any district of the state and to name three men to act as judges in the same. This act permitted the accused to employ counsel and to demand summonses to enforce the attendance of his witnesses.[22]

The radicals were anxious that the property confiscated in the Act of 1779 should be sold, and, in spite of the work of the conservatives, were able to get a law passed in April, 1782, entitled "An Act directing the Sale of Confiscated Property," which accomplished their purpose. By this act all the property confiscated in 1779 was to be sold, together with the property of James McNeil, late of Halifax County, and Alexander Munn, late of Wake County. Archibald MacLaine in a letter to Governor Burke has left a record of the attitude of the conservatives toward this act and confiscation in general. MacLaine considered the property of great importance, but complained that if it was sold according to the old plan the state would never receive any benefit from it. His scheme was to sell only perishable articles and to avoid absolute confiscation. The idea of confiscation of the landed estates of those who had traded with the British Dominions and the confiscation of the debts due to British merchants he thought most obnoxious. However, if the Assembly was determined upon selling the property, he asked that a different mode of selling be adopted and a new set of commissioners be appointed, as those now in charge were profligate scoundrels.[23]

The act as passed embodied many of the ideas of those who labored for conservatism. Seven commissioners were appointed to carry out the sales which were to be held before January 1 of the following year in Hillsboro, Halifax, Salisbury, New Bern, Wilmington, Edenton, and Morgan, but in no case was

[22] *Ibid.*, XXIV, 397.   [23] *Ibid.*, XVI, 247-248.

the sale to be conducted in two districts during the same week. All confiscated lands, Negroes, and horses were included in these sales and were to be sold on condition that the purchasers entered bonds to twice the amount of the purchase money. The deeds were to be issued by the state and to be registered in the county in the same manner as all other grants. One provision of the act acknowledged that certain persons had taken by force, or otherwise, property from the disaffected persons and applied it to their own use. These were required to bring in such property and surrender it to the amount of the value of the article. Section twenty, especially sweeping in its provision for confiscation, read: "Be it enacted by the authority aforesaid, that every person who has been resident of this State, and have heretofore attached themselves in any manner whatsoever to the enemies of this or of the United States, it is hereby fully and entirely expressed that all the property of such persons or person, shall be considered as having been forfeited to and for the use of the State, from the time that such person joined the enemy as aforesaid: and that all bargins and sales, wills, and devices made so as to interfere with this Act is, and is hereby declared to be null and void, to all intents and purposes."[24] The last paragraph of the act might be considered a triumph for the conservatives, for it provided that all the household goods of every estate liable to be sold and as much of the personal household goods as was necessary to support the wives, widows, and children of the owners must be set aside for their own use. In addition, they were entitled to one third of the land or as much as might be necessary for their use.[25]

During this session of the Assembly, Archibald MacLaine, who was a member, wrote a series of letters to his Tory son-in-law, George Hooper, who was living in Charleston, South Carolina. In these letters, which were sometimes hopeful and other times gloomy, he kept his relative informed of what was going on in the Assembly in behalf of their Tory relatives and friends. MacLaine was cheered by the fact that no act of banishment had been passed, and thus hoped the best for his friends.

[24] *Ibid.*, XXIV, 424.   [25] *Ibid.*, XXIV, 429.

He held the opinion that all those who went away at the evacuation of Wilmington might return in safety unless they had done something to exasperate the people, but if they had, there was no knowing what the people might do to them.[26] The fight in the Assembly was a bitter one, for the radicals, led by Griffith Rutherford and Timothy Bloodworth, were emboldened by the surrender of Cornwallis. In this trial of wits between the friends and foes of the Tories, Samuel Johnston with his brother-in-law, James Iredell, relative of the famous Tory, Henry McCulloch, represented the conservative forces in the Albemarle region, while William R. Davie, son-in-law of Allan Jones, and Allan's brother, Willie Jones, represented them in the Halifax section. William Hooper, Signer of the Declaration of Independence, and Archibald MacLaine, brother and father-in-law respectively of George Hooper, came from the Cape Fear section. In season and out, this group worked incessantly for their absent Tory friends and relatives.

This cleavage of the lawmakers of the state into two groups manifested itself as early as the meeting of the first assembly of the state under its new constitution in 1776. At that time the radicals were in control, and elected their candidate, John Penn, to the Continental Congress in place of Joseph Hewes, the conservative choice. The conservatives were generally men of property and accustomed to leadership; they feared to give power to the masses. Since they numbered among their friends and relatives many Tories, they were opposed to legislation which would injure that class. In the election for a governor which came in 1783, the conservative element which came largely from the east supported Caswell, while the west voted for the radical candidate. Thus early did sectionalism manifest itself within the state.

If one were prominent enough, it was possible to obtain an act from the Assembly giving him claim against the confiscated estate of a Tory. This was proved by the act of the Assembly in 1782 which gave Thomas Clarke, John Innis Clarke, and Anne Hooper, wife of William Hooper, a claim on the confiscated

[26] *Ibid.*, XVI, 956-957.

property of James Murray. Seven commissioners were appointed to hear and pass judgment upon these claims.[27]

Many of the Patriots had seized horses, wagons, and provisions of the Tories during the war. Now that peace had been declared, it was feared that suits would be brought by the inhabitants who had been thus despoiled. In order to protect the victors against any such claims, an act was passed by the Assembly in 1783 which provided that all personal actions and all judgments thereupon executed in consequence of, and during the late war with Great Britain until the first of May, 1783, in order to fell the enemy or carry on the war, should be discharged and made void.[28] Unfortunately for the Tories, there was no such law protecting them in similar circumstances.

Shortly after the termination of the war the Assembly passed an "Act of Pardon and Oblivion" for those in the state who had aided the enemy. The following clause from the act must have excluded many from its benefits:

Provided that always this Act or anything therein contained, shall not extend to pardon or discharge, or give any benefit whatsoever to persons who have taken commissions or have been denominated as officers and assisted as such under the King of Great Britain, or to such as are named in any of the laws commonly called confiscation laws, or such as have attached themselves to the British and continued without the limits of this State, and not returned within twelve months previous to the passing of this Act. Provided further that nothing herein contained shall extend to pardon Peter Mallette, David Fanning, and Samuel Andrews, or any person or persons guilty of deliberate and wilful murder, robbery, rape, or houseburning or any of them, anything herein contained to the contrary notwithstanding. Provided nevertheless, that nothing in this Act shall be construed to bar any citizen in this State from civil action for the recovery of debts and other damages. Provided also, that nothing herein contained shall entitle any persons by this law to be received to elect or be elected to any office or trust in this State, or to hold any office civil or military.[29]

This act was much disliked by the conservatives of the Assembly, for it placed their Tory friends in a difficult position. Archibald

[27] *Ibid.*, XXIV, 452.
[28] *Ibid.*, XXIV, 488-489.   [29] *Ibid.*, XXIV, 490.

MacLaine, after the passage of this act, wrote his son-in-law, George Hooper, advising him to become a citizen of South Carolina in order that he might be able to recover his debts in North Carolina.[30]

The Treaty of Peace having been ratified by Congress, the friends of the Tories in the North Carolina Legislature were anxious to secure legislation which would carry out the terms of the treaty and at the same time help their friends. A bill was introduced to reduce to system the confiscation laws then in force. McCulloch, Hooper, Harvey, and A. MacLaine voted with the affirmative but were unable to carry through the measure intended to help their friends. It would have provided that all lands of the men named in the confiscation acts which had not yet been sold would be restored to them on condition that they become citizens of the United States or sell the lands to bona fide citizens of the United States within a specified time.[31] Not yet discouraged, the friends of the Tories introduced a bill to repeal such of the laws of the state as were incompatible with the Treaty of Peace between the United States and His Britannic Majesty. Again, McCulloch, MacLaine, and Hooper voted in the affirmative, but with the minority. The feeling of greed and prejudice was yet too strong among those who hoped to gain still more at the expense of their unfortunate neighbors.[32] Hooper, commenting upon the rejection of the bill, pointed out that, because the carrying of the plan into effect might have some prejudicial consequences to individuals, this was not a reason for sacrificing the national faith and political characters of the state.[33]

In 1784, in spite of the provisions in the Treaty of Peace, a law was passed which provided for the sale of all property both personal and real estate which had been confiscated but had not yet been sold. The state was divided into the districts of Morgan, Salisbury, Hillsboro, Halifax, Edenton, New Bern, and Wilmington, and a commissioner was appointed in each district to conduct the sales. This law was very detailed in its

[30] *Ibid.*, XVI, 964-965. [31] *Ibid.*, XIX, 671-673.
[32] *Ibid.*, XIX, 765. [33] *Ibid.*, XXIV, 661-664.

provisions and made a real attempt to have the sales conducted in an honest manner.[34] The radicals now introduced a measure which disqualified from office every person over twenty-one who at any time had voluntarily aided the British in prosecuting the late war. The desire of the legislators to keep all former enemies out of the state was clearly written in the final clause of the act, which declared: "Nothing contained in this act shall be construed to encourage or permit the return to this state of any person who may have been a resident of the same, and who had at any time during the late war attached himself to the enemy, and who may have acted by commission or otherwise as officers, in any military or judicial department, and who may have not submitted to the laws of the state before the day of the ratification of the definitive treaty."[35] In order to protect the purchaser of confiscated property, an act was put through which provided that those who had bought confiscated property need not assume any suits brought against them by anyone named in the confiscation acts or by anyone representing them.[36] This often worked a hardship on those who had lost property illegally.

Among this mass of legislation, filled with injustices to the defeated and now disgraced Tory class, it is gratifying to find one act passed by the Assembly in 1784 which was for the purpose of mitigating the distress of the orphans of the Tory Thomas Bogg. In accordance with an act of the state in 1777 he had conveyed his property by deed of trust to Benjamin Blount for the benefit and support of Mrs. Bogg and the children. Mrs. Bogg having died, suits were brought against the estate which threatened to impoverish the children. To offset this action, permission was given to Blount to bring suit to recover any debts due to Thomas Bogg or any property of the said Bogg that the people might have in their possession.[37]

The latter part of the year 1785 witnessed several acts of clemency on the part of the state toward individual Tories. The remainder of the confiscated estate of Ralph McNair which had

---

[34] *Ibid.*, XXIV, 683-684.
[36] *Ibid.*, XXIV, 730.
[35] *Ibid.*, XXIV, 730.
[37] *Ibid.*, XXIV, 708.

not been sold was ordered to be held until the next meeting of the General Assembly. The executor of the estate was also authorized to collect all debts which had become due the estate since the expulsion of the said McNair. The same Assembly passed a law which enabled Mary Bedford to sell the personal estate of her husband, Jonas Bedford, who had abandoned her to join the British Army. Likewise, Edward Bridgin, a merchant of London, had restored to him not only his property which had not yet been sold, but also the money received by the state for that which had been sold.[38]

To enable the purchasers of confiscated estates to pay for them the more easily, the General Assembly in 1785 made the currency of the state, certificates granted to the officers and soldiers, final settlement certificates and currency certificates, all legal payment for such purchases.[39]

Sometimes this money was of little value to the state. Finally, an act was passed in 1786 pardoning all Tories who had returned to Washington, Sullivan, Greene, and Hawkins counties. This same group was also permitted to bring suit for the recovery of any property that had been unjustly taken from them.[40] Just what this meant was left for the courts to decide.

Not until the Constitution had been in effect for eight months did the General Assembly of North Carolina finally declare the Treaty of 1783 to be the law of the land.[41] During the same year Hugh Ross had all confiscated lands restored to him and was given the money for any that had been sold. John Coulson was also permitted to return to the state and was allowed to sue and be sued for property. Such suits were not to be permitted to be begun by him unless he should first take the oath of allegiance to the state. This act was not so much to help Coulson as it was to do justice to his grandchildren to whom he had given the land before leaving the state and who were now in danger of losing it because of suits brought against him by his creditors.[42]

[38] Ibid., XXIV, 761-762.
[39] Ibid., XXIV, 803.
[41] Ibid., XXIV, 885.
[40] Ibid., XXIV, 820.
[42] Ibid., XXIV, 993-994.

The acceptance of the Treaty of Peace by the state of North Carolina ended any further attempt to punish those who had placed loyalty to the King above loyalty to the newly formed government. The courts, however, were slow in righting the wrongs that had been committed, and the Tories, both within and without the state, remained resentful until a new generation was born.

CHAPTER VIII

CONFISCATION OF PROPERTY AND DEBTS
OF THE LOYALISTS

THE FIRST LAW IN North Carolina which provided for the seizure of the property of those disaffected to government was enacted in November, 1776.[1] Previous to this time, however, commissioners had been appointed in various counties to inventory the estates of the prisoners who had been sent out of the state. The commissioners for Guilford, Cumberland, Anson, Orange, Bladen, and Chatham counties were appointed by the North Carolina Provincial Congress, May 1, 1776.[2] The women and children were not to be molested, and none of the property except arms and ammunition was to be sold. In addition, any property which had been taken from them was to be returned. On May 6 the commissioners of Pasquotank and Currituck counties were ordered to take over the plantations of Thomas McKnight and James Parker and to rent them for one year. The farming implements were to be taken care of and not sold.[3] The estate of Archibald McArthur was likewise leased for six months.

Mere suspicion of being a Tory was sufficient for the seizure of Thomas Harrison. He was brought before the council and placed in jail until he paid the cost of his being apprehended and was then required to give the sum of £500 as security for his future good behavior. Meantime his estate was inventoried.[4] It was the custom when people were summoned before the council to compel them to pay the cost. In August eight horses which were the property of Loyalists of Cross Creek were brought to Wake County by Colonel Folsom and sold at public auction at the courthouse.[5] In November, 1776, the Provincial Congress resolved that the property of Josiah Martin in the

---

[1] S.R.N.C., XXIII, 985-986.
[2] Col. Rec. of N. C., X, 554.
[3] Ibid., X, 565.
[4] Ibid., X, 689.
[5] S.R.N.C., XI, 348.

palace at New Bern should be sold in February, 1777. The
tabulation of these articles required ten pages in the *State
Records* and their sale brought to the state £894 17s. 5d.[6] Much
Tory property was inventoried during the remainder of the
year, and a few sales of personal property were made.

In April, 1777, a law more stringent than the one of December, 1776, was enacted. Persons guilty of certain crimes
were to suffer death and the confiscation of all their property.
For lesser crimes the penalty was imprisonment for the remainder of the war and the loss of half their property. Still
other groups were required to take an oath of allegiance or to
leave the state at once. Merchants were given three months in
which to dispose of their property, after which it was forfeited
to the state.[7] A law in November required all males over sixteen
who did not take the oath to leave the state. At the same time
the county courts were ordered to seize all property confiscated
under former laws, except enough to support the families of
the traitors.[8] This law also confiscated the property of all persons absent from North Carolina on July 4, 1776, or who had
left since that time and were still absent, unless such persons
came before the Assembly which was to meet after October,
1779, and should be allowed to become citizens.

In January, 1779, the state proceeded with the confiscation
of the property of those who came within the meaning of the
former laws, and specified by name sixty-eight persons whose
property was declared to be confiscated.[9] The merchants, traders,
and others of Cape Fear protested the act. They thought it
would greatly endanger the commercial credit of the state because the merchants were accustomed to carrying on their business by means of credit abroad. It was feared that Great Britain
would consider property which was seized in this way quite
differently from the way in which she would that seized in
war.[10] Commissioners were appointed in the various counties
to sell personal property at public auction and to rent real

[6] *Ibid.*, XXII, 880-889.
[7] *Ibid.*, XXIV, 9-12.
[8] *Ibid.*, XXIV, 84-89.
[9] *Ibid.*, XXIV, 263-264.
[10] *Ibid.*, XIV, 203.

property. Early in 1780 the commissioners sold the property of William McCormick and Company of Pasquotank County for £102,870.[11] Since blankets sold in this sale for £150, one may judge that the real value of the money received at this time was not very great. Part of the property of Samuel Cornell was also sold during the year, while debts due to him to the sum of over £7,000 were paid into the State Treasury.[12]

Early in 1781 an act was passed which nullified the former law under which property was being sold. This may have been done on account of the depreciated condition of the currency or because of the general defectiveness of the law. The Confiscation Commissioners were compelled to pay to the treasurers of their districts all the monies which now remained in their hands and which they had received for selling confiscated property. The commissioners were also requested to return to the next session of the legislature a separate list of the property of every person that came within the confiscation acts. Such lists described all the lands, houses, and other real estate, slaves, horses, hogs, meat cattle, and sheep, and other movable property, and showed how much had been sold under the acts or claimed by other people.[13]

The new law passed in 1782 again provided for the sale of confiscated property. This law as well as those that followed was a compromise between the radicals who wanted to seize everything and the conservatives who wished, if possible, to save the property of their Tory friends and relatives. Iredell, writing in 1783, asserted that not only had the most wanton injury been done to individuals, but that the national character had been disgraced as well, since more than one article of the Treaty of Peace had been expressly violated. He thought the country would not long be a suitable place for residence and that the feeling of the people of sensibility must be deeply wounded.

The law was a triumph for the radicals because it provided

---

[11] The Papers of the Confiscation Commissioners are to be found in manuscript form in two boxes at the North Carolina Historical Commission, Raleigh, and will be referred to as Papers of the Confiscation Commissioners.

[12] Papers of the Confiscation Commissioners.

[13] S.R.N.C., XXIV, 352-353.

for the sale of all property confiscated under the act of 1779 together with that of Alexander Munn and James McNeil. The sale began at once. By a later act the commissioners were required to give an account of all property sold. Some idea of the minuteness of the accounts of the commissioners may be gained from the report of commissioner William McRee. He wrote, "I received from Robert Mylene when I took him, one old bible, one pair of razors, shaving box and bunk, one old shirt, stockings, two or three cravats and one cap."[14]

In November, 1783, fourteen counties reported the sale of Loyalist property amounting to more than £100,000. Griffith Rutherford of the Salisbury District reported £19,520. This amount included money received from personal property, real estate, and debts due to British merchants. The people of Halifax County swore that they owed Archibald Hamilton and Company £10,461 11s. These sums were confiscated and paid to the commissioners for the use of the state. William Moore profited most of all the debtors by the payment to the state of £3,000, which was due Archibald Hamilton and Company, and about the same amount to other merchants. This was all paid in depreciated paper currency. Others who took advantage of the situation to discharge their obligations were former Governor Nash, James Carr, and William Blount. In 1790 there was owing to the state £26,129 29s. 9d. from the commissioners of confiscated property.[15]

In October, 1784, the state enacted legislation to provide for the sale of the remaining Loyalist property in the state.[16] This law closely resembled that of 1782. The commissioners were allowed a commission of from 2 to 3 per cent for their work, and they seem to have acted efficiently. Most of the money for the sales was honestly collected and paid to the state. Under this sale Edenton, one of the seven districts into which the state was divided, reported the sale of £75,277 19s. 10d. The total sales at this time amounted to £284,452 4s., and of this amount

[14] Papers of the Confiscation Commissioners.
[15] S.R.N.C., XXIV, 661-664.
[16] Papers of the Confiscation Commissioners.

over 90 per cent was turned over to the state.[17] Benjamin
McCulloch paid debts amounting to £6,979 18s. 11d. due to
Archibald Hamilton and Company and others; Willie Jones
also satisfied his debt of £1,145 10s. 3d. to the same firm. The
largest loser seems to have been Henry McCulloch, from whom
more than sixty thousand acres were taken, though they did not
bring in as large a return as the lands of Nathaniel Duckenfield.
One of the largest purchasers was James Williams, who in
Orange County alone bought over three thousand, five hundred
acres, most of which had formerly belonged to McCulloch.
On April 29, 1788, there was recorded in the Secretary of
State Office a record of the sales of confiscated property in
thirty counties of North Carolina.[18] These varied in number
from one each in the counties of Camden, Chatham, and Currituck to eighty-three in Orange County. They ranged in size
from city lots of a half acre to tracts of six hundred and forty
acres and in value from £1 to £9,191.[19]

In 1787 an act required the sheriffs of the counties to sell
all Negroes, horses, wagons, and other property that had been
left in the state by the British Army.[20] From the sale of confiscated Loyalist property and from money paid into the State
Treasury in payment of debts due to the Loyalists the state
realized about £600,000. Since these sales took place at different
times and the money received was usually in currency which
was constantly depreciating in value, it is difficult to translate
the figures into real money values.

The sentiment of the people of North Carolina toward
those who had left the country, or who had lost property on
account of their being Tories, is well revealed in the correspondence of the times. During and after the war Henry McCulloch
kept up a correspondence with Marshall Holt, James Iredell,
William Eden, Cornelius Harnett, William Johnston, and

[17] *Ibid.*
[18] Confiscated estates were sold in the following counties: Anson, Beaufort, Bertie, Bladen, Brunswick, Camden, Carteret, Chatham, Chowan, Craven,
Currituck, Dobbs, Duplin, Edgecombe, Guilford, Halifax, Hertford, Hyde,
Nash, Montgomery, Moore, New Hanover, Orange, Randolph, Rowan,
Sampson, Tyrell, Wake, and Wayne. Audit Office, Class 12, Vol. I.
[19] See Appendix B.   [20] *S.R.N.C.*, XXIV, 901.

Willie Jones. In 1783 Willie Jones informed him that he need not ever expect to recover any of his property lost in America, for it was probably his property that brought on the confiscation act. The friends of McCulloch and the wiser and better part of the Assembly (which, Jones said, was the smaller) opposed the passage of the act, but in vain. The representatives of the back country united in favor of the act in order to get possession of the land.[21]

In June, 1784, James Iredell wrote to his Loyalist friend, A. Neilson, that after the peace had taken place he had hoped there might be unreserved communication between old friends regardless of political belief, but that such was not the case at present and that it was not without great danger that any might return who had left the country after the war began.[22] He informed his friend Henry McCulloch in January, 1785, that a petition in his favor had been introduced and rejected and a law had been passed for the immediate sale of all his confiscated property.[23] On account of his very extensive holdings McCulloch appears to have been the victim in a large number of cases. A number of people brought in claims for shares against his father as far back as the time they came over from Ireland with him in 1740. They asked for lands in payment, which they received mostly in Duplin County.[24] A year later Iredell wrote to his friend William Hooper in regard to the confiscation act, that no consideration under heaven would induce him directly or indirectly to support, countenance, or have a part in carrying out so infamous a law. He prophesied that the court at Wilmington would give little heed to the law.[25]

Archibald MacLaine in writing to Iredell gave a good explanation of how the court was evading the peace treaty. The Assembly at this time refused to point out any method to ascertain what had been confiscated, while the juries refused to allow any person whose property had been confiscated to maintain a suit. He explained the action of the juries to be due to

---

[21] McCulloch Letters of North Carolina Historical Society, Raleigh. March 5 and 28, 1783.

[22] McRee, *op. cit.*, II, 104.

[23] *Ibid.*, 116.

[24] *Loyalist Transcripts*, Raleigh.

[25] McRee, *op. cit.*, II, 133-134.

the fact that they were without principle and did not fear the vengeance of the Assembly so long as their actions were aimed at defenseless Tories.[26]

Loyalists were constantly writing to their friends in the state and asking them how they might get back their property. To such an inquiry from William Bayard, Jr., of New York, General Allan Jones replied: "The Assembly to their eternal disgrace have passed a law in which I am told they take away all power of suing for any property sold under any of the Confiscation Acts and direct the judges to dismiss all suits brought for such property. Thus you see all your hopes of justice destroyed by this tyrannical act of the assembly."[27]

Some were so bold as to return in person to collect their debts in accordance with the peace treaty. Alexander McKnight, a merchant, who had been compelled to leave in 1775, returned to New Bern in 1784 in the hope that he might recover his property and debts. He was confident that he had never injured anyone in the state and was not anticipating any trouble. To his surprise he was at once summoned by a mob who threatened him with corporal punishment and drove him back on board his ship. He made two more unsuccessful attempts to recover his property.[28]

A similar effort with almost the same results was made by John MacLellan to recover debts. He returned to Wilmington in 1786 but did not dare to journey to the back country because his life was threatened. His former debtor friends refused to see him, and the courts decided to try him for high treason. In anticipation of conviction and banishment he left the state.[29]

Archibald Hamilton, who was held in highest esteem by both friend and foe, was advised that it would be unsafe for him to return to the state. William Moore, who owed him a sum of money, had it cancelled by the Assembly by proving that his property had been damaged an equal amount by the army commanded by Lord Cornwallis and Lieutenant Colonel

[26] *Ibid.*, pp. 132-138.
[27] *A.O.P.R.O.*, Vol. I. Transcripts of these papers are at Raleigh.
[28] *Loyalist Transcripts.*   [29] *Ibid.*

John Hamilton.[30] In addition to having his lands in America confiscated, his farms in Scotland were sold to satisfy debts which his firm owed to residents of that country.[31] George Parker, a British subject who lived in Wilmington and who fled to England, suffered the confiscation and sale of his house and lot in Wilmington.[32] When Archibald MacLaine attempted to stop the court from taking the property of his friends he was wounded and driven from the courtroom, narrowly escaping assassination. Claims which MacLaine claimed to be false were brought against his estate and were granted. He reported that executions were levied on property which was sold for one fifth or one sixth of its value.[33]

Griffith Rutherford was one Patriot who placed duty to his country above the claims of friendship. When Henry McCulloch asked his advice, he was told that if he had taken it in the past they might now enjoy a friendly correspondence. Pity was extended to McCulloch because of his separation from his friends, but he was reminded that this condition had come about because he had committed the two blackest of crimes, high treason and perjury. Rutherford accused him of being such an inveterate enemy of the United States that with one blast of his mouth he would have annihilated it, had it been possible. He then ended his letter with these words: "My advice is that you send for your family if it suits you and go to Nova Scotia where I understand the Royal Brute of Britain has made provision for all loyalists in North America. For be assured I do not mean to prove traitorous to the laws of my much injured country."[34]

Samuel Johnston responded quite affably when appealed to by his old friend William McCormick, a former planter and merchant. McCormick, who was in England, wrote to Johnston as soon as the Treaty of Peace was signed, to find out about the chance of his returning to North Carolina in regard to his

---

[30] *A.O.P.R.O.*, Vol. I. [31] *Loyalist Transcripts.*
[32] A.O. Class 13, Bundle 100. [33] *Loyalist Transcripts.*
[34] François-Xavier Martin (ed.), *Notes of a Few Decisions in the Superior Courts of the State of North Carolina . . .* (Newbern, N. C., 1797), pp. 48-52.

property. Johnston informed him that all his visible property was gone and that probably his books and bonds had been sold at public auction. He mentioned the fact that the state had received no real benefit from the sales. He advised and entreated McCormick as a friend not to return to North Carolina, because the state was very bitter toward all those who left to avoid taking part in its defense. Since McCormick was one of those who was thought to have influenced the ministry by false or mistaken representation to continue the war longer than they otherwise would have done, he was especially obnoxious.[35] Letters of this nature must have influenced many to stay away from the state.

In spite of the laws which provided that suits would not be permitted against persons who had bought confiscated property, the daughter of Samuel Cornell brought suit against Singleton for the recovery of a house and lot and wharf which had been deeded to her by her father. This suit was known as Bayard and Wife *vs.* Singleton. It was decided by the judges that the plaintiffs were citizens of the United States and of the state and therefore had a right to a decision of their property by trial by jury. It was decided that Cornell was an alien and incapacitated to hold land. The jury found a verdict for the defendant. On the decision of this case, twenty-seven other similar cases were swept off the docket by nonsuits voluntarily suffered.[36]

Another notable case involving confiscation was that brought by Archibald and John Hamilton against John Eaton for the recovery of £800 of proclamation money which he owed them. This case was tried in June, 1792, by which time the state had adopted the Federal Constitution which made the treaty the supreme law of the land, and by statute had declared the treaty to be law in the state and had enjoined the courts of law and equity to render their decisions accordingly. Judgment was given for the plaintiff which showed that British debts, though compulsorily paid into the treasury under an act of the Assembly, might be sued for and recovered.[37]

[35] *Loyalist Transcripts.*
[36] Martin (ed.), *op. cit.*, pp. 48-52.   [37] *Ibid.*, p. 77.

Others who had brought cases earlier had not been so fortunate. Isaac Dubois wrote from Wilmington in 1786 that the people there were more violent then than they had been at any time since the war and that he was under act of banishment to leave the state within twenty days under the penalty of £500. In regard to the Articles of Peace, he said: "One of their worthy judges [Ashe] says he never reads them but with contempt and that he shall pay no more attention to them than he would to a copy of a school boy. Such language as this is in high esteem here and circulates very freely."[38]

Dubois's mother brought suit against John Ashe, Jr. It was argued that Mrs. Dubois was a Tory and thus had no right to sue, and although the court thought the debt was binding, it could not compel Ashe to pay a Tory. Robert Palmer, a famous Tory, who had been a member of the Governor's council and who had held many other offices, returned to North Carolina and in 1785 petitioned the legislature in an attempt to save his estate. He met with failure and was one of those later compensated by England.[39]

The Legislature of North Carolina passed numerous bills from 1784 to 1790 in favor of people who were suffering from the confiscation acts. An act in 1789 declared in favor of Jeremiah and Robert Fields in regard to property deeded them by their father, William Fields, before the confiscation acts were passed. All of the family were notorious Loyalists, yet the sons were now living in the state.[40] In spite of these and other similar isolated cases that might be cited, the vast majority of the Loyalists were never compensated by the state for what they lost. A small minority who possessed wealth or influence secured satisfaction from Great Britain.

Confiscation as first proposed and practiced was for the purpose of punishing and controlling the recalcitrant Tories. It succeeded as a punishment and at the same time drove many from the state. The later acts which provided for the sale of confiscated property and also for the confiscation of debts were

[38] *Loyalist Transcripts.*
[39] *Ibid.*   [40] *S.R.N.C.*, XXI, 269.

for the purpose of gaining money to finance the war in the state and to pay incidental expenses. The money derived from the sale of Samuel Cornell's house was used to pay the expense of the delegates from North Carolina to the Continental Congress.

That the state did not derive the financial benefits from confiscation that were anticipated was due to two causes. The first was the fact that purchases were often allowed to be made in depreciated currency and the second was due to the inefficiency and laxity of the commissioners who were at first in charge of the sales.

Most of the sales of real estate took place in 1786 and 1787. The record of these sales show to whom the property originally belonged, the person to whom sold, price for which sold, number of acres, and date of sale.[41] Some counties and sections of the state benefited more from the sales than did others. In Guilford, Orange, Randolph, and Rowan counties alone, which represent a solid block of territory in the north central part of the state, more than forty thousand acres were confiscated and sold; this land belonged to Henry McCulloch. It was sold in plots which averaged about two hundred acres each. By these sales many acres of land came into the possession of the small planter which indirectly must have been of benefit to the state in addition to the revenue which was realized from the sale. This confiscation in North Carolina tended to make the Revolution economic and social as well as political.

[41] See Appendix B.

CHAPTER IX

EXODUS OF THE LOYALISTS

THE FIRST ACT OF banishment against the Loyalists was passed in April, 1777, and many people began preparations at once to leave the state.[1] Exile could now be legally enforced. Many preferred banishment and the forfeiture of their property to perjury; others took the oath with mental reservations and remained unmolested. The colonel of the militia for Cumberland County reported that over two thirds of the people of the county intended leaving. Those who decided to leave were for the most part prominent in the economic and political life of the state. One of the first to make application to leave was John Hamilton, the senior member of the firm of John Hamilton and Company, prominent merchants. His brig *William* had been seized the year previous on suspicion of trading with the enemy.[2] In August, 1777, he petitioned Governor Caswell for passports for himself and brother and a large number of others who, he thought, would be leaving with them. They planned to leave from Halifax or Edenton in about thirty days and asked that a guard might be appointed to accompany them at that time. It was not until two months after the application that the necessary certificates were received from the Governor which permitted departure. In a friendly letter Hamilton thanked Governor Caswell for his favors and sent him some letters which he had noticed were awaiting delivery.[3] Hamilton went temporarily to Jamaica but soon returned to the states and joined the British forces in Savannah.

In January, 1778, Governor Josiah Martin, who was in New York City, reported that in the last six months not less than one

[1] This act authorized the county courts to require every citizen to take the oath of allegiance or to depart from the state within sixty days. They were privileged to sell their property before leaving, but if they failed to do so, it was forfeited to the state (*S.R.N.C.*, XXIV, 9-12).

[2] *Ibid.*, X, 707. [3] *Ibid.*, XI, 656-657.

hundred and fifty refugees had arrived from North Carolina and that John Hamilton and McLeod were there, the latter a Presbyterian clergyman of good character. At this time Hamilton had pledged over two hundred and seventy Loyalists to join him on summons. These men from North Carolina aided him in the capture of Savannah.[4] In the meantime Hamilton's property was confiscated by the state government, while he entered the British Army as a private. Within a year's time he rose to the rank of colonel. In 1781 he was commander of the Royal North Carolina Regiment, and enrolled many North Carolina Tories in his regiment. Later he joined Lord Cornwallis, served with him throughout his campaign in the South, and surrendered with him at Yorktown.[5] After the Treaty of Peace he lived in England for several years and was later made British consul at Norfolk. While at Norfolk he often visited Halifax and mingled freely with his friends of prewar days. His conduct throughout the war won the respect of those who differed with him in his political views.

Not all of those who were planning to leave with Hamilton succeeded, if we are to judge from the experiences of William Williamson and William Todd. These two men had done nothing detrimental to the cause of liberty, but they had refused to take the oath and were therefore compelled to leave. Before Hamilton's boat sailed for the West Indies their time for forced departure arrived, but the Governor generously extended the time. Feeling secure in this protection, they decided to visit their families once more before leaving and returned to Cumberland County, only to be seized and confined in jail. This made it impossible for them to leave, although they had paid their passage. They offered the magistrates security for their passages but all to no purpose.[6]

New York City, being in the hands of the British, appears to have been the destination of a large number of North Carolinians at this time. In July, 1777, the *North Carolina Gazette*

[4] *Ibid.*, XIII, Prefatory Notes, p. vi.
[5] William Cicero Allen, *History of Halifax County* (Boston, 1918), pp 38-39. [6] *S.R.N.C.*, X, 656-657.

announced that a large vessel had sailed from New Bern with a great number of Tories, their wives and families, mostly Scotch. They were described as men of property, which for the most part they removed with them. Former Chief Justice Martin Howard and his wife and daughter were among them. Josiah Martin, the former governor of North Carolina, who was in New York at this time, described the arrival of the vessel, in a letter to Lord George Germain.[7] He reported that two vessels had arrived from North Carolina within six weeks which contained besides women, children, and Negroes, twenty-two refugee Loyalist subjects from North Carolina, all but three of whom were natives from Scotland. The object of Martin's letter was to intercede for an allowance for Howard, who was now destitute. Another prominent North Carolina refugee in New York at this time was William Knight, former Comptroller of the Customs at Port Roanoke. He was likewise without funds. The rest of the recent arrivals were described as merchants or mechanics, all of whom had been loyal from the beginning except George Miller and Maxwell, who after bearing arms in rebellion, repented and refused to abjure their sovereign. Only one of the group was a native of North Carolina, and he was Brice. He had been loyal from the beginning, and for his devotion Martin thought him worthy of some small help. Martin's pen was kept busy interceding for his former friends.

Regardless of character and conduct, all were required to leave who did not take the oath. Robert Smith interceded with Governor Caswell to facilitate the departure of Alexander Gelately, former register at Edenton, whom he described as a gentleman of high ideals. John Weis, Alexander Clarke, William Knight, James McClain, John Baggs, and James Henderson, who were also included in the request, were described as men of the finest character. On the same day Smith requested that Millen, a merchant of Edenton, might be permitted to depart by ship and to take as his captain James Ferguson, a Loyalist, who had always borne an excellent reputation.[8] During the summer and autumn of 1777 Governor Caswell was in constant

---

[7] *Ibid.*, X, 765-768.   [8] *Ibid.*, XI, 552-553.

receipt of requests from small groups who wished to depart for the West Indies, New York, or Nova Scotia. Others left directly for England and Scotland. The *North Carolina Gazette* for October, 1777, reported that Flora McDonald with a great number of overloyal people had returned directly to their own country.

The eastern counties of the state were well represented in the migrations at this time. One of the most common methods of departure from these counties was for a group of men to purchase a ship, load it with such goods as they might be permitted to take, and set out for the West Indies.[9]

Alexander McKay at this time went to Jamaica for a while and thence to England. From England he desired to go to Nova Scotia. It was difficult for many of them to settle down again. Archibald McKay lived for a while in East Florida, but when that territory was sold to Spain he moved to Nova Scotia and then to England.[10] John McDonald of North Carolina had a similar experience but went directly from East Florida to London.[11]

Many who went to the islands found life agreeable and remained there permanently. The Reverend Francis Johnston of Bertie County was banished as early as 1777, and settled in Jamaica, where he became pastor of a church.[12] John Cruden, one of a large number who went to the islands by way of East Florida, settled at Nassau on the Island of New Providence. He must have been pleased with his surroundings, for he was followed by his Uncle John Cruden, the senior member of the firm, who settled in Exuma in the Bahama Islands.[13]

Since East Florida was the nearest refuge for Loyalists from North Carolina, they began to go there almost from the beginning of the war. With refugees from South Carolina and Georgia they formed the East Florida Rangers, while a later group founded the South Carolina Royalists.[14] Many did not

[9] *Ibid.*, XI, 633.

[10] Wilbur H. Siebert, *Loyalists in East Florida, 1774 to 1785* (2 vols.; DeLand, Fla., 1929), II, 110-111.   [11] *Ibid.*, II, 108-109.

[12] *Loyalist Transcripts.*   [13] Siebert, *op. cit.*, I, 170.

[14] B. F. Stevens (comp.), *Report of the American Manuscripts in the Royal Institute of Great Britain* (London, 1904-1909), III, 322-323.

wait for the evacuation of Charleston to leave the city, and between July and November, 3,340 refugees arrived at East Florida from South Carolina and Georgia. Many of these were refugees from North Carolina.[15] Other refugees went from Charleston to Jamaica and the Bahamas, while many went directly from North Carolina. In 1783 the Assembly of Jamaica exempted former residents of North Carolina, South Carolina, and Georgia from paying imports on any Negroes they might bring in, as well as from all public and parochial taxes except quit rents.

The adventures of some of the Loyalists who sought a refuge in the West Indies early in the struggle were such as to cause them to lament their attachment to the King. Owen Griffin, a tavernkeeper of Ocracoke, found it necessary to leave the state, for his neighbors swore his destruction. In February, 1776, he loaded his goods on a vessel and set sail. He was pursued by two boats with twenty-four men, but the wind came up just in time for him to escape. After a voyage of twenty-six days he put into Dry Harbor in Jamaica. Here he heard of the Restraining Act, which forbade trade between the rebellious subjects in America and His Majesty's Dominions. He was advised to sell or to make over his vessel and cargo or let it be seized. Knowing that he was a loyal subject, he refused to use any collusive subterfuges to save his property but wrote to Charles Hamilton, collector of Montego, and asked for the privilege of entering the harbor. The collector ordered the boat to be seized and carried into the bay. He produced affidavits of all his ill treatment in North Carolina and the necessity of his leaving. The collector was impressed with Griffin's innocence, and gave him a letter to His Majesty's Attorney and Advocate, and he recovered his vessel. He then entered his vessel in due form, paid the fees, and obtained a permit to discharge and load. Having sold a part of his cargo, he took on Jamaica products in exchange and started for Kingston, when he was seized by Captain Douglas of the ship *Squirrel*. His vessel was taken to Kingston, and after a trial the court decided it was a lawful

[15] *Ibid.*, III, 216.

prize. Before the trial he convinced the Governor and council that he was a loyal subject, but they claimed to be without power to help him. His vessel with cargo, apparel, and furniture was sold, and the money divided and distributed among the captors.[16] He afterwards went to England.

The experiences of Griffin were not unusual. James Green received passes from Governor Martin and from Captain Parry, of His Majesty's fleet at Cape Fear, for Antigua. Green knew that the authorities at Antigua had seized many vessels of Loyalists attempting to reach the island, but he considered his passes and the fact that he was engaged in the King's business sufficient protection. He had agreed to bring back supplies for the fleet at Cape Fear. He no sooner arrived in the harbor of St. Johns in March, 1776, than Captain Kuhn of His Majesty's sloop *Lynx* seized his vessel and cargo as a prize. In the Court of Admiralty the seizure was declared legal. He likewise reported to England and presented his claim to the commissioners of confiscated property.[17]

Early in the struggle Tories began leaving North Carolina for Canada and Nova Scotia. Soule MacDonald, of Anson County, went to Shelbourne, Queens County, Nova Scotia, in 1778. He was awarded £616 for the loss of his property by confiscation.[18] At the evacuation of Charleston about five hundred Carolinians left for Canada. Most of these people were members of the Church of England.[19] Thirty-one Loyalists clergymen, of whom ten had been born in America, emigrated to Nova Scotia.[20] This would seem to indicate that as a whole the Church of England clergymen remained loyal.

From the very beginning of the struggle there had been a constant flow of Loyalists to England. The former Crown officials made up a large group, as did also the merchant and planter class. In 1776 perhaps more than two thousand Loyal-

[16] *Loyalist Transcripts.*
[17] *Ibid.*   [18] *Ibid.*
[19] Arthur Wentworth H. Eaton, *The Church of England in Nova Scotia and Tory Clergy of Revolution* (2d ed.; New York, 1912), p. 100.
[20] *Ibid.*, pp. 155-156.

ists from America sought refuge in Great Britain.[21] These people often took a lively pride in the country which they had felt compelled to abandon, and could not endure to hear it slandered. Samuel Curwen, an exiled Loyalist from Massachusetts, on hearing a returned British officer call the Americans cowards, remarked: "It is my earnest wish the despised Americans may convince these conceited islanders, that without a standing army our continent can furnish brave soldiers and judicious and expert commanders, by some knockdown irrefragible argument, for then and not till then may one expect generous and fair treatment. It piques my pride I must confess to hear us called 'our colonies, our plantations,' in such terms and with such airs as if our property and persons were absolutely theirs, like the 'villains' and their cottages in the old feudal system, so long abolished, though the spirit of bravery is not totally gone it seems."[22] This was the sentiment of many Loyalists who partly sympathized with the country of their adoption. The situation of the Loyalists in England was anything but a happy one. Samuel Seawell, also of Massachusetts, declared it to be such as to provoke Job's wife if not Job himself.[23]

A letter written from London in 1779 to George Miller gives an account of another homesick Loyalist in England. This letter was probably written by J. Burgwin, of North Carolina; he complained that outside of his own family he had no friends and that without money it was impossible to make any. His only desire was to return to his native state and he was determined to make the venture, even to stand trial. He declared that he could not be prevailed upon to injure his friends in America in any way.[24] After the war he returned to North Carolina as did many others. Some were allowed to stay, others feared to stand trial, while others were driven out.

The Reverend James Fraser, of Orange County, was living in England at this time and was most active in pressing his

[21] Rev. Jonathan Boucher, "Letters from London," *Maryland Historical Magazine*, VIII, 344.
[22] Samuel Curwen, *Journal and Letters, First Series*, ed. George Atkinson Ward (London, 1842), p. 90.
[23] *Ibid.*, p. 208.   [24] *S.R.N.C.*, XIV, 303.

claim of compensation. The affidavits covering his claim take up thirty-six manuscript pages.[25]

Samuel Cornell, a member of Governor Martin's council and a wealthy merchant of Wilmington, was one of those who did not wait for the Act of Banishment before leaving the colony. In order to avoid giving his credit to the paper money which was about to be emitted by the Provincial Convention as well as the Continental Congress in the summer of 1775, he asked permission of Governor Martin to go to England, since the acceptance of this money would not only be injurious to his interest but also against his conscience.[26] He was given permission to leave. In December, 1777, Cornell and John London, also a merchant of North Carolina, arrived in New Bern from New York on the brig *Edwards* under a flag of truce obtained from Lieutenant General Sir Henry Clinton and Commodore Holtron in order to remove their families and to settle their private affairs in the state. Before they were permitted to come ashore Governor Caswell asked for their flag of truce and sent a man to procure the same. Cornell was then permitted to come ashore in order to make an inventory of his furniture and the names of his family and servants which he wished to take away with him. London was also permitted to land but to proceed no farther than Cornell's residence.[27]

Governor Caswell laid the matter before the Assembly for advice, saying that he did not consider their credentials to be the equivalent to a flag of truce, since they held themselves subjects of the King of Great Britain. The reply of the House was to the effect that these men had come without the requisites required by the Law of Nations and that they ought to be considered enemies, their persons seized as prisoners, and their clothes as prizes of war to be used by the state.[28] From these proceedings we can judge how dangerous it was for Tories to set foot in North Carolina. In this instance it was finally decided that the flag of truce was a proper one, and Cornell and his

---

[25] MS of the claim of the Rev. James Fraser is in the Duke University Library, Durham, N. C.   [26] *Col. Rec. of N. C.*, X, 236.

[27] *S.R.N.C.*, XI, 691-692.   [28] *Ibid.*, XII, 341.

family and servants together with Mrs. Edwards and her daughters were given leave to depart for New York. Household articles and some stores were permitted to be removed. London was also given leave to return to New York and take with him his servants. They were all required to leave within ten days.[29] Prior to setting sail, Cornell conveyed his estates to his children by several deeds of gifts and proved and registered the same. Later on this property was confiscated.[30]

The following year found London back in North Carolina and signifying his willingness to take the oath of allegiance.[31] The justices refused to administer the oath on legal technicalities since he was in the state on parole. In 1779 the House recommended that London's property be restored to him and that he be admitted as a citizen of the state.[32] Before news came of the definite Treaty of Peace, London returned to North Carolina and was arrested and jailed and later admitted to bail.[33] He was in constant danger of being expelled from the state in spite of his many friends. John Walker, one of the justices of the peace, was an especial enemy of London and took every opportunity to harm him, but was unable to gain any support.[34] At the meeting of the court in Wilmington in December, London was indicted for bearing arms and attaching himself to the British Army. The attorney general declared that the state was not ready for trial, though the state's witnesses were present. It was generally supposed that the indictments would never be heard.[35] In June, Archibald MacLaine wrote to George Hooper that he thought it necessary for London and others to produce evidence that they were citizens of South Carolina in order to remain in North Carolina.[36] Thus to return to the state and to remain unmolested, one was required to hurdle many obstacles. The case of London was typical of many others.

When the United States negotiated a victorious treaty of peace with England, the latter attempted to defend the rights

[29] *Ibid.*, XI, 698.
[30] Sabine, *op. cit.*, I, 336.
[31] *S.R.N.C.*, XIII, 477.
[32] *Ibid.*, XIII, 651-652.
[33] *Ibid.*, XVI, 968.
[34] *Ibid.*, XVI, 984.
[35] *Ibid.*, XVI, 991.
[36] *Ibid.*, XVII, 148.

of her loyal subjects in America but in vain. Shelburne did his best to protect them, but the third article of the treaty merely stated "That creditors on either side shall meet with no lawful impediment to the recovery of their full value in sterling money." The fifth article stipulated that Congress should recommend to the states the restitution of the confiscated estates, rights, and properties which belonged to real British subjects and of others who had not borne arms against the United States. All other Loyalists were to be given the privilege to go into any of the states unmolested for a period of twelve months to recover any of their property that had been confiscated. It was also agreed that Congress should recommend to the states that they restore any Loyalist his confiscated estate if the Loyalist paid to the present owner the bona fide price which he had paid for the property. The last paragraph provided that those who had any interest in confiscated lands by debts, marriage settlements, or otherwise should meet with no lawful impediments in the prosecution of their rights.

The sixth article, which the states, especially North Carolina, quite generally violated, was as follows: "There shall be no further confiscation made, nor any prosecution commenced against any person or persons for or by reason of the part which he or they may have taken in the present war; and that no person shall, on that account, suffer any future loss or damage, either in his person, liberty or property; and that those who may be in confinement on such charges, at the times of the ratification of the treaty in America, shall be immediately set at liberty, and the prosecution so commenced be discontinued."[37]

Eden, a member of Parliament, declared that he was shocked that no provision at all was made for the unfortunate Loyalists. He remarked that thousands of them had fled to New York and to St. Augustine, only to find that Great Britain had surrendered both, without making any provision for them. When the time came for discussing the treaty, Lord North especially denounced the articles which left the Loyalists to their fate. He thought

[37] *William Cobbett's Parliamentary Debates*, IX, 178-179.

they should have been provided for in order to save the honor of the British, to say nothing of principle and gratitude.[38]

To the Loyalists in America, the treaty was a sad disappointment: it meant the loss of political power, property, and perhaps even the right to remain in the country. Many of those who had been most sincere in their attachment to the King had no desire to remain. To those who went abroad hoping for only a temporary sojourn it meant perpetual exile. Many of the more inconspicuous ones doubtless remained quietly at home, while a large number now decided to leave. Others sought to return, some to be successful and others to be driven out again.

Some Tories, as we have mentioned, went to Florida and to the British West Indies before finally settling in Nova Scotia. In fact, some appear to have visited nearly all these places before finally finding a resting place. David Fanning was such a man. In September, 1782, he decided to leave Charleston before its evacuation. A number of Loyalists desired to accompany him and they set sail November 6 in the ship *New Blessing* under the command of Thomas Craven. The ship did not live up to its name; it was eight days before it departed. On his arrival in Florida, Fanning was again subject to a delay of eight days before landing, which was finally effected about twenty-seven miles from St. Augustine upon the Matanzeys River. Not being satisfied there, he proceeded to the Halifax River, where he decided to locate his Negro slaves. Soon many of his Negroes died, and Fanning returned to St. Augustine, where he became very ill. Soon after his recovery he learned peace had been declared and that East Florida would be evacuated. Immediately ships arrived to carry all the Loyalists to Nova Scotia, but with all of Fanning's goods at his plantation several miles distant he was loath to leave. When he reached the plantation, near-by settlers desired to leave for St. Augustine, where passage could be had for Nova Scotia, but they had no means of getting there. Fanning now declared that they had all been deserted by the British Government, and advised them to follow him to Fort Noteves on the Mississippi in West Florida. They set out

[38] *Ibid.*, IX, 249.

in open boats and became separated. Fanning finally reached Key West, but was advised to turn back since his ship was too small to cross the Gulf. After various adventures with the captain of a fishing schooner he fell in with a ship which carried him and his wife to Nassau. He remained there but twenty days and set sail for New Brunswick, where he arrived in September, 1784. After a month he journeyed on to Halifax to interview Governor Parr for a tract of land on which he might settle. A new governor was in charge, and it was necessary for him to return to New Brunswick in order to obtain his grant.[39]

Canada was in fact a haven for many of the soldiers from North Carolina at the end of the war. Many of the men of John Hamilton's North Carolina Regiment settled there. After the evacuation of Charleston, Hamilton with his Royal North Carolina Regiment went to St. Augustine and from there to Halifax, Nova Scotia. His company at this time contained 451 men.[40] Seventeen men of the Royal North Carolina Regiment with eight women and children settled on the St. Johns River in 1784.[41] Major Wright secured a grant of 61,250 acres at a cove east of Country Harbour, Nova Scotia, for 329 officers and soldiers of the King's Carolina Rangers, the South Carolina Regiment, and the Royal North Carolina Regiment. The returns of disbanded troops taken in November, 1784, and November, 1785, respectively show that only 201 of these actually settled there.[42]

During the early months of 1783, thousands of emigrants from the American states arrived in Nova Scotia. In a single day in April, 1783, twenty vessels sailed from New York City carrying 7,000 people to St. Johns.[43] These same vessels returned to New York City for more, and it was estimated that by the end of September 18,000 would have arrived. About

[39] David Fanning, *op. cit.*, pp. 37-46.
[40] *Loyalist Transcripts.*
[41] William Odber Raymond (ed.), *Winslow Papers, A.D. 1776-1826* (St. John, N. B., 1901), p. 224.
[42] *Land Papers of Nova Scotia.* These papers are to be found in the building of the Historical Society at Halifax, Nova Scotia.
[43] *Reports on Canadian Archives*, ed. Douglas Brymner (Ottawa, 1894), p. 404.

35,000 Loyalists found homes in Nova Scotia, Cape Breton, and Prince Edward Island, and of these about 20,000 came from New York State.[44]

The liberal grants of land to be had in Canada induced many to go to that region. Captains were given 3,000 acres; lieutenants, 2,000 acres; field officers, 500 acres; disbanded soldiers, 300 acres; all other Loyalists, at least 200 acres. William Dummer, a justice of the King's Bench, was granted 1,200 acres for his wife and 1,200 for each of his seven children.[45] By 1787, 3,200,000 acres had been given to Loyalists in Upper Canada alone. Many of the army officers, public officials, and churchmen were given pensions and also positions in the army, state, or church.[46]

A detachment of the North Carolina Volunteers was one of nineteen Loyalist military companies disbanded at the mouth of the St. John's River on the shores of the Bay of Fundy in September, 1783. Stores as well as tracts of land were allotted them.[47] The settlers in the various districts complained much of favoritism and unjust treatment. James Dole, who had been chosen by the Loyalists at Port Roseway, Nova Scotia, to represent them in their dealings with the government, complained to Sir Guy Carleton in the autumn of 1783 that after they had spent sixty thousand guineas developing the town, Governor Parr of the Province had reserved two miles of the best land in the town and had given it to all sorts and ranks of men who had settled there. At this time there were about two hundred and eighty settlers in Nova Scotia from North Carolina.[48]

The Scotch officers and soldiers went to Canada in preference to the West Indies. Archibald McDugald along with many of his brother Loyalist officers settled at Country Harbour, Nova Scotia. A number of Scottish families who had emigrated to New York from North Carolina reached Nova Scotia before the

[44] *Ibid.* (Ottawa, 1895), p. 61.
[45] *Ontario, Bureau of Archives* (1930), p. 81.
[46] *Ontario, Bureau of Archives, Report for 1904*, ed. Alexander Fraser (2 vols.; Toronto, 1905), pp. 12-13.
[47] B. F. Stevens (comp.), *Report on the American Manuscripts in the Royal Institute of Great Britain*, VI. [48] *Ibid.*, VI, 543.

end of the war. These families settled on the farms and proved a valuable asset to the country.[49]

Men who had fought and suffered together often wished to settle together as neighbors. Sergeant Daniel McDonald, Alexander McDonald, Murdock McCloud, Roger McDougall, and Jacob Shepherd, all petitioned Governor Carleton for land on the south side of the Miramicki River. They had been disbanded on the river St. Johns and had already settled on vacant land which they hoped to get permission to occupy.[50] These newcomers to Nova Scotia did not always receive a cordial welcome from the older inhabitants. Colonel Dundas declared that the old inhabitants of Nova Scotia were more disaffected toward the British Government than were any of the original thirteen states.

The new settlements seemed to thrive in spite of the lazy habits of the settlers. For the first year they received free supplies from the government which broke down their initiative for work.[51] Many of them had endured great hardships during the voyage from New York. Some women and children perished during the trip.[52]

Life in the new country was especially difficult for those who wished to live like gentlemen on small means. The disbanded army officers on half pay were of this class. They desired their sons to become army and navy officers and meantime got into debt. Their children and grandchildren were brought up with a high sense of their importance, but without money to support this exalted idea. In a new country they were called upon to compete with young men who had no hopes of prosperity except by hard work.[53]

Those who desired to work made rapid progress. In January, 1785, Governor Parr of Nova Scotia wrote that the Loyalists were contented and making good progress in culti-

[49] *Loyalist Transcripts.*

[50] *Original MSS in the Archives at Toronto.*

[51] James Hannay, *History of New Brunswick* (2 vols.; St. Johns, N. B., 1909), p. 197.

[52] *Haldimand Papers,* Vol. B, 148, p. 167.

[53] Hannay, *op. cit.,* I, 199.

vating their fields. The settlements in Nova Scotia alone required an expenditure on the part of the British Government of more than $4,500,000 before they became self-sustaining.

Loyalists were going to Quebec in great numbers at the same time that others were on their way to Nova Scotia. Communication with England was slow. Therefore, the officials at Quebec were often compelled to act on their own judgment. In the spring of 1784 Governor Haldimand, who had succeeded Sir Guy Carleton as governor in 1778, had supplies and transportation ready but no orders. As the Loyalists arrived, they were given their choice of location and also transportation and supplies. There appeared to be some rivalry between Quebec and Nova Scotia for the Loyalists as settlers. Among the first to arrive was a number of Negroes who appear to have been fighting under the New York Tory, Sir John Johnston.[54]

Some of the Loyalists went straight to England from New York and later asked for transportation to Canada. Most of them settled at Kingston on the St. Lawrence and the adjoining township of Pittsburgh. Simcoe, who was governor of Upper Canada when these people arrived, declared that many of them were not entitled to the indulgences and protection of government and had never been in America. Others remained at Nova Scotia as long as the provisions were given them, and then left.[55]

The officials at Quebec made strenuous efforts to supply the needs of ever-increasing arrivals. The more the Loyalists received, the more they demanded. Some of them asked that their farms be stocked and that certain changes in the form of government be granted. They were told that if they were not satisfied, vessels would be provided to take them to Nova Scotia.[56] Again and again Governor Haldimand ordered the men in charge of the various settlements to aid the refugees in the building of huts and to have provisions and materials ready for them upon their arrival.[57] Whenever possible, bedding and

[54] *Haldimand Papers*, Vol. B, 63, p. 342.
[55] Ernest Alexander Cruikshank (ed.), *The Correspondence of Governor John Graves Simcoe* . . . (5 vols.; Toronto, 1923-1931), I, 10.
[56] *Canadian Archives* (1886), p. 391.
[57] *Ibid.* (1886), p. 404.

utensils as well as food were provided. Supply masters exceeded their orders in giving out rations, but the ill-disposed constantly poisoned the minds of the credulous. Those who settled at Martreche in Quebec were especially unhappy. The Canadian officials blamed the discontent on the few troublemakers. The settlers demanded an increase in the rations and complained of being ill. Besides food, they were being furnished with clothing and blankets. It was decided that those who came after 1784 would not receive provisions and other advantages which had been extended to the earlier arrivals.[58] Evidently it was thought that these late-comers were coming more for profit than on account of their loyalty to the Crown.

There was much land in Quebec owned by the French, who were very anxious to get their seigniories settled. They held out special inducements, such as stock and tools, to entice the Loyalists from the King's lands. Those who chose to settle the seigniories were not felt to be entitled to the same indulgences as those who took the land that had been set aside for them by the government.

Some of the earlier arrivals in Quebec secured the maximum allowance of a town, a country, and a water lot, and after selling them returned to the states.[59] In Nova Scotia and Upper Canada (Ontario) some secured entire townships and then sold them.

As late as 1793 large numbers were still leaving New England to take up lands in Canada. In the year 1791 by an act of Parliament, Canada was divided into Upper and Lower Canada, and Lieutenant Colonel Simcoe, former commander of the Queens Rangers, a Loyalist company in the Revolution, was made lieutenant governor. In 1793 George Hamilton, of Cambridge, Washington County, Massachusetts, wrote to Governor Simcoe that he would be in Niagara by July 1, to have his township run into lots and would bring enough of his associates with him to occupy every lot. Evidently Governor Simcoe had issued a proclamation about lands to be had in Canada, for Hamilton assured him that he had trumpeted his proclamation all over

[58] *Ibid.* (1886), p. 423.   [59] *Ibid.* (1894), p. 424.

New England. At the same time Simcoe was warned that many of them would come with no other desire but to extort money from their associates and to impose on him and other Crown officials.[60] These men who settled Canada were actuated by every motive from that of excessive patriotism to Great Britain to the desire for selfish gain.

A settlement made by a small number of soldiers sometimes led to the migration of others from their state. In 1793 a few disbanded soldiers settled on the Niagara frontier in Ontario. They were soon joined by settlers from the different states and even from faraway North Carolina. These people traveled from North Carolina with their goods loaded on wagons. From the mouth of the Genesee River they transported their wagons, horses, and goods to Niagara by boat.[61] An English firm of Pultney, Hornby, and Company bought of the Indians a large tract of land in the Genesee Valley in central New York State, which they offered for sale to new settlers. Simcoe thought that on the surface this looked like British capital working against the interests of the British nation, but that actually it would work out to the detriment of the land speculators. He reasoned that the proprietors of this tract would advertise for settlers; but when they arrived and saw the ease with which they could pass into Upper Canada with its superior climate and soil and there could obtain farms for practically nothing, they would emigrate into the King's dominions.

A number of Loyalists from North Carolina were attracted by the Genesee scheme, since they wished to escape from the animosities which still existed even as late as 1794. They traveled by wagon from North Carolina to the mouth of the Genesee River on Lake Ontario and then by boat to the Niagara frontier. As Governor Simcoe had predicted, they continued on to Upper Canada and were followed by their friends and associates. Governor Simcoe rejoiced at this and thought that after all the government land was sold, the settlers attracted to Genesee would furnish a market for the land which the officers

[60] Cruikshank (ed.), *op. cit.*, I, 312.
[61] *Ibid.*, III, 193.

wished to sell.[62] Many officers who had received large tracts of land in what is now Ontario were holding them in anticipation of selling them to the newcomers.

As late as 1817 the sons and daughters of former Loyalists in North Carolina were moving to southern Ontario and receiving grants of two hundred acres each. Governor Simcoe, who was made lieutenant governor of Ontario in 1791, and who during the war had commanded the Queen's Rangers in which many Loyalists of North Carolina were enrolled, was the attraction that called many people to Ontario during this period. Solomon Austin, who had served in the Rangers and who greatly admired Simcoe, decided in 1794 to leave North Carolina and to move to Ontario to be near his old friend. Austin with his wife and nine children was well received by Simcoe and granted six hundred acres of choice land. He chose a site on Patterson Creek, now called river Lynn. In the War of 1812 he and his four sons fought under General Brock, two of the sons holding the rank of captain. Before 1886 the direct descendants of the original Solomon Austin numbered seven hundred and thirty-four.[63] These figures suggest what a loss the United States sustained in the migration of such stock.

One of the strange requests for lands in Canada was that made by the traitor Benedict Arnold. In 1797 he petitioned for a grant of 10,000 acres for himself and of 5,000 acres for his wife and seven children. He was given 13,400 acres. In support of his petition he gave his loss in real and personal property as £16,000, and loss of half pay as an officer as £4,050. Arnold desired the land for speculation, since he did not wish to be compelled to go to Canada to live. He also asked for the grant to be a general one in order that he might make his selection in any province where land might be available. In answering the request General Simcoe told Arnold that there was no legal impediment to his and his children's having the land, provided that they had not already received a grant in the Province of New Brunswick. At the same time he informed Arnold that he

[62] *Ibid.*, III, 56.
[63] *Ontario Historical Society, Papers and Records*, II, 112.

was a character extremely obnoxious to the original Loyalists of America. The fact that Arnold did not intend to live in Canada removed in part the objection to his being granted the land.[34]

The Loyalists who went to Canada were proud of their exile and considered themselves superior to the early settlers. In November, 1789, Lord Dorchester requested the council at Quebec to put a mark of honor upon the families who had adhered to the unity of the Empire and joined the Royal Standard in America before the treaty of separation in the year 1783. The council convened, and thereafter all Loyalists were to be distinguished by the letters "U.E." affixed to their names, alluding to their great principle—the Unity of Empire. A register of the U.E. Loyalists was ordered kept, and for twenty years names were added to this list.[65]

The distinction of being a descendant of the U.E. Loyalists has continued to the present day. In 1884 United Empire Loyalists' Centennial celebrations were held at Adolphostown, Toronto, and Niagara. The tenor of the celebration may be gathered by an excerpt from the speech of Lewis L. Bogart at Adolphostown:

But while I may not today place in the balance the motives which influenced the two parties,—the Whigs and Tories—of that day, I do maintain whatever reason the Whigs may have had for the course they took, the Tories, the Loyalists were actuated by a noble sense of duty, of patriotism, of christian fidelity and the Crown. They could not discover a sufficient reason for raising the standard of revolt and engaging in civil strife. During the hundred years that the Loyalists have been engaged in converting the wilderness into comfortable homes, the press of the United States has occupied itself, the thousands of Americans abroad have been assiduously at work educating the world to the effect that the American Tories of 1776 were the off-scourgings of the land, the vilest of the vile, worthy of only being executed by mankind. Not only the daily and weekly press has been thus engaged but the school books used by the young people in the United States and sometimes in Canada have contained the most outrageous partial accounts of the struggle of the participants on either side. Never has history been so perverted, never did misrepresentations so effectually deceive. Not only have the

[64] *Canadian Archives* (1891), Introduction, pp. xiv-xv.
[65] *Ontario Archives*, p. 12.

children of the United States been imbued with hate toward the Loyalists, but the modern Englishman, Scot, not to say Irishman has accepted the teaching of partisan American writers.[66]

Bogart was a man over eighty years of age. This speech was typical of those given in the other towns that day and reveals the feelings of many of the Loyalists' descendants of today.

No definite date can be given as the time when the migration of the Loyalists ended. Lands were still being given to the Loyalists in Nova Scotia in 1792. We have already mentioned in this chapter that some left North Carolina for Canada as late as 1817. But are we justified in calling them Loyalists at this late date? Likewise, there is no way to tell how many migrated from the country. During the twelve years from 1775 to 1787, sixty thousand sailed from New York City to various parts of Great Britain, of which nearly twenty-five thousand were from New York State.[67] How many sailed from the other ports we have no way of knowing.

The migration of Loyalists to Nova Scotia, Canada, and the West Indies had a lasting influence on those regions. So many went to what is now the Province of Ontario, Canada, that they became the most influential element in the history of the Province. This was almost equally true of Nova Scotia and that part of the Province which became New Brunswick. Their descendants are a powerful factor in determining the attitude of those provinces toward the United States even down to the present time.[68]

Those who went to the West Indies with their Negroes were more progressive than were the English planters, and there was constant friction between the two groups.[69] By 1786 the newcomers from America outnumbered the original British inhabitants in the Bahamas.

[66] A copy of this speech may be found in the Grosvenor Library, Buffalo, N. Y.

[67] Force (ed.), *American Archives*, IV, 359.

[68] Sir Robert A. Falconer, *The United States as a Neighbor from a Canadian Point of View* (Cambridge, England, 1926), p. 12.

[69] Wilbur H. Siebert, *The Legacy of the American Revolution to the British West Indies and Bahamas* . . . (Columbus, Ohio, 1913), p. 26.

The exact number of Loyalists who left North Carolina for Canada, the West Indies, and the British Isles will never be known. Since the state has no important seaports, the departures were usually made from Charleston, Norfolk, or New York. It would be safe to say that the majority of the Loyalists who were serving in the regularly enrolled Loyalist companies in the British Army at the close of the war went either to Canada or the West Indies. Many of these later went to England. Wherever one comes across a list of Loyalist settlers, he is almost certain to find North Carolina represented.

CHAPTER X

COMPENSATION AND PENSION ALLOWED TO LOYALISTS

THE SIGNING OF THE Treaty of Peace between the United States and Great Britain brought home to the Loyalists for the first time a realization of their true position. A perusal of the fourth, fifth, and sixth articles of the treaty afforded them little comfort, and they realized that for recompense for their losses they must depend upon the liberality of the British Parliament. The House of Commons on February 27, 1783, passed a resolution (immediately preceding the resignation of Lord North) against the further prosecution of the war and the attempt to reduce the colonies by force.

In the peace negotiations Strachey strongly supported Oswald, the leading British commissioner, in his efforts to safeguard the rights and property of the Loyalists. The American commissioners were loath to grant these demands; more than once it seemed as if the negotiations would be wrecked on this issue.[1] The American commissioners finally compromised by the provisions of the fourth, fifth, and sixth articles. James Iredell, in describing how the treaty had been violated in North Carolina, declared that more than one article of the treaty had been expressly violated. He considered that this had not only done the most wanton injury to individuals but had disgraced the national character as well.[2]

By October, 1782, there were three hundred and fifteen American Loyalists receiving aid from Parliament to the amount of £40,280 yearly, in addition to between £17,000 and £18,000 yearly in occasional sums.[3] Among this group was Josiah Mar-

[1] Francis Wharton (ed.), *The Revolutionary Diplomatic Correspondence of the United States* (6 vols.; Washington, D. C., 1889), V, 848-850.
[2] McRee, *op. cit.*, II, 51.
[3] John Eardly-Wilmot, *Historical View of the Commission for Enquiring into the Losses, Services, and Claims, of the American Loyalists, at the Close*

tin, late Governor of North Carolina, who had claimed £500 a year from July 5, 1777; Henry McCulloch, Junior and also Senior, who had received £200 a year since April 5, 1777; Martin Howard, £250 a year since midsummer 1777; and Neil Snodgrass, £100 a year since January 5, 1778. These sums had been voted by Parliament for temporary support in 1778.[4] In the summer of 1782 Lord Shelburne wrote to Wilmot that the sum being paid the Loyalists had become enormous and that it was necessary to establish a limit in regard to the amount given. He was called upon to make a judgment of their claims and permitted to choose his assistant.[5]

John Wilmot chose another member of Parliament, Daniel Parker Coke, to assist him. Their task was "To enquire into the cases of all the American sufferers, both of those who already received assistance from the Public, and of those who were claiming it; and to report their opinion thereon to their Lordships."[6] Both of these men had been voting independently in Parliament. That they might not be accused of accepting any ministerial job they agreed to serve without pay. They had generally voted against the American war.

They began their work by examining the three hundred and fifteen persons who were receiving temporary support. The period from October, 1782, to January, 1783, was consumed in the examination. Fifty-six persons receiving £5,595 per year failed to appear, and their allowance was suspended. Twenty-five of the remaining two hundred and fifty-nine were found to be ineligible for relief on the grounds for which relief was to be granted: namely, being deprived of their means of subsistence and thereby reduced to present distress on account of the loyal part they had taken in the recent contest. Ninety persons who received £16,885 per year had their allowance reduced by £6,385 per year because they appeared to be receiving too much in comparison with the others. Ten of those

of the War between Great Britain and her Colonies, in 1783; with an Account of the Compensation Granted to Them by Parliament in 1785 and 1788 (London, 1815), p. 19.   [4] Loyalist Transcripts.
[5] Eardly-Wilmot, op. cit., p. 17.   [6] Ibid., p. 18.

examined who were receiving a total of only £1,480 per year
had their allowance increased to £2,080 per year. The total
saving independent of those who were suspended amounted to
£8,295.[7] These allowances were made for only three months
at a time, since it was intended at the close of the war to make
a more careful investigation.

Meanwhile fresh claims were accumulating. In the spring
of 1783, four hundred and thirty-eight new claims were examined, so that in June, £17,445 were added to the amount
given to the Loyalist refugees. In the meantime peace had been
made between Great Britain and the United States, and at once
great numbers of Loyalists left their old homes for Great
Britain. In still greater numbers did they leave for Nova Scotia
and the Bahamas.[8]

The North Carolina Loyalists who were living in London
were active in their own behalf, while the committee on Loyalists was in session the early part of 1783. In March they held
a meeting in the London Coffee House under the chairmanship
of James Parker. The purpose of the meeting was to give to
the agent, Henry McCulloch, their representative in London,
their opinion of the claims of the sufferers from their states.
A committee composed of Thomas McKnight, Lewis Henry
De Rosset, Alexander Morrison, James Monroe, and Arthur
Benning, decided that the property losses amounted to £256,000.
Four months later a similar meeting was held at the same place
with Lewis H. De Rosset in the chair. At this time they were
attempting to aid the commissioners in distinguishing between
those who were legitimate objects of bounty and those who were
pretenders.[9] Their decision in most cases was favorable.[10]

[7] *Ibid.*, pp. 20-22.   [8] Sabine, *op. cit.*, I, 90.
[9] A.O.P.R.O., I, 124. These transcripts are in Raleigh.
[10] At this time the committee decided that the following were entitled to
compensation: Howard Murchison, Connor Dowd, Captain Maurice Nolan,
Major Alexander McDonald, Captain Kenneth Stewart, Lieutenant Donald
McDonald, a Mr. Pennington, Andrew Sprowles, Murdoch McDonald, Robert
Palmer, James McNeil, Henry McCulloch, George Miller, William McCormick, McCormick & Company, Norman Morrison, Benjamin Booth, Frederick Gray, Alexander Telfair, James Parker, Robert Gilmour, William
Caldenhead, John Dunlop's heir, Neil Snodgrass's heir, James Cotton, Colonel
Edmund Fanning, Owen Griffin, Robert Nelson, Samuel Marshall, John

The new ministry in which Fox was secretary of state and Lord John Cavendish was chancellor of the exchequer not only approved of the temporary provision which had been made for the American Loyalists, but also introduced a bill for appointing a new commission to carry on the work. The commission consisted of Wilmot and Coke, the two former members of the commission, and three assistants. The examination was to last for two years. At this time loyalty to the British Government was made the cornerstone for compensation. One part of the act provided that anyone who presented a fraudulent claim and attempted to claim more than a just compensation should be absolutely excluded from any compensation whatsoever.[11] For purpose of investigation the Loyalists were placed in six classifications.[12] Claimants were requested to state specifically in writing the nature of their losses. Compensation was not allowed for estates bought after the war began, rents, incomes, offices received during the rebellion, anticipated professional profits, losses in trade, labor, or by the British Army, losses through depreciated money, captures at sea or debts.[13]

The payment of money to the Loyalists at this time was not without precedent in English history. In the reign of King William in 1689, £1,500 had been voted for the relief of the Irish nobility who had lost their estates in Ireland.[14] In 1715 money was voted for those who had lost their property by the rebels in Scotland in the reign of George I.[15] As late as 1739 the sum of £60,000 was voted for the relief of those who had

---

Lowry, John McKay's widow, J. E. Tomlinson, a Mr. Brimmage, the Reverend John Agnew, Richard Conway, Edward Brice Dobbs, F. Williamson's widow, Josiah Martin, and Captain Alex McLeod's widow. Presumably all these were at this time living in England.

[11] Eardly-Wilmot, *op. cit.*, p. 44.

[12] The commission opened their investigation in October, under the following classification: (1) those who had rendered services to Great Britain; (2) those who had borne arms against the revolution; (3) uniform Loyalists; (4) Loyalists, resident in Great Britain; (5) those who took oaths of allegiance to the American states but afterwards joined the British; (6) those who armed with the Americans but afterwards joined the British Army or Navy (Alexander Fraser, ed., *Second Report of the Bureau of Archives for the Province of Ontario*, Toronto, 1904, p. 14).

[13] *Ibid.*, p. 14.

[14] *Commons Journal*, X, 217-259.   [15] *Ibid.*, XIX, 54.

suffered by the Spanish depredations in America during the reign of George II.

The commission began its sessions in August, 1783, and, according to the act, was to hear claims until March 25, 1784. They published a notice of the place and purpose of their meeting in the London *Gazette*, and in the British and Irish newspapers. Notice was also sent to the Commander-in-Chief of His Majesty's forces in New York and to the Governors of the Provinces of Canada, Nova Scotia, and East Florida.[16] The various committees or agents of the American Loyalists were sent for and examined in order to get a general knowledge of their losses. The commissioners met with a great variety of veracity and candor from these people examined and also from most of the Loyalists themselves.[17]

When March 25, 1784, arrived, the time set as the limit after which no claims would be received, 2,063 claims to the amount of £7,046,278 for real and personal property had been presented, while those presented for debts amounted to £2,234,125. This was a large sum of money. By July, 1784, claims to the amount of £534,745 had been examined and had been settled for £201,750. The most essential part of the inquiry revolved about the loyalty and general conduct of the claimant. At first a distinction was made between those who had favored Britain from the beginning and those who had joined the Loyalists after having first favored the Revolution. Ultimately, however, this classification did not affect the amount of compensation that was allowed.

The committee presented its second report on December 23, 1784, consisting of 128 cases who had asked for £693,257 and had later been allowed £150,935. A few months later a report followed which showed the claims of 122 cases for £898,186, which had been settled for £253,613. Since the Act of 1783 was to expire in July, 1785, it was renewed with the provision for a committee to meet in Nova Scotia and to consist of Jeremy Pemberton and Colonel Thomas Dundas. The Canadian com-

---

[16] Fraser (ed.), *op. cit.*, p. 15.
[17] Eardly-Wilmot, *op. cit.*, pp. 46-48.

mittee was to take care of the claims of those people who could not easily come to England. This act also empowered the commissioners to appoint a person to be sent to America to substantiate the claims which the Loyalists were making.[18]

The Canadian commissioners carried on their deliberations in the same manner as did those of England. They began their hearings November, 1783, and concluded them in 1789. During this time 2,235 claims were presented, of which 135 were from North Carolina. For various reasons 834 claims were rejected. A sum of £2,745,000 was granted to the 1,401 successful claimants.[19]

In fixing the amount of compensation that should be paid, the commissioners considered three things: loyalty, service, and the extent of the losses. The early claimants, not knowing what claims would be accepted and rejected, were very comprehensive in their reports and included too much rather than too little in their demands.[20] There was the greatest disproportion between the claims made and the sums allowed. Of the North Carolina claimants this ranged all the way from the claims that were entirely rejected, such as that of Colin Clarke for £2,471, to that of Robert Nelson, who asked for £2,100 and received £2,080. The largest single claim in the state was that made by the trustees of the Earl of Granville, deceased, for £365,749, for which they were allowed £40,000. Among other large claimants of the state was the merchant firm of Hamilton for £105,591, which was allowed only £8,000. The heirs of Kenneth Campbell asked for £20,283 and received £8,300, while James Cotton was allowed but £2,032 4s. of a claim for £11,241 16s. Henry McCulloch, who put up a claim for £54,265 and received £11,747 16s., was the most highly compensated single individual from North Carolina. On the other hand, there were eight individuals from the state who were allowed less than £50 each.[21]

The tendency of the commissioners was to refuse to allow claims which would have been suffered by the individuals

[18] Ibid., p. 56.   [19] Canadian Archives (1904), p. 20.
[20] Eardly-Wilmot, op. cit., p. 54.   [21] See Appendix C.

whether they had been Loyalists or not. These included such
things as trading ships captured during the war by the Americans, or goods captured by the Americans; damage suffered
from British troops; crops destroyed or stolen by the American
troops and a host of other things.[22]

The chief and only general complaint against the commissioners was their examining the claimant and his witnesses apart
and not making it an open and public hearing. The dissatisfied
for this reason branded it an inquisition. Because the claimants and witnesses were in their turn parties and witnesses for
each other, it was naturally feared that in an open hearing they
would be intimidated to support each other's claims.[23]

The claims of the honest Loyalists were aided by the reports
which arrived during 1786 and 1787 from Anstey, who had
been appointed by Parliament to check their losses in America.
He was able to procure evidence for many of the Loyalists
which they had not been able to secure for themselves.[24] The
closeness with which the claims were scrutinized is shown by
the application of Archibald Hamilton of North Carolina. He
left the state and went to England in 1777, rather than take
the oath of allegiance. He was in partnership with his brother
and uncle in trade and estimated his loss at £85,813. Upon his
arrival in England he was held responsible for debts which his
firm owed to creditors in Scotland. He was compelled to sell
his two farms in Scotland to meet this payment. In spite of all
his arguments, and he was in England to present his own case,
his claim was denied under the following pretense:

This is one of of those intricate and difficult cases which in the time
alloted for our Enquiry it is impossible to state with accuracy. It is
an obscure account stating immense losses in trade and making the
balance probably too great without any intention to deceive.

This man had no great merit on the score of loyalty. He admits
that in the plight of war he meddled in no politics but took care of
his business. He acted like a sensible man, but he certainly has not
so great a claim upon government as if he had been a partisan.

All the property however appears to be lost, and probably from

[22] *Loyalist Transcripts.*
[23] Eardly-Wilmot, *op. cit.*, p. 66. [24] *Ibid.*, p. 67.

the activity of this gentleman's relations most of them took part actively in favor of Great Britain.

These seem to us to be reasons against granting a very considerable allowance, but there is a circumstance which puts it out of our power to grant any allowance whatever to him. We find upon a former application to the Treasury that they determined it not to be the case, and we never act in opposition to such a minute unless we have a very strong reason for so doing. Having no reason of that sort in this case, we find ourselves concluded by the former minute of the Treasury and report this to be in no case for an allowance.[25]

For the average Loyalist this would have ended his claim. Fortunately for Archibald Hamilton he had a brother who was a lieutenant colonel in the King's Army who stood in high favor at this time. This brother, John Hamilton, succeeded in having Archibald's claim again brought before the commissioners, with the result that he was awarded a pension of £80 a year. The commissioners gave as a reason for reversing their decision, the fact that Hamilton was no longer able to make a living as an insurance broker as he had been formerly. Another reason was that he had a very large family. Three years later his allowance was increased £70 per annum and in four months again by £50, making a total of £200 per year.

The petition of Duncan McNabb, who escaped capture after the Battle of Moore's Creek and reached Philadelphia, is typical of a large number. He presented a statement of his claims, which is a good illustration of those filed by the average small planter.[26] Like many others in their petitions, he gave a careful

---

[25] *Loyalist Transcripts.*
[26] Three hundred acres of land in Anson County, 150 pds. Dwelling houses and out houses, 50 pds. Three hundred acres of land Buffalo Creek, 150 pds. Four likely horses, 40 pds. Twelve head of horned cattle, 28 pds. Twenty hogs, 6 pds. One likely negro man, 40 pds. Two feather beds, 10 pds. Eight pair double Scotch blankets, 10 pds. Six pair of sheets, six table cloths and twelve hand towels, 8 pounds—2. Twenty yards of drugget, 1 pound—10. Two hundred fifty yard of linen, 25 pounds One fine cloth great coat, 2 pounds. Five suits of men's clothes, 15 pounds. Six waist coats, three pair of breeches, 3 pounds—18. Six pairs of overalls and sixteen pairs of stocking, 4 pounds—16. Sixteen fine shirts, 8 pounds. One pair of gold sleeve buttons, one set of knee and stock buckles, 3 pounds, —10. One silver salt pot, one and a half dozen silver waist coat buttons, 4 pounds—1. One hundred fifty bushels of Indian Corn, 15 pounds. One rifle gun, two fine prizes, one pair of pocket pistols, 6 pounds—1. Women's

account of his services. In spite of all he had sacrificed, the commissioners saw fit to allow him only £162 on his claim for £593 18s.

The final and twelfth report of the Board of Commissioners was made on May 15, 1789. Since the inquiry into the claims was not yet completed, the commission was renewed once more, and it was not until the spring of 1799 that the business was finally settled.

The final report of the Canadian commissioners showed that they had taken evidence at Halifax, St. John, Quebec, and Montreal and had heard 1,401 claims. To these claimants they made awards of £2,745,000. The commissioners for some reason or other refused to listen to the claims of 834 petitioners.[27] The average amount received by the petitioners in Canada was small because those who had large fortunes at stake went directly to Britain to have their claims adjusted.

A total of 5,072 claims was presented in Canada and Britain for the sum of £10,358,413. Of the claims presented, 954 were withdrawn or not prosecuted. The amount claimed by those who were examined was £8,216,126, of which £3,033,091 was allowed. Parliament immediately provided £2,096,326 18s. of this amount, which left £936,764 to be voted.

One set of claims was of such magnitude that it was dealt with separately, according to a scheme proposed by William Pitt, which met with general approbation on the part of Parliament. There were the claims of the Proprietors of Pennsylvania for £944,000 which were liquidated by the commissioners at £400,000, of the Fairfax Proprietors in Virginia for £96,000, to whom £60,000 were allowed, for Granville heirs of North Carolina who claimed £365,000 and received £60,000, of the Proprietors of Maryland who asked for £447,000 and were allowed £210,000. Pitt thought that these amounts were too generous inasmuch as the state of Pennsylvania had allowed the heirs of Penn to retain their private estates and had voted them the

---

apparel, kitchen furniture, tea equippage, 16 pounds. Plantation utensils, 10 pounds. Total 593 pounds—18.

[27] *Canadian Archives* (1904), p. 20.

sum of £130,000 in addition. He suggested that a pension of £3,000 a year should be allowed to one heir and likewise £1,000 a year to another heir. He proposed that the claimants under the will of Lord Granville should receive the full amount allowed them not exceeding £10,000, and 60 per cent of as much as would exceed that sum. This gave them £40,000 instead of the original £60,000 which had been allowed them. The sum allowed to the Fairfax heirs was reduced from £60,000 to £13,000, and to the heirs of the Maryland Proprietors from £210,000 to £100,000.[28] All of these recommendations were accepted by the commissioners and by Parliament.

In addition to the claimants on account of loss of property, there were a large number who sought compensation for loss of office or profession in the rebellious colonies. Pensions amounting to £25,785 per year were granted to 204 such claimants, besides annual allowances to 588 persons, mostly widows, orphans, and merchants, who had no means of livelihood, but had no loss nor real or personal property except debts.

The Loyalists from North Carolina were not backward in pressing claims for pensions for loss of their offices and professions. In 1784 not less than sixty-two men and women from that colony were receiving regular yearly pensions. Their sums varied from £16 per year to Joseph Johnston to £500 per year paid to former Governor Joseph Martin. When the original recipients of the pensions died, payments were made to the widows and children down to and including the year 1831.[29]

Not only do the pension lists for North Carolina differ from year to year, but also the rosters to be found for the same year in different volumes of the Treasury Reports. The names on the earlier pension rolls were mostly those of colonial officers or professional people, while those of a later date contained a greater number of widows, orphans, merchants, and planters. Three men, Murdock McDonald, John McRae, and William McQueen, drew pensions continuously from 1786 to 1831.[30]

[28] Eardly-Wilmot, *op. cit.*, p. 199.
[29] Treasury 50, Vol. 28, E. R. 16.
[30] Treasury 50, Vol. 2, p. 28, E. R. 16.

Compensation and caring for the Loyalists was an expensive process. Food, clothing, temporary relief, and annuities in establishing them in Canada cost the British Government not less than $30,000,000. This was exclusive of the value of the land given to them.[31]

Of the £3,033,091 allowed by the commissioners for loss of property in America, the claimants from North Carolina received £134,175. This sum was unequally divided among the successful 139 claimants, many of whom received pensions in addition to this cash settlement for their loss of property. A total of 205 people from North Carolina asked for either a pension, indemnity for loss of property, or both. The applicants from this state met with more success in pressing their claims than did the Loyalists from the nation as a whole.[32]

Liberal as was the policy of the British Government in rewarding the petitioners, the sums allowed were often woefully small in comparison with what had been asked. Jonas Bedford asked for £6,837 and received £413, Dorothy Booth for £3,368 and received £212 10s., David Fanning for £1,625 and received £36. It is not to be expected that the Loyalists accepted these reductions without bitter and continuous complaints.

In 1786 the agents of the committee of Loyalists, who were chosen from each province for their character and ability, petitioned Parliament for the immediate payment of the sums that had been allowed them. They knew that a report had been made to the Lords of the Treasury but had not yet been presented to Parliament.[33] The same year James Delancey, as general agent for the committee looking after the Loyalist claims, petitioned for information in regard to the basis on which reductions were made in the sums asked. The claimants thought that the value and amount of their claims had been substantiated by the evidence given, and that a reduction was being made according to some arbitrary rule concerning which they had a right to know.[34] The proposal made by Pitt to Parliament in 1788,

[31] *Canadian Archives* (1894), p. 21.   [32] *Loyalist Transcripts.*
[33] Eardly-Wilmot, *op. cit.*, p. 143.   [34] *Ibid.*, p. 148.

which provided for the payment in full of all claims that had been allowed to the amount of £10,000 or less, brought general satisfaction to the petitioners.

The last communication of the agents of the Loyalists was addressed "To the King's Most Excellent Majesty," in which they thanked him for his very liberal treatment of them. They closed their petition by asking him to believe them, at all times and on all occasions, equally ready as they had been in the past to devote their lives and properties to his services and the preservation of the British Constitution.

APPENDICES

APPENDIX A

Lists of Loyalists

The following lists contain a large number of names of both soldiers and civilians in North Carolina who supported the Crown throughout the Revolution. In many instances added interest is given by including their residence and profession. While these lists do not claim to include the names of all the Tories of the state, they are representative of that group who were interested enough to take an active part. Prior to the making of these transcripts it was impossible to locate by name or profession any considerable number of Tories in the state. The names given here and in the following appendices probably include the greater number of the more prominent Loyalists. The sources from which these documents are derived, are indicated in brackets at the end of each document. The reproduction of these documents without editorial changes accounts for any unusual spelling of proper names and the crude wording of the reports of some of the Loyalist officers.

I

Abstract of Subsistence for His Majesty's Regiment of North Carolina Loyal Militia, under the Command of Colonel Samuel Campbell, Stationed on James's Island Commencing as Undermeath, and Ending the 5th of May 1782 both Days Inclusive

Field Officers
Colonel Samuel Campbell
Lieut. Colonel Graham
Major Archibald Taylor

Captains
James Ashworth
Donald McKeithan   Second
Duncan Morison   Second
Lewis Lowry   Second
Thomas Evans   Second
William Lane
Sam'l. Campbell

Lieutenants
David Crocker
William Maultsby
John Campbell   Second
Alexander Ballentine   Second
Charles Robison   Second

Isaac Falkinburgh   Second
Andrew Riddell   Second
Sam'l. Campbell

Adjutant
John McKenzie

Sergeants
Conrod Whisenhunt
Peter Snider
Alexander McColl
Donald McFattar Junior
James Carraway
James Langford
Zachariah Faircloth
Richard Teer

Piper
Douglas Blew

Qur. Master

Archibald Campbell

Privates

Henry Masters
David Harmon
John Landiss
George Reynolds
Isaac Leppo
Edmund Folling
William Wood
Daniel Boilstone
Thomas Swarford
Caspar Rickart
Philip Airhart
Henry Hately
Austin Yansey
James West
Mattison Hunt
Martin Keener
Peter Whisenhunt
John Justice
Philip Whisenhunt
Adam Abernethy
William Owens
Thomas Reynolds
John Thomas
James Anderson
Simon Jones
Martin Benson
Jobb Dill
Samuel Evans
Robert Gates
Fredrick Hegar
Benjamin Morre
Ralph Thompson
James Pemberton
Dugald Duncan

Privates *(Continued)*

Dugald Ray
John Campbell Senr.
Donald Downie
Archibald McKeithan
Donald McFatter Senr.
Gilbert Taylor
John Morrison
Neil Curry
Donald McAlister
Jeremiah Simpson
John Simpson
Jonathan Coats
Joshua Moses
Aaron Dixson
David West
James Wade
William Underhill
Solomon Cormack
Enoch Tootle
Mark Ridghill
Josiah Artis
Arthur Johnston
John Bailey
Thomas Bailey Senr.
Thomas Bailey Junr.
James Bailey
John Beleu
Michael Berry
George Lifener
Robert Key
Gabriel Moore
Robert Bradley
John Fereby
Richard Hall
Thomas Teel
Moses Downer
John Murphy
John Blew

[North Carolina Historical Commission, English Records, Treasury Papers, Miscellanea, North and South Carolina Refugees, 1781-1782, P.R.O. Treasury 50, Bundle 5.]

II

North Carolina Volunteers

Rank	Name	Country	Age
Lieut. Colonel	John Hamilton	Scotland	36
Major	Daniel Manson	do	44
Captains	William Hamilton	do	27
	John Legget	America	40
	Daniel McNiel	do	28
	Thomas Hamilton	Scotland	25
	John Wormley	America	22
	John Martin	Scotland	56

Rank	Name	Country	Age
Captains	William Chandler	America	25
	Neil McArthur	Scotland	42
Lieutenants	Donald Campbell	do	48
	John Shaw	America	21
	James Campbell	Scotland	25
	Alexander Campbell	do	25
	James Hamilton	do	26
	Alexander Foderington	America	23
	Donald McAlpine	Scotland	48
	Thomas Coffield	America	26
	John McDonald	Scotland	23
	Rodrk. McLeod	do	36
Lieutenants	Dugald McKeathan	do	24
Ensigns	Rodk. Hamilton	Scotland	36
	Dugald McKeathan	do	24
	Robert Simpson	Ireland	21
	Donald Campbell	Scotland	27
	Thomas Manson	do	24
	Thomas McDonald	do	26
	Robert Hamilton	do	26
	Archd. McDugald	do	27
	Alexr. McCaskel	do	21
	Archd. McEachron	do	34
	William Campbell	do	—
	——— Weeks	America	16
Chaplain	——— Browne	—	—
Adjutant	James Stevenson	Scotland	30
Qur. Master	Neil Currie	do	25
Surgeon	Mrud. McLeod	do	40
Mate	John Piper	do	23

[North Carolina Historical Commission, English Records, War Office Papers, Army Lists, Annual Army Lists, Printed. 1777-1783. Vol. 165, p. 17. P.R.O.]

III

Abstract of Pay Due to Subaltrons and Privates Belonging to Anson County Regiment Commanded By Duncan Ray Collonel

Those men Came Lately to Charlestown from North Carolina

Lieutenant	Daniel McColl	Anson
Ensign	Alexr. McLennan	Do
Privates	Murdoch McDonald	Anson
	James McLennan	Do
	Hector McLean	Do
	Norman Shaw	Do
	John McCaskil	Do
	Donald McDonald	Do
	Duncan Ray Collonel Loyal Militia	

Endorsed North Carolina Militia

No. 16   McColl

Abstract

[North Carolina Historical Commission, English Records, Treasury Papers, Miscellanea, North and South Carolina Refugees, 1781-1782, P.R.O. Treasury 50, Bundle 5.]

IV

Abstract of pay Due to Capt. Stephen Scarborough and Mathew Parker Ensn. of the No. Carolina Militia who came to this Town in the Course of a Few days past

Rank	Name	County	Commencing
Captain	Stephen Scarbourgh	Bladden	1st May 81
	Mathew Parker	Do	Do
		To receive 6 months pay	
		A Leslie	

I Hereby Certify the Above Written have Served in Bladden County under my Command from the 27th Septr. 1781

Hector Mac Neill Colo.
N.C.L. Militia

Endorsed No. Carolina Militia
Vouchers for No. 17
Abstract

[North Carolina Historical Commission, English Records, Treasury Papers, Miscellanea, North and South Carolina Refugees, 1781-1782, P.R.O. Treasury 50, Bundle 5.]

V

No. 3. North Carolina Anson County Militia.

We the subscribers Officers and Privates of Anson County, North Carolina Militia, have received in Charlestown of Colo. Gray Paymaster of Militia, the sums annexed to our respective Names, in the right hand Column below, upon the Dates prefixed thereto, having also signed a duplicate hereof, the same being for the several periods affixed to our names, as per certified Abstract No. 3 ordered by the Commandant to be paid the 17th of January 1782.

Rank	Names	
Colonel	Duncan Ray	
Major	John Watson	
Captains	McLean John	
	Ray Duncan	
	Ray Daniel	
	Watson John	
Privates	Armour James	
	Keith Duncan	Endorsed North Carolina Militia
	Lane Laughlan	Receipts No. 3.
	McRae John Senr.	of Abstract No. 3.

[North Carolina Historical Commission, English Records, Treasury Papers, Miscellanea, North and South Carolina Refugees, 1781-1782. P.R.O. Treasury 50, Bundle 2.]

VI

No. 4. North Carolina Militia Colo. Faithful Graham's Regiment who came to Charlestowm

We the Subscribers Field Officers of Colo. Graham's Regiment of North Carolina Militia have received in Charlestown of Colo. Gray Master of Militia, the sums annexed to our names in the right hand Column below, upon the dates prefixed thereto, having also signed a Duplicate hereof being the Balance due us to rectify a mistake made on our pay in Abstract No. 1, the same having been there, under-rated in the following proportions, viz a Colonel's £ 20 and a Major's £ 10 P Annum, as P Abstract No. 4 ordered to be paid the 4th February 1782

Rank	Name
Colonel	Faithful Graham
Major	Archibald Taylor
	Thos. Torrans

Endorsed No. Carolina Militia
        Receipts No. 4
        of Abstract No. 4

[North Carolina Historical Commission, English Records, Treasury Papers, Miscellanea, North and South Carolina Refugees, 1781-1782, P.R.O. Treasury 50, Bundle 2.]

VII

Abstract of Pay due sundry Officers and Privates of the Royal North Carolina Militia of Bladen County, now in Charlestown

Lt. Colonel	Hector McNiel
Captain	Patrick McNiel
Privates	Finlay McRae Senr.
	Archibald McEachran
	Niel Murphy
	John Cameron
	John Duff
	Patrick McNiel
	John McLaughlan
	John McPhaul

Hector MacNeill
Lt. Colo.

Charlestown 17 January 1782 The ranks and dates in the above Abstract are agreable to a Certificate from Major Craig now in my hands

Robert Gray P.MM.

[North Carolina Historical Commission, English Records, Treasury Papers, Miscellanea, North and South Carolina Refugees, Cash Book of money received by the Commandant of Refugees, 1781-1782, P.R.O. Treasury 50, Bundle 2.]

VIII

Abstract of Pay due sundry Officers and Privates of the Royal Militia of Cumberland County, North Carolina now present in Charlestown

Lieut. Colonel	Archibald McKay
Commissary	John McIntyre

Charleston 17 January 1782 The Ranks and dates in the above Abstract are agreable to a certificate from Major Craig now in my hands

Robert Gray P. M. M.

Ensign McQueen must produce a certificate from Major Craig

R. G. P. M. M.

[North Carolina Historical Commission, English Records, Treasury Papers, Miscellanea, North and South Carolina Refugees, P.R.O. Treasury 50, Bundle 2.]

IX

Abstract of Subsistance for the No. Carolina Royal Militia Commanded by Colo. Samuel Campbell, on James Island
Comencing and Ending

Rank and Names	Rank and Names
Surgeon	Dun: Morison :B:
John Gibson	Private
Alex. Gordon	William Milton
Clark	John Campbell

Rank and Names	*Rank and Names*
Private	Private
John Thompson	John Owens
James McDaniel	John Jackson
William Coner	Issac Conduff
John Griffis	William Courtes
John Champion	John Patcheon
John Nixon	Mathew Bailey Jr.
Duncan McIntosh	Joseph Ashworth Capt.
William Ferebee	Daniel Blevins
Frederick Hughes	

Endorsed No. Carolina Militia No. 24, Abstract.

[North Carolina Historical Commission, English Records, Treasury Papers, Miscellanea, North and South Carolina Refugees, 1781-1782. P.R.O. Treasury 50, Bundle 5.]

X

We the underwritten do hereby Certify that the men mentioned in the within Roll, have Served in the North Carolina Militia during the Time Specify'd therein, and under the Officers Set against their Respective Names.— Given under our Hands this 6th. March 1872

Archd. Mc Dugald Collo. Loyal Militia
Hector Mac Neill
Colon Militia
Danl. Ray Captn.
Donald Molloy Capt.
N.C.L.M.

[P.R.O. Treasury 50, Bundle 5.]

XI

Roll of Soldiers belonging to the No. Carolina Highland Regt. who served in the No. Carolina Militia before their Enlistment, with the time that each served—

Names	*County they formerly lived in*
Murdoch Mac Leod m	Anson County
Donald Mac Ra Weaver m	Cumberland
James Mac Ra Jr. m	do
Hugh Mac Donald m	Anson County
Duncan Mac Ra m	do
Archibald Mac Donald Deserted	Cumberland
Malcom McCuaig m	do
Malcom Mc Quin m	do
Alexander Mac Donald m	do
Farquhar Mac Ra Jr. m	do
Alexander Mac Arthur m	Bladen
John Currie Taylor Xm	Cumberland
Ronald Stewart m	do
Archd. Mac Donald Deserted	Bladen
John Mc Ra m	Anson
Neill Peterson m	Cumberland
Stephen Saunders m	Anson
Archibald Carmichaell Xm	Cumberland

Names (Continued)	County they formerly lived in
Finlay Mc Ra m	Cumberland
George Lyons m	Bladen
Dugald Blue Piper m	do
Donald Mc Kenzie	Anson
John McLennan	Anson
George Mac Kay	Cumberland
Donald Patterson Deserted	do
John McCallman m	Cumberland
Malcom Black m	do
Bartholomew Murphy m	Anson
Nichael Stanly m	Cumberland
John McPherson Jr. m	do
Archd. McPherson m	do
Ronald MacDugald	Bladen
John Mc Lean m	Anson
Peter Mc Lean m	Cumberland
Donald Mc Donald m	Anson
John Mc Donald 1st	Cumberland
John Mc Donald 2nd	Anson
John Mc Ra Senr. m	Cumberland
Archd. McArthur m	do
Norman Mc Leod m	do
Malcom Mc Neill	do
Alexr. McAlister	do
John Leslie	Bladen
Kenneth Mc Lennan m	Cumberland

Endorsed Roll of Soldiers in the No. Cara.
        Highlanders that Served in the
        North Carolina Militia

[North Carolina Historical Commission, English Records, Treasury Papers, Miscellanea, North and South Carolina Refugees, 1781-1782. P.R.O. Treasury 50, Bundle 5.]

XII

A Return of the time of Service, of the Refugees from No. Carolina, Under their Different Militia Commanders,—Charlestown Decr. 1st 1781—

Names	Names (Continued)
Colo. Faith. Graham	Robert Mc Ewen
Capt. Archd. Taylor	John Mc Viccar
Major Archd. Taylor	Dond. Mc Alister
Capt. Duncan Morison	Archd. Sellers
Capt. Dond. Mc Keithen	Jmo. Blew
Leut. Dond. Mc Keithen	Capt. Dond. Mc Keithens Co.
Ensign Wm. Maultsby	Archd. Campbell Comisary
Leut. Wm. Maultsby	Malcom Mc Fatter Sergt.
Capt. Jn. Smilie	Dond. Mc Fatter Jr.
Capt. Neil Mc Phail	Dond. Mc Fatter Senr.
Capt. Robt. Hendry	Dun. Taylor
Leut. Andrew Riddle	Jno. Campbell
Capt. Thos. Private	Gilbert Taylor

Names (Continued)

Leut. Wm. Lane
Ensign Benjam Lamberth
Major, Thos. Torrants
Capt. Archd. Sellers
Leut. Charles Robeson
Ensign Wm. Henry
John Smilie leut.
Capt. Thos. Moore
Jas. Smilie Ensigh
Neil Mc Nair Ensigh
Capt. Dun. Morrisons C.
Alexr. Ballantine Sergt. Majr. acted also Leut.
Jno. McKinzey Adjut.—of the Bladen Militia
Alex Mc Cole Sert.
Dugd. Blew Piper
Neil Curry
Parlan Mc Farlan
Alexr. Mc Donald
Jas. Watson
Jno. Martin
Neil Martin
Jno. Murphy
Neil McNeil
Dond. Ferguson
Miles McInish
Colin McLelland
Dond. McLennand
Archd. Morison
Jno. Morison
Normond Morison
Finley McRae

Names (Continued)

Archd. Mc Keithen
James Pemberton
Wm. Rylie
Jas. Campbell
Archd. Campbell Jr.
Dugd. Ray
John Munn, Wounded
Dond. Downie, Do
Dugd. Duncan
Neill Campbell
Ronald Mc Dugald

Capt. Jno. Smilies Co.
Jno. Curry Sergt.
Angus Brown
Dond. McKay
Capt. Neil McPhaule wounded
John Hart
Dugald McLachlan
Duncan McIntosh
Capt. Jno. Moore
Dond. Campbell Sergt.
Duncan Graham
Peter McLean
Neil Mc Inish

[North Carolina Historical Commission, English Records, Treasury Papers, Miscellanea, North and South Carolina Refugees, 1781-1782. P.R.O. Treasury 50, Bundle 5.]

XIII

Abstract of Subsistence for His Majesty's Regt. of North Carolina Militia under the Command of Colonel Samuel Campbell Stationed in James's Island— Commencing as Underneath, & Ending the 1st of April 1782 Inclusive.

Names and Rank

Officers shown on list of
    5th of May 1782
Field Officers
Captains
Lieutenants
Adjuts.
Qur. Mr.

    Sergeants
John Plowman
Malcolm McFatter

Names and Ranks (Continued)

Privates

William Henderson
Horatio Griffin
Benj. Biggerstaff
John Peterson Deserted
Archibald Morison
Donald McFatter Jr.
Angus McDonald
Archibald Campbell X (Not in the
                    Regiment)
Duncan Taylor   X
Endorsed North Carolina Militia
        No. 9
        Abstract

Privates *(Continued)*

Daniel Madden
Jacob Picwman
John Plowman
George Egner
Willian Kapley
Daniel Shooltz
Skoggin King
Henry Sites

[North Carolina Historical Commission, English Records, Treasury Papers, Miscellanea, North and South Carolina Refugees, 1781-1782, P.R.O. Treasury 50, Bundle 5.]

XIV
No. 6 North Carolina, Bladen County Militia

We the Subscribers Officers and Privates of Bladen County North Carolina Militia, have received in Charlestown of Colo. Gray Paymaster of Militia, the sums annexed to our respective names, in the right hand Column below, upon the Dates prefixed thereto, having also signed a duplicate hereof, the same being for the several periods affixed to our Names, as per certified Abstract No. 6. ordered by the Commandant to be paid the 17th January 1782.

Names & Ranks

Privates 1782
McDuffee John
    Abstract No. 6.
        Robert Gray P. M. M.
                [P.R.O.   Treasury 50, Bundle 1.]

XV
No. 8. North Carolina Militia Lt. Colo. John Moore. Payroll

Names and Ranks 1782

Lieut. Colonel
Moore John
    Captains
Harmon Anthony
Manow, John

    Lieut.
Perkins Benjan.

Names and Ranks

Privates
Bedford Jonas
Copley Conrod
Miller George
Snider Titus

                [P.R.O.   Treasury 50, Bundle 1.]

XVI
No. 11. North Carolina Militia now enlisted in Governor Martins Corps in Charlestown.

We the subscribers Officers and Privates formerly of the North Carolina Militia, but now enlisted in Governor Martin's Corps have received in Charlestown by Order of General Leslie, of Colo. Gray Dy. P.M.M. the sums annexed to our respective Names in the right hand Column below upon the Dates prefixed thereto, having also signed a duplicate hereof, the same being for services previous to the evacuation of Wilmingtown.

1782	*Names & Ranks*	*From whence*
	Privates	
	Donald Innis	Anson
	Archd. McDonald Senr.	Anson

For the foregoing per Order of 20 April 1782
Donald Ray Capt.

[P.R.O. Treasury 50, Bundle 1.]

XVII

No. 12. Sergeants McLeod and McLellan of the Anson County Militia

Sergeant Roderick McLennan In full for services in North Carolina. Charlestown 28 May 1782 Received by order of Lt. General Lesly of Rt. Tray Dy. P.M.M. the sum of Seven Pounds Stg. each as above for which we have signed two receipts of this tenor and date.

Rory McLennan

[P.R.O. Treasury 50, Bundle 1.]

XVIII

No. 15. North Carolina Militia who served in South Carolina under Major Ferguson &c.

We the Subscribers Officers and Privates of the No. Carolina Militia who served in So. Carolina under Major Ferguson &c have received in Charlestown by order of Lt. General Leslie of Colo. Gray P.M.M. the sums annexed to our respective Names in the right hand column below, upon the Dates prefixed thereto, having also signed a duplicate hereof the same being for our services in South Carolina under Major Ferguson

August 14	Daniel Doty	Captain

[P.R.O. Treasury 50, Bundle 1.]

XIX

No. 21. North Carolina Militia Colo. Samuel Bryan

We the subscribers Officers and Privates of Colo. Bryan's Regiment of North Carolina Militia, have received in Charlestown by order of Lt. General Leslie, of Robert Gray P.M.M. the sums annexed to our respective Names in the right hand column below, upon the Dates prefixed thereto, having also signed a duplicate hereof, the same being for the several periods undermentioned as per Abstract No. 21.

Nov 21   Capt. Henry Shouse

[P.R.O. Treasury 50, Bundle 1.]

XX

No. 24. North Carolina Regiment of Militia Colo. Samuel Campbell

Names & Rank

Privates
Curtis William
Sites Christian

[P.R.O. Treasury 50, Bundle 1.]

XXI

No. 25. North Carolina Militia, Colonel Samuel Campbell

We the subscribers officers & privates of Col. Samuel Campbells Regimt. of No. Carolina Militia have received in Chas. town by order of Genl. Leslie of Robt. Gray P.M.M. the sums annexed to our respective names in the right hand Column below upon the dates prefixed thereto, the same being our pay for the several periods affixed to our names as p North Carolina Abstract No. 25.

Names & Ranks 1782	Names & Ranks (Continued)
Privates	Privates
Blewer Jacob	Justice John Jr.
Bowman Peter	Holeman Thos.
Fritz Jacob	Richard Gasper
Goldsmith Jesse	Johnson Henry
Healiy Henry	Shuford Jacob

A true copy of Abstract No. 25

Robert Gray P.M.M.

[P.R.O. Treasury 50, Bundle 1.]

XXII

North Carolina Independent Company

Rank	Name	Country	Age
Captain	Eli Branson	America	40
Lieutenant	Samuel Jones	do	26
Ensign	John Bloxham	England	28

[North Carolina Historical Commission, English Records, War Office Papers, Army Lists, Annual Army Lists. War Office, Vol. 65, p. 23.]

XXIII

Seconded Officers

Regiments they belonged to:	Rank	Name
No. Caro. Loyalists	Ensign	Angus McDonald
Independent Corps	Surgeon	John Clarke
North Carolina Hilanders	Captain	Alexr. McRa
	Lieutenant	Duncan McNab
	Ensigns	Malcolm McRay
		Allen Stewart

[North Carolina Historical Commission, English Records, War Office Papers, Army Lists, Annual Army Lists, Printed. 1777-1783. P.R.O. War Office, 65. Vol. 165, p. 28.]

XXIV

No. 2. List of the Militia from Different County's in North Carolina Neglected in the former Return for pay.

Names & Ranks	Countys
Capt. Donald McInnes	Anson
Lieut. Miles McInnes	Do
John Morrison	Do
Neil McLeoud	Do
Duncan McPherson	Anson
Torkle McLeoud	Do

Names & Ranks	Countys
Duncan McRae	Do
John McRaw	Do
Ferquhard McRaw	Do
John McLeoud	Do
James Monk	Do
George McRay	Do
Lieut. Donald Shaw	Cumberland
John McLeoud	Do
Alexr. McLeoud	Do
John Stewart Sergt.	Do
Angus McDonald	Do
John McLelland	Do
Dond. McKenzie	Do
Malcolm McNeil	Do
Alexr. McLeoud	Do
Malcolm McQueen	Do
Robert Sellers	Bladen
John Leslie	Do
Neil Colbreath Sergt.	Do
Sergt. John Campbell	Bladen
Ensign John Campbell	Do
Sergt. Angus Taylor	Do
Adjut. John McKenzey	Do
Archd. Campbell Quarter Master	Do
Alexr. Murkinson	Do
James Caraway	Do
Jesse Brown	Do
Lee Brown	Bladen
Jeremiah Holeman	Do
George Harman	Do
Daniel Cameron	Do
John McDonald	Do
Alexr. McAlister	Do
Niel McNiel	Do
Archd. Campbell	Do
John Smith	Anson
John Robeson	Hanover Do
Archd. Campbell	Bladen Do

Endorsed No. 2 North Carolina Abstract

[North Carolina Historical Commission, English Records, Treasury Papers, Miscellanea, North and South Carolina Refugees, 1781-1782. P.R.O. Treasury 50, Bundle 5. Books 4 and 5.]

XXV

A list of men from No. Carolina bound for Augustine Who Acted in the Militia Service never Recd. pay for their Service Vizt.

Names and Ranks	Names and Ranks (Continued)
Captain	Privates
John Stradfort	Robt. Hays
Wm. Strickland	Saml. Branton
James Precy (?)	Lewes Hardick
	Solomon Glass

Names & Ranks (Continued)

Lieut.
Caleb Biggs
Weill Smylie
Neill Ransey

Names & Ranks (Continued)

James Baker
Wm. Baker
Perqd. Belton
Nandol McDougald

Headquarters 6 Octr. 1782
The General desires the above
officers and men may receive
three months pay in full of
all demands except Capt.
Strickland who has been already
paid

Robert Anderson
Asst, Secy.

Endorsed   No: Carolina Militia
              Voucher for no. 19
              Abstract

[North Carolina Historical Commission, English Records, Treasury Papers,
Miscellanea, North and South Carolina Refugees, 1781-1782. P.R.O. Treasury
50, Bundle 5.]

XXVI

Abstract of pay Due to officers & privates belonging to Colonel David Fannings Regiment of North Carolina Militia Commencing 1st March 1781 &
Ending 30th Septr. 1782 Being five hundred & forty nine Days

Names & Ranks

Captain
Joseph Curry
Abner Smally

Lieutenant
Absolom Authry
James Ellet

Names & Ranks (Continued)

Private
Abram Back
Thomas Ellet

David Fanning
Colo. No. C. L. M.

[North Carolina Historical Commission, English Records, Treasury Papers,
Miscellanea, North and South Carolina Refugees, 1781-1782. P.R.O. Treasury
50, Bundle 5.]

XXVII

Abstract of Pay Due William Beans for Duty done in Behalf of Government in North Carolina under the Command of Colnl. David Fanning Commencing the 22th of November 1781 and Ending the 5th July 1782

Names & Ranks
William Beam Private

David Fanning Colo.

Abstract of pay Due Captn. Merediath Edwards of the North Carolina
Militia in Colonel David Fannings Regiment Comenceying the 16th July
1781 and Ending the 5th of July 1782

Merediath Edwards Capt.

David Fanning Colo.

[North Carolina Historical Commission, English Records, Treasury Papers,
Miscellanea, North and South Carolina Refugees, 1781-1782. P.R.O. Treasury
50, Bundle 5.]

XXVIII

Abstract of pay due to officers and privates belong to Colonel David Fannings Regiment of Loyal Militia Who came Lately from North Carolina Commencing the 1st March 1781 & Ending 24th Augt. 1782 being five Hundred & forty two days

Ranks & Names	Ranks & Names (Continued)
Capt. Ben Underwood	Privates Jno. Mezey
Jno. Irven	Saml. Wamble
Lieutt. Wm. Carr	Christian Morris
Mm. Hilles	Jno. Johnes
Thos. Danelley	Hendry Johnston
Hendry Ramsour	

David Fanning Colo.
N.C.L.M.

Endorsed Col. Fanning

[North Carolina Historical Commission, English Records, Treasury Papers, Miscellanea, North and South Carolina Refugees, 1781-1782. P.R.O. Treasury 50, Bundle 5.]

XXIX

Charlestown July 29, 1782

This is to Certify that Bazel Owings and his Son Wm. Owings joined my Ridgment June 22d. 1780 and that William Owings was wounded in the action at the hanging Rock the 6 of August and that his father Bazel Owings Decesed this Life abought January the 15 1781

Samuel Bryan Coln.

Endorsed

The Commandant desires Col: Gray will please to pay Wm. Owens the Wages due himself & Father, as Specifyed on the within receipt Augt. 9th

1782   J Blucke
                                                   Secy.

[North Carolina Historical Commission, English Records, Treasury Papers, Miscellanea, North and South Carolina Refugees, 1781-1782. P.R.O. Treasury 50, Bundle 5.]

XXX

Abstract of Pay due Lieutenant Colinel John Hampton & Captn. Nicholas White of Colonel Samuel Bryans Regiment of the North Carolina Militia on Duty under the command of the Right Honourable Lord Cornwallas And the Said Colonel Bryan Comenceying the 24th day of June 1780 and Ending the 5th day of July 1782 Being 744 Days—

Names & Ranks	
Samuel Bryan	Colonel
John Hampton	Lieut. Colo.
Nicholas White	Capt.

Endorsed North Caro. Militia
No. 21
Abstract

[North Carolina Historical Commission, English Records, Treasury Papers, Miscellanea, North and South Carolina Refugees, 1781-1782. P.R.O. Treasury 50, Bundle 5.]

XXXI

This is to Sartify that Roger Turner Sarved as a Capt. of the Melisa in My Ridgment For tha bove mensaned time

Samuel Bryan Coln. N. Car.

Colo. Gray will please pay Roger Turner for his Services as represented

J Blucke

Secy.

Augt. 12th 1782

[North Carolina Historical Commission, English Records, Treasury Papers, Miscellanea, North and South Carolina Refugees, 1781-1782. P.R.O. Treasury 50, Bundle 5.]

XXXII

18th March—1781

Sir,

The Commandant desires you will pay the two wounded Men Norman McLeod & Roger McLellan from North Carolina two Guineas each

Yours &c

J. Blucke

Capt: 23d Regt.

[North Carolina Historical Commission, English Records, Treasury Papers, Miscellanea, North and South Carolina Refugees, 1781-1782, P.R.O. Treasury 50, Bundle 5.]

XXXIII

North Carolina Apl. 5th 1776

A General Return of Prisoners in Halifax Goal for carrying Arms in suport of the Regall Authority in this Province, under the Command of General Donald Mack Donald

Names & Ranks	*Names & Ranks (Continued)*
Colo.	Captns
Allen McDonnell	Neal McCarty
Capts.	John Legate
Allexander Morison	Allexander McCoy
James McDonnell	Enas McDonnell
Allexander Miara	James News
Murdock McCaskle	Thomas Wair
	Moris Nolan
Lieuts.	Lieutenants
Daniel McCleoad	Archebald McAchrin
Keneth McDonnell	John Mykes
	Lauglin McKinan
Chapln.	Kiniard Stewart
John Bethune	James Munro
Chirurgn.	Ensign
Murdoch McCleoad	Daniel Morison
Wagr. Mr. Gl.	
Aaron Verdien	Volunteer
Adjutt.	Duncan St. Clair
Francis Frasier	Major
Qr. Master	Samuel Sneed
Daniel McCleaod	

Names & Ranks (Continued)

Commissary
Allexander McClean
  Volunteers
Roard Mack Kinan
Darcey Fowlet
  Colo.
Thomas Rutherford
  Lieut. Colo.
Allexander McDonnell
  Colonel
William Fields
  Lieut. Colo.
Robert Fields
  Captn. Lt. Horse
Joseph Dobson
  Do of Foot.
Jeremiah Fields
Joseph Fields
Robert Turner
Wm. Aromfield
Seymour York
Wm. Draper
Mathias Sattinfield
  Ensigns
Wm. Shannon
Saml. Divony
Stephen Civnay
  Serjt. Major
Wm. Craft

Names & Ranks (Continued)

Capts.
William Gardiner
Nathanl. Steed
Lewis Lowrey
Jacob Pope
  Ensign
Thomas Brafford
  Adjutant
John Smyth
  Captn.
David Jackson
  Colonel
John Pilas
  Chirurgn. & Capt of Lt. Horse
Robison York
  Captain Lt. Horse
John Pilas Jr.
  Lieut.
Wm. Bradford
  Captn. Lt. Horse
Eenoe Bradley
  Lieut.
Daniel McDonnell
  Ensign
John Downing
  Volunteer
Stephen Barker

[North Carolina Historical Commission, Revolutionary War Prisoners.]

XXXIV

To the Right Honorable Lord Sidney,
  His Majestys principle Secretarys of State
    for the home department.

> The Memorial of the North Carolina
> Loyalists, who have borne arms,
> during the late War in America

Most humbly Sheweth

That your Memorialists conceiving it their indispensible duty as good & Loyal Subjects to support the right of their Sovereign, and the constitutional authority of the British Government in North America, did in conformity to such sentiments take up arms in the late civil War, and urged many of their friends to pursue the same laudable conduct in support of the Royal authority . . .

That severals of your Memorialists went to Nova Scotia soon after the Treaty of Peace with a view of Settling in that Country, but found it altogether impossible in the present State of their finnances, to clear the ground, and raise the necessarys of life, in a Climate to Southern Constitutions inhospitable, and severe**

That your Memorialists humbly concieve the Bahama Islands to be the only places at present within the British dominions in America the most likely to afford them, an opening the most promising, for present, and future advantages—

That your Memorialists, without presuming to dictate, humbly recommend John Hamilton Esquire late Colo. of the Royal North Carolina Regiment, for the Government of the Bahama's when the same becomes vacant, a circumstances they are well convinced, would prove the means of giving particular satisfaction to all the Southern Loyalists, as well as to the Inhabitants of those Islands in general . . .

Your Memorialists will ever
Pray &c &c &c

Neill McArthur Capt.	Wm. Fortune Colo.
John Martin Capt.	Maurice Nowlan Capt.
Alexr McKay Capt.	Donald McAlpine Capt.
Alexr. Morison Capt.	Alexr. McDonald Capt.
Alexr. McLeod Capt.	Kenneth Stewart Capt.
Archd. McKay Capt.	Willm. McLeod Ensign
Malcom McKay Ensn.	Roderick Mackinnon Lt.
Dond, Shaw Lieut.	Dond. Morrison Ensn.
Norman McLeod Lieut.	Dunn. McNabb Lt.
John McLeod Lut.	Dun. McRa Ensn.
Conner Dowd	Angus Martin
Murdoch Martin	John Macleod
Martin Martim	J. McKean
Donald McKinnin	Collin Clark
Norman Morison	Eli Branson Capt.
Alexander Morison	James Monro Majr.
John Morison	John MacIver
Kenneth Morison	John Halbert Capt.
Roderick Morison	John Macdonald Lt.
Allen McDonald	W. Hamilton Capt.
Kenneth Cameron	Angus Campbell Capt.
Thos. Clark	Alexr. Campbell Lt.
Sam Marshall	Donald McDugd. Senr.
J. Bedford Captn.	Farqd. McCallum
Neill McGeathy Lt.	Dond. McDonald Lieut.
James McAlpine	John Stewart Lieut.
D. Drumd. MacGregor	George Lyon
Archd. McArthur	Neill Colbreath
James Munro Lt.	James Tory
John Hamilton McAlpine	John McCulloch
John Maclellan	Joseph McCulloch
Archibald McCoal	Edward Mclellan
George McCoal	Dugall Duncan
Joseph McLellan	Alexander MacAlister
William Mclellan	

[North Carolina Historical Commission. English Records, Foreign Office—America Miscellaneous, 1783-1794. P.R.O. Foreign Office, Class 4, Vol. I.]

XXXV

Account of Stoppages due from the North Carolina Militia to His Majesty's Hospital at Wilmington between the 9th and 24 April 1781 both days inclusive. North Carolina.

Company of Col. Jo. Hunt

Names	Names (Continued)
Issac West	Stophel Wright
Isaac Paine	James Tommilin
John Jones	Willm. Gronis
Thomas Jones	James Cooley
John Bryant	John Pyle
Robert Bryant	Samuel Pyle
Thomas Bryant	James Anderson
John Tinney	William Pyle
Robert Tinney	John Hunter
John Linley	Nathl. Abner
Benjamen James	Thomas Craton
Joseph Kirk	Thomas Blair
Henry Strador	Alexr. Sutherland
Jacob Graves	Charles Jones
Peter Fogleman	James Hunt
John Somers	

Endorsed   North Carolina Militia
Stoppages to 24th April 1781
£ 1;16.8 Sterling

[North Carolina Historical Commission, English Records, Treasury Papers, Miscellanea, North and South Carolina Refugees, 1781-1782. P.R.O. Treasury 50, Bundle 5.]

XXXVI

Account of Stoppages due from the Independant Dragoons to His Majesty's Hospital at Charleston, between the 25 Decr. 1781 & 24 February 1782 both days inclusive.

Mens Names	Men's Names
Gerry Holiman	Jacob Walls
Jona. Jenkins	Wm. Gillow
Thomas Roberts	Wm. Wadsworth
Wm. Jackson	James Truit

Endorsed Independant Drags.

[North Carolina Historical Commission, English Records, Treasury Papers, Miscellanea, North and South Carolina Refugees, 1781-1782. P.R.O. Treasury 50, Bundle 5.]

XXXVII

Account of Stoppages due from the North Carolina Indept. Dragoons to His Majesty's Hospital at Charlestown, between the 21st. & 24 October 1781 both days inclusive.

Men's Names	Men's Names
Mathw. Dunavan	Anthy. Murphy
Thomas Whitesides	Joseph Howell

Danl. Madden
Endorsed   No. Carolina Indep. Dragoons
              to 24h. October 1781
              £ —;6/

[North Carolina Historical Commission, English Records, Treasury Papers,
Miscellanea, North and South Carolina Refugees, 1781-1782. P.R.O. Treasury
50, Bundle 5.]

XXXVIII

Account of Stoppages due from the No. Carolina Indept. Dragoons in His
Majesty's Hospital at Charleston, between the 25th Octr. & 24h Decr. 1781
both days inclusive

Men's Names	*Men's Names*
John Godfrey	John Boid
Sergt. Roberts	Thos. Murphy
John Jenkins	James Green
George Holiman	Richard Hath
James Holiman	James Trust
Lee Brown	Wm. Higworth
George Brown	

Endorsed: No. Carolina Indept. Dragoons—
              to 24h. Decr. 1781

[North Carolina Historical Commission, English Records, Treasury Papers,
Miscellanea, North and South Ca-olina Refugees, 1781-1782. P.R.O. Treasury
50, Bundle 5.]

XXXIX

Account of Stoppages due from the North Carolina Militia to His Majesty's
Hospital at Wilmington, between the 25h Augt. & 24 Octobr. 1781.
Both days inclusive.

Men's Names	*Companies*
James Crosby	Col. McNiels
Aaron Lambert	C. Cox
Ezekal Loftan	do
William Russull	do
John Mann	Col. Slingsby
Capt. Goddan	Bladen County
Jonathn. Allen	C. Brevalts
John Murphy	C. McCarty

Endorsed   North Carol: Militia
              Stoppages between 25th Aug: &
              24 Oct. 1781
                   —inclusive—
              £3:8:8: sterlg.

[North Carolina Historical Commission, English Records, Treasury Papers,
Miscellanea, North and South Carolina Refugees, 1781-1782. P.R.O. Treasury
50, Bundle 5.]

XL

Account of Stoppages due from the North Carolina Militia to His Majesty's
Hospital at Wilmington, between the 25th April, & 25th June 1781.
North Carolina—both days inclusive

Men's Names	*Companies*
Thomas Williamson	Col. McNiel
Seth Hayes	of Duplin County

Benjn. Hinds of Duplin County
Endorsed North Carolina Militia
Stoppages to 24th June 1781—
£ 1:19 — Sterling

[North Carolina Historical Commission, English Records, Treasury Papers, Miscellanea, North and South Carolina Refugees, 1781-1782. P.R.O. Treasury 50, Bundle 5.]

XLI

Account of Stoppages due from the North Carolina Militia to His Majesty's Hospital at Wilmington between the 24th June, & 24th Augst. 1781. No. Carolina—both days inclusive.

Men's Names	Companies
Michael Killion	Col. Field
Christian Morris	Col. Field

Endorsed No. Carolina Militia
Stoppages to 24th. August 1781
£ 1:4:4: Sterling

[North Carolina Historical Commission, English Records, Treasury Papers, Miscellanea, North and South Carolina Refugees, 1781-1782. P.R.O. Treasury 50, Bundle 5.]

XLII

A Return of the time of Service of the Refugees from No. Carolina Under the Command of their Different officers, Charleston, Decr. 1st. 1781.

Names	Names (Continued)
Capt. Robt. Hendry Co.	Thos. Murphey
Jas. Hendry Sergt.	Jas. Green
Alex. Hendry, Corpl.	Thos. Brown
Charles Hendry	Aaron Dickson
Finley Murphey	David West
William Hendry	William West
Charles McAlester	
	Capt. Archd. Sellers Co.
Capt. Thos. Private Co.	Jno. McAlister Sergt.
Jno. Taylor Sergt.	Saml. McAlister Corpl.
Abraham Taylor Do	Malcom Robeson Senr.
Danl. Carmick Corpl.	Danl. Mcfee
Solomon Carmick	Malcom Robeson Jr.
Richd. Calton	Hugh Murphy
Levy Kent	Gilbert McKenzey
Wm. Underhill	Amgus McAlister
James Weade	
Jacob Wills	Capt. Joseph Brinkley
Richard Tear	George Harrison
William Gilgow	Cornilious Lery
Dick Hall, a (Negro)	Durham Leigh
Alexr. Morkinson	

Endorsed A Return of the No. Carolina Refugees Decr. 1st 1781.
Endorsed also— North Carolina Militia

No. 1
Abstract

[North Carolina Historical Commission, English Records, Treasury Papers, Miscellanea, North and South Carolina Refugees, 1781-1782. P.R.O. Treasury 50, Bundle 5.]

XLIII

Abstract of pay due to Officers and Men belonging to Colln. Hector MacNeills Regiment of North Carolina Militia,—Who came to Charleston in Course of this Week Ending Feby. 15th, 1782

Names and Ranks	Names and Ranks
Major	Sergt.
Samuel Andrews	Archibald MacKay
Captain	Neill Little
Damiel McPhater	Private
John McNair	Damiel McPhater
Daniel MacNiell	John MacNair
Samuel Andrews	Hector MacNeill
William Rhodes	William Strickland
Lieut.	Paul McCoule
William Strickland	
Hector MacNeill	

Endorsed   North Carolina Militia No. 10 Abstract

[North Carolina Historical Commission, English Records, Treasury Papers, Miscellanea, North and South Carolina Refugees, 1781-1782. P.R.O. Treasury 50, Bundle 5.]

XLIV

No. 23. Refugees as now in Charlestown

We the Subscribers Refugees of the Second Class now in Charlestown by the order of Lt. General Lealy, of Robert Gray Dy. P.M.M. the sums annexed to our respective names in the right hand Column below upon the dates prefixed thereto, having also signed a duplicate hereof, the same being pay allowed us for the several periods undermentioned, as by the following abstract

Date	Names	From whence
May 28	John Colson	North Carolina

No. 24. Militia Officers at present Refugees in Charlestown

We the subscribers Officers of the South and North Carolina Militia at present Refugees in Charlestown, have received by order of the Commt. Lt. Genl. Lealy of Robert Gray Dy. P.M.M. the sums annexed to our respective Names in the right hand column below upon the dates prefixed thereto, having also signed a duplicate hereof the same being in part pay allowed us as Refugees for the several periods undermentioned as per the following Abstract no. 24.

Date	Names and Rank	From whence
1782	Colonels	
	Wright Gideon	North Carolina
	Majors	
	Torrence Thomas	North Carolina

[P.R.O. Treasury 50. Bundle 3. Book 11.]

XLV

No. 26. Refugees of the Third Class now in Charleston.

We the subscribers, Refugees of the Third Class have received in Charlestown by order of Lt. General Leslie of Robert Gray Dy. P.M.M. the sums annexed to our respective Names in the right hand Column below upon the Dates prefixed thereto, having also signed a duplicate hereof, the same being pay allowed us for the several periods undermentioned as by the following Abstract.

Dates	*Names*	*From whence*
1782		
May 28	James Temples	North Carolina

No. 28. Rifugee Women and Children going back to the Country

We the subscribers Refugee Women going into the country have received in Charlestown by order of the honle. Lt. General Leslie of Gobert Gray P.M.M. the sums annexed to our respective names in the right hand column below upon the dates prefixed thereto, having also signed a duplicate hereof, the same being our voluntary acceptance of the same to go into the country and for ever to renounce all future claims of support from the British Government.

1782	*Names*	*Women*	*Children*	*From whence*
	Edy Johnston	1	2	North Carolina

No. 31. Quarter Masters of the Refugees from different Districts

We the subscribers Quarter Masters of the Refugees from different Districts, have received in Charlestown by order of the Commandant, of Colo. Gray P.M.M. the sums annexed to our respective Names in the right hand column below upon the dates prefixed thereto, having also signed a duplicate hereof, the same being for the periods undermentioned as per Abstract No. 31.

	Quarter Masters	*Periods Inclusive*	
District	Names	From	To
North Carol.	Wm. McQueen	15 Jan. (82)	30 June 82

No. 33. Refugees of the Second Class in Charles Town

We the subscribers of Refugees the second Class, have received in Charles Town by Order of the hon. Lt. General Leslie of Robert Gray P.M.M. the sums annexed to our respective Names in the right Hand Column below, upon the Dates prefixed thereto having also signed a duplicate hereof, being our Pay for the

No. 38 (cont'd)

Date	*Names & Classes*	*Names and Class (Continued)*
1782	Norton John	Patrick Mary
	Price William	Pope George
	Petrie Andrew	Riddle Ann
	Rogers Andrew	Tiel Mary Ann
	Robertson Malcom	Thomson Charlotte
	Saunders John	Thomson Mary
	Sandal Peter	Whisenhunt Mary
From North Carolina &c recommended		Wasden Mr.
by Colo. Samuel Campbell		Whitley Rachel
	Bowman Sarah	Yansey Mayville
	Beverly's Orphans	Yansey Widow
	Baily Mary	Laird Jane Senr.
	Baily's Orphans	Murril Mrs.
	Baily Elizabeth	Rees Mr.
	Cunduff Eliza.	Russel Mr.
	Dill John	Joiner Mr.
	Dill's Orphans	King Wilma
	Davis Nancy	King Winy
	Davis Margaret	
	Egner Elizabeth	Prescott Rebecca

No. *38 (Continued)*

Date	Names & Classes	Names & Classes
	Ferrabee Mary	Bennet William
	Hughs Sarah	Skinner Johannes
	Hunt Ann	Bowen Hannah
	Herman Eliza.	McNiel Margt.
	Jackson Susannah	Prescott Mary
	Kee Elizabeth	Prescott Fanny
	Lifner's Orphans	Shields Eliz.
	Maultsby Margt.	Mills Widow
	McDaniel Susanh.	Pack Benjamin
	McKenzie Anny	Nash Mrs.
1782	Hames Mrs.	Gentry Sarah
	Palmer Mrs.	Nelson Anne
	Jones Mrs.	Conway Nancy
	Smith Mrs.	White Jerusha
	Lavender Mrs.	Griffin Martha
	McClintock Mrs.	Williams Mary
	Garret Mrs.	Sneed Mary
	Wilson Nath	Huffman Daniel
	Tilman Prudence	Garret Mrs for her other children

The above is made out from a number of separate orders sent me by the Commandant which are folded up together and marked vouchers for Abstract No. 38

Robert Gray P.M.M.

[North Carolina Historical Commission, English Records, Treasury Papers, Miscellanea, North and South Carolina Refugees, 1782. P.R.O. Treasury Class 50, Bundle 3. Book 11.]

XLVI

No. 21. Distressed Refugees from different places

1782	Names	From whence
	Elizabeth Brooks	North Carolina
	Margaret Evans	North Carolina

[P.R.O. Treasury 50. Bundle 3. Book 11.]

APPENDIX B

LAND CONFISCATED

Appendix B contains a list of the real estate that was confiscated and sold in North Carolina. Some counties contained a large number of tracts, while others possessed comparatively few. Henry McCulloch was the largest loser. A surprisingly large number of small planters lost their holdings, and for the most part before the Treaty of Peace had been signed.

State of North Carolina ⎫ I do hereby certify that this and the foregoing
Secretarys Office ⎭ sixteen sheets of Paper contain a true Extract
of all the Grants of Confiscated property recorded in this office. Given under my Hand this 29 day of April 1788-

W. Williams D. Sec.

[North Carolina Historical Commission, English Records, Treasury Papers, ... Reports on land grants of confiscated property, 1787-1788. Audit Office. Class 12, Vol. 91.]

EXTRACTS OF ALL SUCH GRANTS OF CONFISCATED PROPERTY AS ARE RECORDED IN THE OFFICE BY THE SECRETARY OF THE STATE OF NORTH CAROLINA

Date of Grant	County in Which Situated	Names of Former Proprietors	Number of Acres	Names of the Purchasers	Sum Sold for
	Anson	Henry E. McCulloch	64	William Bowman	30:—:—
	"	" " "	58	" "	20:—:—
	"	Walter Cunningham	100	Samuel Younge	57:—:—
	"	James Cotton	300	" "	50:—:—
	"	Walter Cunningham	200	Benjamin Robenson	61:—:—
'84 June 5th	"	Robert Palmer	200	Spruce McCoy	80:—:—
5	"	" "	300	" "	100:—:—
'85, Ap. 23rd	"	James Cotton	640	Thomas Gillaspie	105:10:—
'87, Ju. 29th	"	Henry E. McCulloch	—	Thomas Clark	52:—:—
29	"	" " "	—	" "	28:—:—
29	"	" " "	—	" "	83:—:—
29	"	" " "	100	" "	20:—:—
29	"	" " "	64	" "	35:—:—
29	"	" " "	30	" "	12:10:—
'87 Nov. 5	Anson	Robert Boyd	300	Patrick Boggin	100:—:—
5	"	John Coleson	400	William Wood	303:—:—
5	"	Thomas Bailey, Jr.	150	Sampson Lanier	30:—:—
5	"	Robert Boyd	300	Anthoney Sharp	213:—:—
'86, Oct. 24	Beaufort	Robert Palmer	128	Joseph Leech	65:—:—
8	"	" "	241	William McCabe	76:—:—
'86, N. 1	"	Andrew Sprourl	168	Richard Blackledge	100:—:—
'87, N. 15	Bertie	Nathl. Duckenfield	333	Simon Totevine	3335:—:—

Date of Grant	County in Which Situated	Names of Former Proprietors	Number of Acres	Names of the Purchasers	Sum Sold for
'87, N. 15	Bertie	Wallace & Company	166	John Pouns	260:—:—
15	"	Nathl. Duckenfield	475	William Asburn	1805:05:—
15	"	—— McKitrick	2	John Pouns	225:—:—
15	"	Nathl. Duckenfield	400	Humphrey Hardy	329:—:—
15	"	William Lother	100	George Ryan	451:—:—
15	"	Nathl. Duckenfield	213	William Ashburn	515:10:—
15	"	—— McKitrick	/	Benjamin Bryan	530:10:—
5	"	Nathl. Duckenfield	462	Jonathan Jacocks	332:—:—
'87, N. 15	Bertie	Nathl. Duckenfield	425	George Ryan	5802:—:—
15	"	" "	225	Thomas W. Pugh	75:—:—
15	"	" "	640	George Ryan	766:—:—
15	"	" "	579	Jeremiah Fleetwood	426:10:—
15	"	" "	425	John Capeheart	310:—:—
15	"	" "	193	Christopher Clark	1120:—:—
15	"	William Buchannon and Co.	203	George West	430:—:—
15	"	Henry E. McCulloch	506	John Johnston	700:—:—
15	"	Nathl. Duckenfield	225	William Ashburn	104:05:—
15	"	" "	290	John Hagan	123:—:—
15	"	" "	280	Humphrey Hardy	101:10:—
15	"	Henry E. McCulloch	506	John Johnston	621:—:—
15	"	—— McKitrick	2	Benjamin Baar	362:10:—
15	"	Nathl. Duckenfield	374	George Ryan	4953:—:—
15	"	" "	550	" "	9191:—:—
15	"	" "	235	Jonathan Jacocks	1620:—:—
15	"	" "	518	Elisha Ashburn	5053:15:—
'86, O. 24	Bladen	Thomas Christie	/	Henry E. Lutterloh	83:—:—
24	"	" "	/	" " "	80:—:—
24	"	" "	/	William Watson	200:03:—
24	"	" "	/	Daniel Shaw	1:—:—
24	"	" "	/	Jarrell Ervin	2:—:—
24	"	William Campbell	/	" "	2:—:—
24	"	Thomas Christie	/	" "	2:—:—
'87, N. 15	"	Daniel Leggett	100	Jacob Rhodes	10:05:—
15	"	David Godwin	239	" "	315:—:—
15	"	Neal McFall	50	" "	76:—:—
15	"	David Leggett	150	" "	22:—:—
15	"	Kennee Stewart	50	" "	28:03:—
15	"	David Godwin	88	" "	121:—.—
15	"	Neal McFall	100	" "	85:—:—
15	"	Peter McFarland	100	William Watson	95:—:—
15	"	David Godwin	50	Alexander Goddin	50:—:—
15	"	Jacob Kersey	150	Elias Barnes	87:—:—
'87, N. 15	Bladen	David Leggett	77	Robert Raiford	20:—:—
15	"	David Godwin	51	Curtis Ivey & G. J. McRee	10:10:—
15	"	Jacob Kersey	180	" "	160:05:—
15	"	David Godwin	577	John Yates	221:—:—

Date of Grant	County in Which Situated	Names of Former Proprietors	Number of Acres	Names of the Purchasers	Sum Sold for
'87, N. 15	Bladen	David Godwin	100	John McMillan	6:01:—
15	"	" "	100	Mathew R. White	14:—:—
15	"	David Leggett	100	" " "	15:—:—
15	"	John McDonald	½	William K. Patrick	20:—:—
15	"	Matterine Calvin	½	Robert Raiford	6:10:—
15	"	David Godwin	50	Richard Brown	12:10:—
15	"	John McDonald	½	Jesse Lassiter	9:15:—
15	"	" "	½	G. J. McRee & Curtis Ivey	100:—:—
15	"	David Godwin	118	Alexander Goddin	50:—:—
15	"	John McDonald	½	Robert Scott	9:10:—
15	"	Mark Robeson	288	Jarrell Ervin	102:04:—
15	"	George Parker	300	John Russ, Jr.	54:—:—
15	"	Randol McDugald	350	Allen McDugall	110:—:—
'87, N. 15	Bladen	David Leggett	143	Peter Smith	14:10:—
15	"	" "	117	David Flowers	12:—:—
15	"	Archibald McEachan	100	Elias Barnes	25:05:—
15	"	David Godwin	100	Jacob Reads	12:13:—
15	"	Faithful Grayham	640	Griffith J. McRee	2505:—:—
15	"	Hector McNeel	100	James Spiller	22:03:—
15	"	George Parker	195	William Bryant	753:01:—
15	"	David Leggett	243	Curtis Ivey & G. J. McRee	40:—:—
15	"	Noah Mercer	148	William Moore	105:05:—
15	"	Jacob Kersey	100	G. J. McRee & Curtis Ivey	40:10:—
15	"	David Leggett	100	James White	20:—:—
15	"	Joseph Mercer	124	Jesse Lasseter	83:10:—
15	"	Archibald McEachan	100	Robert Raiford	30:—:—
15	"	John Colvill	314	" "	20:—:—
15	"	Mark Robertson	304	" "	60:—:—
15	"	" "	280	" "	60:—:—
15	"	Randol McDugall	200	Daniel Shaw	201:—:—
'87, N. 15	Bladen	Mark Robertson	320	Jarrett Ervin	111:03:—
15	"	Daniel Southerland	120	" "	101:01:—
15	"	William Palmour	320	" "	120:03:—
15	"	John Colvin	344	G. J. McRee & Curtis Ivey	16:—:—
15	"	David Godwin	87	" "	57:—:—
15	"	" "	130	" "	72:—:—
15	"	Jacob Kersey	290	" "	220:10:—
15	Brunswick	Thomas Hooper	591	John McKinsey	848:10:—
15	"	" "	391	" "	500:—:—
15	"	" "	353	" "	570:—:—
15	"	" "	268	" "	390:—:—
15	"	" "	429	" "	500:—:—
15	"	" "	448	" "	500:—:—
15	"	" "	625	" "	570:—:—
15	"	" "	225	" "	848:10:—
15	"	" "	300	Griffith John McRee	424:—:—

Date of Grant	County in Which Situated	Names of Former Proprietors	Number of Acres	Names of the Purchasers	Sum Sold for
'87, N. 15	Brunswick	William Tryon Esq.	/	Howell Tatum	45:05:—
15	"	Christopher Cains	525	James Chairs	1065:—:—
15	"	William Tryon	492	Robert Howe	3080:—:—
15	"	The Rev. McDowell	—	Jacob Leonard	20:10:—
15	"	Christopher Cains	160	Lewis Dupree	100:—:—
15	"	" "	350	James Chairs	105:—:—
15	"	" "	550	" "	100:—:—
15	"	Hope & Buck Willets	52½	Robert Bell	14:05:—
15	"	Eborn & Reynolds	/	William Gause	13:—:—
15	"	Christopher Cains	640	James Chairs	1605:—:—
15	"	James White	½	Nathaniel Wooten	6:10:—
15	"	Eborn & Reynolds	½	Benjamin Mills	10:—:—
15	Camden	Andrew Sproul	310	Hardy Murphrey	130:—:—
15	Carteret	William Brimmage	/	Nathan Smith	103:—:—
15	"	William Low	276	William Dennis	100:—:—
15	"	George Harrison	50	" "	1:14:—
15	"	William Low	200	" "	31:—:—
'87, N. 15	Carteret	George Harrison	27	Eli West	1:10:—
15	"	Samuel Cornell	136	" "	23:—:—
15	Chatham	Ralph McNair	177	John Montgomery	183:—:—
'86, O. 24	Chowan	Mrs. Clark	—	Selby Harney	3100:—:—
'87, N. 15	"	Clark & Weir	/	Michael Pain	1151:10:—
15	"	John Henley	/	William Little John	353:—:—
15	"	——— Honey	/	John Pouns	460:—:—
15	"	John Henley	/	Frederick Rampkey	425:—:—
15	"	" "	/	" "	205:—:—
15	"	Thomas Wright	/	Edmund Blount	97:—:—
15	"	——— Honey	/	John Pouns	380:—:—
15	"	John Henley	118	William Roberts	850:—:—
15	"	Thomas Wright	½	John Mare	100:—:—
15	"	John Henley	½	William Barrett	342:—:—
15	"	Weir & Clark	½	Michael Payne	342:10:—
15	"	Thomas Wright	½	John Mare	150:—:—
15	Craven	Thomas Tyer	100	James Arants	37:—:—
'87, N. 15	Craven	James Cleatherell	640	Edward Parker	203:—:—
15	"	Robert Palmour	65	John Gray Blount	15:—:—
15	"	Francis C. Dobbs	225	" " "	70:—:—
15	"	Edward Brice Dobbs	512	James Arants	141:—:—
15	"	Patrick Clary	/	John Craddock	3975:—:—
'84, N. 13	"	Samuel Cornell	/	Spere Singleton	2160:—:—
'86, O. 21	"	Martin Howard	—	Elizabeth Cook	1100:—:—
'87, N. 5	"	Thomas Brown	200	John Davis	135:—:—
5	"	Richard Fur	100	William Griffith	51:—:—
5	Currituck	John Bennett	129	Griffith Dauge	1225:—:—
5	Dobbs	Arthur Dobbs	300	Richard Caswell	43:—:—
5	"	Curnelius Larey	300	" "	100:—:—
5	"	Thomas Torrance	200	Samuel Chapman	35:10:—
5	"	" "	200	John Gray Blount	26:—:—

Date of Grant	County in Which Situated	Names of Former Proprietors	Number of Acres	Names of the Purchasers	Sum Sold for
'87, N. 5	Dobbs	Thomas Torrance	200	Samuel Chapman	111:—:—
'85,Dec. 14	"	John Hambleton	371	James Glasgow	69:—:—
Mar. 23	"	Thomas Terans	220	James Armstrong	20:—:—
'85,Apr. 25	Dobbs	Thomas Terans	130	James Armstrong	46:—:—
25	"	Thomas Dick	150	Richard Caswell	37:—:—
'86,Oct. 24	Duplin	William Tryon Esq.	—	William Jones	100:—:—
24	"	" " "	—	" "	118:—:—
24	"	" " "	—	Curtis Ivey & J. G. McRee	113:05:—
24	"	Frederick Gregg	—	Joseph T. Roads	115:—:—
24	"	William Tryon Esq.	60	David Jones	22:01:—
24	"	" " "	555	Curtis Ivey & J. G. McRee	113:05:—
24	"	" " "	585	" "	112:—:—
'86,Oct. 24	Edgecombe	James Hill or McClelen	./	Jonathan Loomas	325:—:—
24	"	William McClellan	./	" "	130:—:—
24	"	Timothey Nocholson	./	Abner Robertson	70:—:—
Mar. 14	"	William McClelans	50	Edward Hall	760:10:—
14	"	Anthoney Bachon	460	" "	784:—:—
14	"	Benjamin Vickers	114./	Noah Sugg	201:—:—
14	"	Anthoney Bachon	123	Amos Johnston	411:—:—
14	"	Benjamin Vickers	400	Charles Garrard	752:—:—
'86,Mar.14	Edgecombe	Anthoney Bachon	78	Solomon Sessoms	212:—:—
Oct. 24	"	Robert Mackie	./	John Ingles	252:—:—
Oct. 24	"	James Moire	./	William Tuton	406:—:—
24	"	Timothey Nicholson	./	Richard Blakledge	76:—:—
24	"	Andrew Little	./	" "	15:—:—
24	"	William Lowther	./	John Gray Blount	580:—:—
24	"	William McClellan	./	" " "	302:—:—
24	"	Andrew Little	./	Richard Blackledge	7:—:—
24	"	Joseph Tuton	—	" "	33:—:—
24	"	James Moire	—	James Armstrong	210:—:—
24	"	William McClellan	—	Richard Blackledge	1160:—:—
24	"	" "	—	Edward Hall	600:—:—
24	"	Joseph Tuton	—	Archibald Thompson	53:—:—
24	"	John Agar	./	Edward Hall	40:—:—
24	"	Lawrence Obey	355	John Deloach	309:—:—
24	"	Alexander Godwin	225	Andrew Greer	199:—:—
'86,Sept.25	Guilford	Henry E. McCulloch	—	John Willis	615:15:—
'86,Sept.25	Guilford	Henry E. McCulloch	—	John Willis	637:—:—
25	"	" " "	—	James Williams	728:—:—
25	"	" " "	—	John Willis	700:—:—
25	"	" " "	—	" "	725:—:—
25	"	" " "	4	" "	1400:—:—
25	"	" " "	328	" "	1400:—:—
25	"	" " "	256	" "	256:—:—
25	"	" " "	350	" "	350:—:—

Date of Grant	County in Which Situated	Names of Former Proprietors	Number of Acres	Names of the Purchasers	Sum Sold for
86, Sept. 25	Guilford	Henry E. McCulloch	234	John Willis	453:—:—
25	"	" " "	234	" "	453:—:—
25	"	" " "	324	" "	623:—:—
25	"	" " "	147	James Lyne	356:—:—
25	"	" " "	150	" "	326:—:—
25	"	" " "	270	" "	457:—:—
25	"	" " "	130	" "	206:—:—
25	"	" " "	330	James Williams	741:—:—
Oct. 24	"	" " "	223	Robert Shew	600:—:—
24	"	" " "	156	William Dick	513:—:—
86, Oct. 24	Guilford	Henry E. McCulloch	268	James Hambleton	801:—:—
24	"	" " "	2—	Daniel McKindley	250:01:—
24	"	" " "	240	James Bell	560:—:—
24	"	" " "	416	Samuel McDill	417:—:—
24	"	" " "	200	Daniel McKindley	201:—:—
24	"	" " "	—	Roddy Hanna	550:01:—
24	"	" " "	141	John Alcon	283:01:—
'87, Nov. 5	"	" " "	216	Henry Ghiles	1050:—:—
86, March 14	Halifax	John Hambleton	275	James Casthstarphen	105:—:—
14	"	Andrew Miller	105	John Clayton	606:05:—
14	"	" "	3—	Nicholas Long	350:—:—
14	"	" "	./	John Pouns	1651:—:—
14	"	James McNeel	140	Fanney McNeel	2000:—:—
14	"	Andrew Miller	(torn)	John Geddy	382:—:—
14	"	Andrew Miller & Co.	(torn)	" "	290:—:—
14	"	" " " "	(torn)	John Pouns	320:—:—
25	"	" " " "	(torn)	" "	636:—:—
'86, March 25	Halifax	James Milner	478	Henri Gerrard	400:—:—
25	"	" "	½	Lunsford Long	85:—:—
25	Hertford	Hartley & Nicholson	640	Josiah Collings Jr.	1360:—:—
25	"	John Agner	½	Thomas Brittle	130:—:—
25	"	" "	½	Hardy Murphrey	30:—:—
25	"	Hartley & Nicholson	102	Josiah Collins Jr.	405:—:—
'86, Oct. 24	Hyde	Robert Palmer	640	Joseph Leech	370:—:—
24	"	" "	—	" "	91:—:—
24	"	" "	6—	" "	76:—:—
'87, Nov. 5	"	" "	640	James Alderston	340:—:—
5	"	" "	200	James Jasper	302:—:—
5	"	" "	300	John Cooper	59:—:—
5	"	William Palmer	400	" "	401:—:—
5	"	Robert Palmer	500	" "	150:—:—
5	"	" "	260	" "	205:—:—
'86, March 14	Nash	James McNeel	384	James Armstrong	2600:—:—
14	"	James Greenlie	750	Dixon Marshal	150:—:—
'86, March 14	Nash	George Brown	673	Dixon Marshal	240:—:—
14	"	James McNeel	208	Fanney McNeel	304:—:—
14	"	James Cary	—	Micajah Thomas	121:—:—
14	"	William Brimmage	—	Wright Stanolee	278:—:—
14	"	" "	—	" "	30:—:—

Date of Grant	County in Which Situated	Names of Former Proprietors	Number of Acres	Names of the Purchasers	Sum Sol for
'87, June 29	Montgomery	Henry E. McCulloh	174	Thomas Clark	62:—:—
Nov. 5	"	" " "	222	Jesse McClendon	500:10:—
5	"	Josiah Martin	160	Alexander Frazer	31:15:—
5	"	" "	300	John Hopkins	121:—:—
5	"	" "	160	Mark Allen	10:—:—
5	"	" "	160	" "	17:17:—
5	"	" "	160	" "	20:—:—
15	"	Henry E. McCulloch	35	William Sanders	17:—:—
15	"	" " "	54	" "	29:—:—
15	"	" " "	120	" "	40:—:—
15	"	" " "	56	" "	37:—:—
15	Moore	Laughlin Beaton	100	Griffith J. McRee	5:—:—
'87, Nov. 15	Moore	John McKeal	200	G. J. McRee & Curtis Ivey	91:—:—
15	"	Conner Doud	100	" "	10:—:—
15	"	Frederick Grigg	100	" "	13:—:—
15	"	John McNeill	100	Milton Glass	10:01:—
15	"	Frederick Gregg	400	Griffith J. McRee	40:—:—
'86, Oct. 24	New Hanover	William Tryon Esq.	180	David Jones	65:—:—
24	" "	" " "	2—	" "	345:—:—
24	" "	" " "	45—	" "	345:—:—
'87, Sep. 14	" "	Edward Bridgin	—	Peter Bacote	2100:—:—
11	" "	Daniel Sutherlin	—	John Kingsborough	5050:—:—
Nov. 15	" "	George Parker	—	" "	3000:—:—
'84, June 5	Orange	Henry E. McCulloch	212	James Williams	324:—:—
5	"	" " "	258	" "	363:—:—
5	"	" " "	159	" "	175:—:—
5	"	" " "	325	" "	420:—:—
5	"	" " "	230	" "	151:—:—
5	"	" " "	204	" "	443:—:—
'84, June 5	Orange	Henry E. McCulloch	1270	James Williams	202:—:—
5	"	" " "	132	" "	75:—:—
5	"	" " "	270	" "	270:—:—
5	"	" " "	117	" "	170:—:—
5	"	" " "	184	" "	102:—:—
5	"	" " "	180	" "	180:—:—
5	"	" " "	214	" "	124:—:—
5	"	" " "	270	" "	356:—:—
5	"	" " "	152	" "	153:—:—
5	"	Governor Tryon	1	" "	83:—:—
5	"	Henry E. McCulloch	226	" "	161:—:—
5	"	" " "	461	" "	233:—:—
5	"	" " "	208	Thomas Clark	305:—:—
5	"	" " "	357	" "	
5	"	" " "	140	Henry Cook	60:—:—
5	"	" " "	560	Thomas Burke	
5	"	Millers & Comp.	—	Patrick St. Lauranse	—

Date of Grant	County in Which Situated	Names of Former Proprietors	Number of Acres	Names of the Purchasers	Sum Sold for
'84, June 5	Orange	James Miller	1	James Allison	
5	"	Henry E. McCulloch	380	Jacob Richards	301:—:—
5	"	James Miller	1	" "	101:—:—
'85, Apr. 25	"	Henry E. McCulloch	120	Thomas H. Perkins	70:—:—
25	"	" " "	350	" " "	130:—:—
25	"	" " "	156	" " "	302:—:—
25	"	" " "	232	" " "	155:—:—
25	"	" " "	325	" " "	113:—:—
'86, Aug. 25	"	" " "	560	William Lytle	1270:—:—
25	"	" " "	115	James Williams	122:—:—
25	"	James Milner	180	Tilghman Dixon	1110:—:—
25	"	Henry E. McCulloch	102	" "	206:02:—
25	"	" " "	33	James Thompson	100:—:—
'86, Aug. 25	"	" " "	208	Samuel Parker	401:—:—
25	"	" " "	200	William O'Neal	325:—:—
25	"	James Milner	64	William Cabe	450:01:—
25	"	Henry E. McCulloch	115	Michael Mozer	227:—:—
'86, Aug. 25	Orange	James Milner	186	John Flintham	841:—:—
25	"	Henry E. McCulloch	170	William Sheppard	311:—:—
25	"	" " "	292./	George Dauhorty	307:—:—
25	"	" " "	112	Phillip Mozer	150:—:—
25	"	" " "	640	Martin Cole	305:—:—
25	"	" " "	90	William Rea	166:—:—
25	"	" " "	225	William Lytle	325:—:—
25	"	" " "	240	John Counts	305:10:—
25	"	" " "	—	Samuel Campbell	80:—:—
25	"	" " "	230	Joseph Noey	231:—:—
25	"	" " "	23	John McDaniel	100:—:—
25	"	" " "	69	William McCauley	125:—:—
25	"	" " "	108	James Williams	110:—:—
25	"	" " "	155	Henry Cooke	51:—:—
25	"	" " "	60	Henry Thompson	120:—:—
25	"	" " "	—	James Thompson	102:—:—
25	"	Edmund Fanning	—	Roswell Huntington	501:—:—
'86, Aug. 25	Orange	Edmund Fanning	—	Memucan Hunt	1001:—:—
25	"	" "	—	William Lytle	1022:—:—
25	"	" "	1	Josiah Watts	726:—:—
25	"	" "	1	William Waters	535:—:—
25	"	" "	1	William Sheppard	550:—:—
25	"	" "	1	George Daugherty	601:—:—
25	"	" "	1	William Sheppard	405:—:—
25	"	" "	¾	George Daugherty	835:—:—
25	"	Young Miller & Co.	1	" "	4558:—:—
'84, June 5	"	Governor Tryon	1	James Williams	36:04:—
5	"	Henry E. McCulloch	111	" "	105:—:—
5	"	Governor Tryon	1	" "	18:04:—
5	"	" "	1	" "	27:01:—
5	"	Henry E. McCulloch	270	Thomas Mulholland	101:—:—

Date of Grant	County in Which Situated	Names of Former Proprietors	Number of Acres	Names of the Purchasers	Sum Sold for
'84, June 5	Orange	Henry E. McCulloch	100	Jas. Mebane & Thos. Mulholland	41:—:—
5	"	" " "	295	" "	105:—:—
5	"	" " "	253	" "	85:—:—
5	"	" " "	264	Andrew Ross	151:—:—
'84, June 5	Orange	Henry E. McCulloch	163	Andrew Ross	151:—:—
5	"	James Miller	1	" "	60:—:—
5	"	Henry E. McCulloch	530	" "	300:—:—
5	"	" " "	1	" "	60:—:—
5	"	" " "	400	Jn. Taylor & Jas. Mebane	467:—:—
5	"	" " "	296	" "	161:—:—
5	"	" " "	225	" "	151:—:—
5	"	" " "	347	" "	382:—:—
5	"	" " "	225	James Thackston	803:—:—
5	"	" " "	335	" "	472:—:—
'85,Apr. 25	"	" " "	120	Thomas H. Purkins	70:—:—
25	"	" " "	350	" " "	130:—:—
25	"	" " "	156	" " "	302:—:—
25	"	" " "	232	" " "	155:—:—
25	"	" " "	325	" " "	113:—:—
25	Randolph	Francis Arnold	260	John Clendenen	324:—:—
25	"	Robert Palmour	272	John Standfield	356:—:—
'84,Nov.13	Randolph	Henry E. McCulloch	298	Britain Fuller	:—:—
'85,Apr. 25	"	" " "	298	James Roberts	100:—:—
25	"	" " "	357	William Bailey	105:13:—
'86,Aug.25	"	" " "	243	Patrick Travers	410:—:—
25	"	" " "	243	William Lytle	215:—:—
25	"	" " "	250	" "	501:—:—
25	"	" " "	136	James Clark	181:—:—
25	"	" " "	243	William Bailey	252:—:—
25	"	" " "	243	" "	452:01:—
25	"	" " "	397	Samuel Park	761:—:—
25	"	" " "	243	Samuel Travers	501:—:—
25	"	" " "	243	William Pickett	471:—:—
25	"	" " "	243	Patrick Travers	534:—:—
25	"	" " "	243	" "	381:—:—
25	"	" " "	75	William Bell	151:—:—
25	"	" " "	272	" "	403:03:—
25	"	" " "	250	Patrick Travers	1000:—:—
'86,Aug.25	Randolph	Henry E. McCulloch	243	Patrick Travers	381:—:—
25	"	" " "	75	William Bell	151:—:—
25	"	" " "	272	" "	403:03:—
25	"	" " "	250	Patrick Travers	1000:—:—
25	"	" " "	160	John Stanfield	355:—:—
25	"	" " "	250	Alexander Nelson	315:—:—
25	"	" " "	260	Francis Arnold	452:—:—

Date of Grant	County in Which Situated	Names of Former Proprietors			Number of Acres	Names of the Purchasers	Sum Sold for
'86, Aug. 25	Randolph	Henry E. McCulloch			169	Patrick Travers	276:11: 6
25	"	"	"	"	290	" "	400:03:—
25	"	"	"	"	200	William York	231:—:—
25	"	"	"	"	260	Patrick Travers	360:01: 6
25	"	"	"	"	270	John Clark	212:—:—
'87,Nov.15	"	"	"	"	381	" "	1905:—:—
15	"	"	"	"	250	William Lytle	1366:13: 4
15	"	"	"	"	438	" "	1481:—:—
15	"	"	"	"	282	William Bell	1031:—:—
15	"	"	"	"	282	" "	1005:—:—
15	"	"	"	"	438	William Lytle	1405:—:—
'87,Nov.15	Randolph	Henry E. McCulloch			282	William Bell	1151:—:—
15	Rowan	"	"	"	310	Joseph Cunninham	201:—:—
15	"	"	"	"	218./	Andrew Bostain Sr.	204:—:—
15	"	"	"	"	154	John Ford	200:—:—
15	"	"	"	"	216	Andrew Bostain	282:—:—
15	"	"	"	"	167	David Smith	117:—:—
15	"	"	"	"	237	Humphrey Brooks	392:—:—
15	"	"	"	"	96	David Craig	52:08:—
15	"	"	"	"	231	Benjamin Roundseval	151:—:—
15	"	"	"	"	287	John Lopp	348:—:—
15	"	"	"	"	155	Beacham Hiltom	115:—:—
15	"	"	"	"	400	Joseph Cunningham	351:—:—
15	"	"	"	"	152	William Strange	170:—:—
'84, June 5	"	"	"	"	126	Spruce McCoy	301:—:—
'85,Mar.23	"	"	"	"	200	Francis Lock	200:10:—
9	"	"	"	"	217	Francis Lock Sr.	200:—:—
23	"	"	"	"	365	Francis Lock	266:—:—
'84, June 5	Rowan	Henry E. McCulloch			159./	Spruce McCoy	168:—:—
5	"	"	"	"	2—	" "	301:—:—
'85,Mar.23	"	"	"	"	(torn)	Francis Lock Sr.	303:—:—·
23	"	"	"	"	(torn)	David Woodson	150:—:—
23	"	"	"	"	(torn)	Mathew Lock	204:—:—
23	"	"	"	"	193	" "	258:—:—
'82,Dec. 16	"	"	"	"	299	John Steel	300:—:—
'85,Mar.23	"	"	"	"	263	David Woodson	420:—:—
23	"	"	"	"	213	" "	300:—:—
31	"	"	"	"	115	Peter Frost	117:—:—
27	"	"	"	"	200	Anthoney Numon	227:—:—
23	"	"	"	"	377	Samuel Cummens	502:—:—
23	"	"	"	"	193	Andrew Beard	71:01:—
23	"	"	"	"	247	James Crage	126:40:—
27	"	"	"	"	175	Anthoney Numon	277:—:—
30	"	"	"	"	375	John Lewis Beard	301:—:—
30	"	"	"	"	28—	David Crage	291:—:—
'85,Mar.30	Rowan	Henry E. McCulloch			37—	John L. Beard	200:—:—
30	"	"	"	"	380	James Crage	385:—:—
28	"	"	"	"	336	Valentine Beard	826:—:—
23	"	"	"	"	375	David Crage	150:10:—

Date of Grant	County in Which Situated	Names of Former Proprietors	Number of Acres	Names of the Purchasers	Sum Sold for
'85, Mar 28	Rowan	Henry E. McCulloch	2—	Robert Martin	231:—:—
30	"	" " "	425	Jacob Wootsman	100:—:—
30	"	" " "	340	Radford Ellis	341:—:—
25	"	" " "	343	Benjamin Abbott	43:09:—
25	"	" " "	139	Maxwell Chambers	236:—:—
25	"	" " "	366	" "	428:—:—
9	"	" " "	102	John L. Beard	175:01:—
9	"	" " "	305	Conrod Brim	392:—:—
9	"	" " "	482	John L. Beard	200:—:—
'87, June 29	"	" " "	202	James Meeley	525:—:—
29	"	" " "	220	" "	515:—:—
Nov. 5	"	Edward Turner	162	James Armstrong	125:—:—
5	"	Henry E. McCulloch	200	John Armstrong	1160:—:—
'87, Nov. 5	Rowan	Henry E. McCulloch	218	John Armstrong	1015:—:—
5	"	Mathias Sappenfield	216	Edward Scarborough	475:—:—
5	"	" "	69	" "	320:—:—
5	"	Henry E. McCulloch	124	Henry Ghiles	1000:—:—
'86, Oct. 24	Sampson	Thomas Christie	106	John Wester	40:10:—
24	"	Edward Brice Dobbs	571	Curtis Ivey & J. G. McRee	107:—:—
24	"	" " "	—07	Thomas Carr	32:—:—
24	"	Thomas Christie	461	James Spiller	203:—:—
24	"	William Forbes	—	Hardy Homes	150:—:—
24	"	Edward Brice Dobbs	—	James Moore	16:—:—
24	"	" " "	—	James Spiller	21:—:—
24	"	Thomas Christie	—	" "	91:—:—
24	"	Edward Brice Dobbs	—	Jonathan Taylor	14:—:06
24	"	Thomas Christie	—	Samuel Cates	12:—:—
24	"	" "	—	James Spiller	22:—:—
24	"	Edward Brice Dobbs	—	Jonathan Taylor	80:06:—
24	"	" " "	—	Thomas Carr	32:—:—
'86, Oct. 24	Sampson	Edward B. Dobbs	49	Jonathan Carr	50:01:—
24	"	" " "	407	Curtis Ivey & J. G. McRee	340:—:—
24	Tyrell	Governor White	200	Nehemiah Long	2096:—:10
24	"	" "	250	" "	2620:01:—
24	"	" "	206	Hardy Murfree	2013:13:—
24	"	" "	360	Humphrey Hardy	3519:—:—
24	"	John Hooker	161	Nathan Hooker	961:—:—
24	"	James Craven	320	James Baker	1860:—:—
'87, Nov. 15	"	" "	320	" "	15:—:—
'84, June 5	Wake	Henry E. McCulloch	372	William Moore	471:—:—
5	"	" " "	372	" "	463:—:—
5	"	" " "	330	" "	238:—:—
5	"	" " "	200	" "	141:—:—
5	"	" " "	164	" "	80:—:—
5	"	" " "	330	" "	281:—:—
5	"	" " "	244	" "	491:—:—
'84, Jan. 9	"	" " "	291	Nicholas Long Jr.	363:—:—
9	Wayne	Robert Palmer	640	Samuel Chapman	380:—:—

APPENDIX C

Loyalist Claims

This appendix includes a list of those Loyalists of North Carolina who made application to Great Britain for compensation for loss of office or property in the state. Sometimes the claims were made by the brother, sister, or heir of the original person who lost the property or office. Both the sum asked for and the sum received have been given to show the great discrepancy that sometimes existed between the two. The names indicate that a great number of the claimants were of Scotch descent.

The great number of people in North Carolina who lost property is but partially represented in this list, as will be seen by comparing it with Appendix B, which contains an account of the owners of land confiscated in the various counties.

Loyalist Claims

Name of Applicant	Province or County	Sum asked for	Sum allowed
Bedford, Jonas	N. C.	6,837.	413.
Benning, Henrietta	N. C.	1,135.	105.
Blewer, Jacob	S. C.	262.	54.
Blewer, John	N. C.	156.10	36.
Blewer, Peter d	S. C.	457.15	118.4
Boote, Dorothy w.	N. C.	3,368.	212.10
Branson, Eli	N. C.	750.	450.
Brice, Rigdon	N. C.	1,000.	39.12
Brimage, William [E. R. 18.]	N. C.	1,180.	120.
Campbell, Angus	N. C.	765.	382.16
Campbell, Kenneth	N. C.	1,392.	700.
Chadds, Sush. Wife of Cap't. Henry Chadds & admix. of Saml. Cornell deced	N. C.	20,283.	8,300.
Clarke, Colin	N. C.	2,471.	...
Cobham, Thomas [E. R. 19.]	N. C.	1,895.	1,627.
Bath, Thos. Marquis of, & George Wm. Earle of Coventry, Trustees named in the Will of John Earl of Granville decd.	N. C.	365,749.	40,000.

LOYALIST CLAIMS

Name of Applicant	Province or County	Sum asked for	Sum allowed
Colbreath, Neil	N. C.	279.	144.10
Collett, John	Va.	560.	400.
Colvill, Matthew's Heirs	N. C.	12,350.	1,500.
Cotton, James (Col. Militia)	N. C.	11,241.16	2,032.4
Crosby, James	N. C.	394.	246.
Cruden, James Surviving partner of John Cruden and Co.	N. C.	9,621.	2,400.
Cunningham, Walter	N. C.	1,822.	198.10
De Rossett, Lewis Henry [E. R. 20.]	N. C.	10,153.	2,695.
Dobbs, Conway Richard	N. C.	21,200.	1,000.
Dobbs, Edward Brice	N. C.		1,000.
Dowd, Connor	N. C.	5,524.12	1,077.18
Dubois, Isaac	N. C.	487.	50.
Dukenfield Sr. Nathl. Bart.	N. C.	8,762.	3,000.
Dunlop, Colin Son & Co.	Va.	1,764.	750.
" " "	"	1,423.	921.
Dunlop, William	N. C.	700.	400.
Fanning, David	N. C.	1,625.	36.
Fanning, Colonel Edmd.	N. C.	17,396.1	3,098.3
Fitzsimmons, Margt. formerly Evans	N. C.	606.	255.
Wilson, James Senr. James Wilson Junr., Cumberland Wilson and Wm. Wilson Copartners with Colin Dunlop Son and Co. do. [E. R. 21.]	Va.	2,750.	1,000.
Gammell, James	N. C.	3,046.	2,150.
Graham, Faithful	N. C.	1,299.	414.
Gray, Mary (Widow)	S. C.	340.13	167.
Gray, Mary Wd. as Guardian to her Son Donald Gray	S. C.	340.13	167.
Gray, Mary Wd. as Guardian to her Daughter Mary Gray [E. R. 22.]	S. C.	340.13	167.
Green, James	N. C.	1,480.6	279.10
Gregg, Frederick	N. C.	14,708.	5,970.
Griffin, Owen [Box 23.]	N. C.	3,427.	366.10

LOYALIST CLAIMS

Name of Applicant	Province or County	Sum asked for	Sum allowed
Hamilton, Archibald John and William	N. C. & Va.	105,591.	8,000.
Hamilton, James	N. C.	790.	381.2
Hamm, Andrew	N. C.	726.13	100.16
Harkey, David [E. R. 24.]	N. C.	700.	35.8
Kerr, James	N. C.	2,007.	913.
Leggett, Capt. John	N. C.	2,435.	741.12
Love, Malcolm	N. C.	814.9	115.12
Low, William	N. C.	481.	200.
Lowther, Wm. & (Barbara his wife)	N. C.	309.	250.
Lyon, George [E. R. 25.]	N. C.	1,945.	800.
McArthur, Neil	N. C.	4,056.18	1,434.4
McCormick, William	N. C.	460.	168.10
McCormick, Wm. Thomas McKnight & James Parker Survivors of the Firm of William McCormick and Co.	do.	5,192.10	2,119.16
McCormick, William. Thomas McKnight and James Parker survivors of the Firm of William McCormick and Co. for the loss of the Ships Belville and Betsy	do.	7,800.	1,968.
McCrumen, Donald	N. C.	735.	108.
Wallace, Michael	Va.		23.16
Do. on behalf of Margt. Wallace	do.		46.18
Do. on behalf of James Wallace	do.		186.18
Do. on behalf of the Children of Mary Norris Wife of Alexander Norris of Glasgow [E. R. 26.]		1,200.	262.10
McCulloch, Henry E.	N. C.	54,265.	11,747.16
McDonald, Alexander	N. C.	1,093.	340.16
McDonald, Allen [E. R. 27.]	N. C.	1,341.	276.

LOYALIST CLAIMS

Name of Applicant	Province or County	Sum asked for	Sum allowed
McDonald, Angus	N. C.	1,909.	614.12
McDonald, Donald	N. C.	940.	300.
McDonald, Donald	N. C.	721.	74.
McDonald, Isabella	N. C.	800.	100.
McDonald, John	N. C.	752.	206.10
MacDonald, Murdock	N. C.	604.12	156.1
McDonald, Soirle	N. C.	2,047.10	369.12
McEacharn, Archibd.	N. C.	198.18	51.
McGeachy, Neil	N. C.	466.	124.
McGuire, Thomas	N. C.	645.	. . .
McInnes, Donald [E. R. 28.]	N. C.	414.12	60.
McInnes, Miles	N. C.	424.9	138.
McKay, Alexander	N. C.	1,224.10	309.12
McKenzie, John	N. C.	985.	270.
McKenzie, Revd. Wm.	N. C.	843.	210.
McKinnin, Roderick	N. C.	358.	71.8
McKinnon, Donald	N. C.	435.	123.
McKnight, Thomas [E. R. 29.]	N. C.	23,183.	3,638.
McKnight, Thomas	N. C.	8,671.9	2,749.16
McLean, Major Alexander	N. C.	743.	144.
McLean, Lilias	N. C.	738.14	134.
McLenan, Roderick	N. C.	201.5	60.
McLeod, Mr. Alexander	N. C.	2,280.	337.12
McLeod, Alexander	N. C.	620.	247.12
McLeod, Ann	N. C.	998.	120.13
McLeod, Alexander Son of Capt. Alexander McLeod deceased	N. C.	454.	
McLeod, John (Son of Capt. Alex.)	N. C.		50.
McLeod, Mary daughter of Cap't Alexr. McLeod	do	Claim includd. in that of the	50.
McLeod, Catherine daughter of do.		other Childn	50.
McLeod, John	N. C.	363.15	148.16
McLeod, John	N. C.	660.	161.
Mackleod, Murdock [E. R. 30.]	N. C.	348.	162.
McLeod, Normand	N. C.	424.	125.4
McLeod, Torquil	N. C.	221.	50.
McLeod, William	N. C.	441.	119.
McNabb, Duncan	N. C.	593.18	162.
McQueen, William	N. C.	395.10	225.15
McRae, Capt. Alexr.	N. C.	721.1	159.
McRae, John	N. C.	203.	118.
McTier, William	N. C.	1,749.	600.
Marshall, Samuel [E. R. 31.]	N. C.	2,049.	200.

LOYALIST CLAIMS

Name of Applicant	Province or County	Sum asked for	Sum allowed
Martin, Angus	N. C.	1,519.	150.
Martin, Alexander	S. C.	267.	68.
Martin, John	N. C.	755.	165.
Martin, Josiah Esqr. Govr.	N. C.	3,500.	1,260.
Monro, Major James	N. C.	9,895.10	2,983.
Munro, Ensign James	N. C.	378.	100.4
[E. R. 32.]			
Moore, William	N. C.	1,026.	266.
Morrison, Alexander	N. C.	1,288.10	411.12
Morrison, Donald	N. C.	344.	60.
Morrison, Duncan	N. C.	1,395.	150.
Murchison, Janet	N. C.	1,398.	193.16
Nelson, Robert	N. C.	2,100.	2,080.
Nowlan, Maurice	N. C.	3,687.	920.
[E. R. 33.]			
Palmer, Robert	N. C.	8,103.	78.8
Pemberton, James	N. C.	793.	555.
Pemington, William	N. C.	941.	105.
Ray, Daniel	N. C.	398.15	39.
Riddell, Andrew	N. C.	661.	234.
Rogers, James	N. C.	151.	82.4
Ross, John	N. C.	680.	300.
[Box 34.]			
Rutherford, John and Wm. George	N. C.	600.	500.
Shaw, Donald	N. C.	637.8	178.
Stewart, Kenneth (late of Cumberland County)	N. C.	364.	141.
Stewart, Kenneth (late of Bladen County)	N. C.	1,147.17	310.8
Taylor, Archibald	N. C.	1,078.	380.
Telfair, Alexander	N. C.	3,578.	395.8
[E. R. 35.]			
Tomlinson, John Edge	N. C.	6,583.	344.
Torry, James	N. C.	232.10	43.8
Tucker, Dr. Robert	N. C.	1,260.18	234.
Vardy, Aaron	N. C.	367.15	226.16
Welsh, Nicholas	N. C.	1,154.	448.10
Williams, Major Henry	N. C.	1,704.	630.12
Do. as Repre. of his Father Samuel Williams deceased)	do	1,299.5	860.
Williams, Jacob	N. C.	588.	50.
Wilson, Richard	N. C.	702.	180.
[E. R. 36.]			

[North Carolina Historical Commission. English Records, American Loyalist Claims.]

APPENDIX D

Pension Rolls

These lists of North Carolinians who received pensions from the British Government are believed to be complete for the years given. Not only did the names constantly change as older members died and new names were added, but the amount allowed to the same individual varied from time to time. The names certify to the loyalty of certain families within the state to the King's cause.

I

Loyalists Quarterly Pension Lists Allowances 1786

McCulloh, H. Eustace	300	McNicholls, P.A. A E.	30
Macknight, Thomas	230	Martin, Angus	30
MacCormick, William	100	McArthur, Neil	30
McKenzie, Rev. William	100	Mackay, Archibald	30
Marshall, Samuel	100	McQueen, William	26
McLeod, Major Alex.	96	McLeod, Ann	20
Miller, George	70	Morrison, Duncan	30
McNeil, James	50	McInnes, Lt. Miles	20
Murray, Margaret	50	McDonald, John	20
Morrison, Capt. Alex.	42	Martin, Alex.	20
McKay, Mrs. Mason	40	McDonald, Murdoch	18
Murchieson, Jennet	40	McLean, Lilias	15
McRae, John	30	Moore, William	30
McGeachy, Neil	30		

[Treasury 50, Vol. II. E. R. 16.]

II

Loyalists Quarterly Pension Lists Allowances 1790

Bedford, Jonas	20	McNicholl, P.A. & E.	30
Benning, Henrietta W.	30	Neilson, Archibald	60
Boote, Dorothy W.	34	Johnston, Joseph	16
Cotton, Ann widow	50	Knight, William	30
Green, James	24	Love, Malcolm	20
Griffin, Owen	24	McCormick, Will.	65
Hamilton, Col. Archibald	50	McDonald, Murdoch	18
Hamilton, Archibald	200	McDonald, John	30
Howard, Abigail	50	McDougal, Ann W. late	16
Howard, Ann	50	McGilvra	16
Hamilton, James 4 Daughters	30	McInnes, Miles	16
McRae, John	30	McKnight, Thomas	50
Marshall, Samuel	100	McLean, Lilias	16
Martin, Angus	30	McQueen, William	20
Murcheson, Jannet	30	Parker, Elizabeth	30
McKay, Mrs. Mason	40	Phillips, Rev. Jn. Lott	60

Rutherford, John	50	Torrey, James	16
Telfair, Paulina	50	Williams, Jacob	30
Thomlinson, J. E.	60		

[Treasury 50, Vol. II. E. R. 16.]

III

Loyalists Quarterly Pension Lists Allowances 1790

Bedford, Jonas	20	McDonald, Murdock	18
Benning, Henrietta Wd.	30	McDonald, John	30
Boote, Dorothy	34	McDougal, Ann (now McGilvra)	16
Colbreath, Neil	12	McInnes, Miles	16
Cotton, Ann Wid.	50	McKnight, Thomas	50
Crosby, James	30	McLean, Lilias	16
Green, James	24	McQueen, William	20
Griffin, Owen	24	McRae, John	30
Hamilton, Col. Archibald	50	Marshall, Samuel	100
Hamilton, Col. John	30	Martin, Angus	30
Hamilton, Archibald	200	Murchieson, Jannet	30
Howard, Abigail	50	Neilson, Archibald	60
Howard, Ann	50	Parker, Elizabeth	30
Hamilton, James 4 Daughters	30	Phillips, Rev. John Lott	60
Johnson, Joseph	16	Rutherford, John	50
Knight, William	30	Telfair, Paulina	50
Love, Malcolm	20	Thomlinson, J. E.	60
McNicholl, A. & E.	30	Torrey, James	16
McKay, Mrs. Mason	40	Williams, Jacob	30
McCormick, William	65		

[Treasury 50, Vol. XII. E. R. 16.]

IV

Loyalists Quarterly Pension Lists Allowances 1790

Brimage, William	120	McGuire, Thomas	280
Mackenzie, Rev. Wm.	100	Palmer, Robert	300
McCormick, William	15	Pennington, William	60
Macknight, Thomas	90		

[Treasury 50, Vol. XXXI. E. R. 16.]

V

Loyalists Quarterly Pension Lists Allowances 1794

Benning Henrietta	30	Green, James	24
Boote, Dorothy	34	Griffin, Owen	24
Brimage, Elizabeth, widow		Hamilton, Col. Archibald	50
of William, and 4 children,		Hamilton, Col John (96)	30
Thos. West, born 15 July		Hamilton, Archibald	200
1775		Howard Abigail	50
Elizabeth Tollock and Mary		Hamilton, James 4 Daughters	30
Frances born 21st Oct. 1777,		Knight, William	30
Harriet, born 12th April 1782	59. 13.7	Mc Nicholl, Annabella	10
Cotton, Ann widow	50	McKay, Mrs. Mason	40
Cunningham, Cath. wid.	21.4	McCormick, William	65
Crosby, Frances wid. 2 chiln.	23.19.7	McDonald, Murdock	18

258

APPENDICES

McDougal, Ann (now McGilvra)	16
McInnes, Miles	16
McKnight, Thomas	50
McQueen, William	20
McRae, John	30
Martin, Angus	30
Murcheson, Janet	30

[Treasury 50, Vol. XIV. E. R. 16.]

WIDOWS AND CHILDREN

Neilson, Archibald	60
Parker, Elizabeth	30
Phillips, Rev. John Lott	60
Telfair, Paulina	50
Torrey, James	16
Williams, Jacob	30

VI

Loyalists Quarterly Pension Lists Allowances 1794

Benning, Henrietta wid.	30
Boote, Dorothy	34
Cotton, Ann wid.	50
Green, James	24
Griffen, Owen	24
Hamilton, Col. Archibald	50
Hamilton, Col. John (96)	30
Hamilton, Archibald	200
Hamilton, James 4 Daughters	30
Knight, William	30
McNicholl, Annabella	10
McKay, Mrs. Mason	40
McCormick, Wm.	65
McDonald, Murdock	18
McDougal, Ann (now McGilvra)	16
Mackenzie, Rev. Will	100
McCormick, William	15
McKnight, Thomas	90

[Treasury 50, Vol. XXXIII. E. R. 16.]

McKnight, Thomas	50
McQueen, William	20
McRae, John	30
Martin, Angus	30
Murcheson, Jannet	30
Neilson, Archibald	60
Phillips, Rev. John Lott	60
Telfair, Paulina	50
Torrey, James	16
Williams, Jacob	30

WIDOWS & CHILDREN

Cunningham, Cath.	21.4
Crosby, Frances 2 child.	23.19.7
Mc Guire, Thomas	280
Pennington, Will.	60
Palmer, Robert	300

VII

Loyalists Quarterly Pension Lists Allowances 1798

Benning, Henrietta	30
Boote, Dorothy	34
Brimage, Eliz. widow of	
William and 3 children	
Eliz. Tollock A Mary Frances,	
born 21st Oct. 1777, &	
Harriett born 12th April 1782	
Cotton, Ann widow	50
Howard, Abigail	50
Hamilton, James 4 Daughters	30
Knight, William	30
Mc Nicholl, Annabella	10
McKay, Mrs. Mason	40
McCormick, William	65
McDonald, Murdoch	18
McInnes, Miles	16

[Treasury 50, Vol. XVI. E. R. 16.]

Cunningham, Cath.	21.4
Crosby, Frances and 1 child	23.9.91/2
Green, James	24
Griffin, Owen	24
Hamilton, Col. John	30
Hamilton, Archibald	200
McKnight, Thomas	50
McQueen, William	20
McRae, John	30
Martin, Angus	30
Murcheson, Jannet	30
Neilson, Archibald	60
Phillips, Rev. Jn. Lott	60
Torrey, James	16

VIII

∴ Loyalists Quarterly Pension Lists Allowances 1798

Mackenzie, Rev. William	100	McGuire, Thomas	280
McCormick, William	15	Pennington, William	60
McKnight, Thomas	90	Palmer, Robert	300

[Treasury 50, Vol. XXXV. E. R. 16.]

IX

Loyalists Quarterly Pension Lists Allowances 1802

Benning, Henrietta	30	Hamilton, Archibald	200
Boote, Dorothy	34	Hamilton, James 4 Daughters	30
WIDOWS AND CHILDREN		Knight, William	30
Brimage, Eliz.		McCormick, William	65
Brimage, Harriet her child		McDonald, Murdoch	18
born 12th April 1782	4 .18.4¾	McInnes, Miles	16
Cotton, Ann	50	McKay. Mason	40
Cunningham, Catherine	21.4	McKnight, Thomas	50
Crosby, Frances & 1 child	23.9.9½	McNicholl, Annabella	10
Green, James	24	McQueen, William	20
Hamilton, Col. John	30	McRae, John	30
Murcheson, Jannet	30	Martin, Angus	30
Neilson, Archibald	60	Palmer, Helen, widow of Rob.	
WIDOWS AND CHILDREN		Palmer from 18 Nov. 1802	60
Phillips, Mary widow		p Min 12 Dec 1803	
of John Lott Min 9th		Torrey, James	16
April 1802	36		

[Treasury 50, Vol. XVIII. E. R. 16.]

X

Loyalists Quarterly Pension Lists Allowances 1802

Mackenzie, Rev. William	100	McGuire, Thomas	280
McCormick. William	15	Palmer. Robert	300
McKnight, Thomas	90	Pennington, William	60

[Treasury 50, Vol. XXXVIII. E. R. 16.]

XI

Loyalists Quarterly Pension Lists Allowances 1806

Benning, Henrietta	30	McInnes, Miles	16
WIDOWS AND CHILDREN		McKay, Mason	40
Brimage, Eliz.	44	McKnight, Thomas	50
Cotton, Ann	50	McNicholl, Annabella	10
Cunningham, Cath	21.4	McQueen, William	20
Crosby, Frances & 1 child	23. 9.9½	McRae, John	30
Green, James	24	Martin, Angus	30
Hamilton, Archibald	200	Murcheson, Jannet	30
Hamilton, James 4 Daughters	30	**WIDOWS AND CHILDREN**	
Knight, William	30	Phillips, Mary	36
McCormick, William	65	Torrey, James	16
McDonald, Murdoch	18		

[Treasury 50, Vol. XX. E. R. 16.]

XII

Loyalists Quarterly Pension Lists Allowances 1806

Mackenzie, Rev. Will.	100	McKnight, Thomas	90
McCormick, William	15	Pennington, William	60

[Treasury 50, Vol. XL. E. R. 16.]

XIII

Loyalists Quarterly Pension Lists Allowances 1810

Benning, Henriatta	30	McInnes, Miles	16
WIDOWS		McKay, Mason	40
Brimage, Eliz.	44	McKnight, Thomas	50
Cotton, Ann	50	McNicholl, Annabella	10
		McQueen, William	20
WIDOWS AND CHILDREN		McRae, John	30
Cunningham, Cath.	21.4	Murcheson, Jannet	30
Cro'sby, Frances	23	WIDOWS	
Green, James	24	Phillips, Mary	36
Hamilton, Archibald	200	Palmer, Helen	60
Hamilton, James 4 Daughters	30	Torrey, James	16
Knight, William	30		
McCormick, Will.	65		
McDonald, Murdoch	18		

[Treasury 50, Vol. XXII. E. R. 16.]

XIV

Loyalists Quarterly Pension Lists Allowances 1810

McCormick, William	15	Pennington, William	60
McKnight, Thomas	90		

[Treasury 50, Vol. XLII. E. R. 16.]

XV

Loyalists Quarterly Pension Lists Allowances 1814

McCormick, William	15	Pennington, William	60

[Treasury 50, Vol. XLIV. E. R. 16.]

XVI

Loyalists Quarterly Pension Lists Allowances 1818

Pennington, William	60

[Treasury 50, Vol. XLV. E. R. 16.]

XVII

Loyalists Quarterly Pension Lists Allowances 1822

Pennington, William	60

[Treasury 50, Vol. XLVI. E. R. 16.]

XVIII

Loyalists Quarterly Pension Lists Allowances 1826

Pennington, William	60

[Treasury 50, Vol. IV. E. R. 16.]

XIX

Loyalists Quarterly Pension Lists Allowances 1818

Benning, Henrietta	30	McKay, Mason	40
Cunningham, Cath.	21.4	McNicholl, Annabella	10
Crosby, Frances	23	McQueen, William	20
Green, James	24	McRae, John	30
Hamilton, James 4 Daughters	30	Murcheson, Janet	30
Hamilton, Henrietta	74	Macknight, Christian	56
Knight, William	30	(crauford)	
McDonald, Murdoch	18	McCormick, Eliz.	38
McInnes, Miles	16	(crauford)	
		Phillips, Mary	36
		Palmer, Helen (now Troward)	60

[Treasury 50, Vol. XXV. E. R. 16.]

XX

Loyalists Quarterly Pension Lists Allowances 1822

Benning, Henrietta	30	McNicholl, Annabella	10
Crosby, Frances	23	McQueen, William	20
Green, James	24	McRae, John	30
Hamilton, James Daughters	30	McCormick, Eliz.	38
Knight, William	30	(crauford)	
McDonald, Murdoch	30	McInnes, Christiana	16
McKay, Mason	18	Palmer, Helen (now Troward)	60

[Treasury 50, Vol. XXVI. E. R. 16.]

XXI

Loyalists Quarterly Pension Lists Allowances 1826

Benning, Henrietta	30	McQueen, William	20
Crosby, Frances	23	McRae, John	30
Green, James	24	McInnes, Christiana	16
Hamilton, James 4 Daughters	30	Palmer, Helen (now Troward)	60
Knight, William	30		
McDonald, Murdoch	18		
McNicholl, Annabella	10		

[Treasury 50, Vol. XXVII. E. R. 16.]

XXII

Loyalists Quarterly Pension Lists Allowances 1830

Crosby, Frances	23	McQueen, William	20
Hamilton, Jane Daughters	30	McRae, John	30
McDonald, Murdoch	18	McInnes, Christiana	16
McNicholl, Annabella	10		

[Treasury 50, Vol. XXVIII. E. R. 16.]

XXIII

Loyalists Quarterly Pension Lists Allowances 1831 —last

Crosby, Frances	23	McNicholl, Annabella	10
Hamilton, Jane Daughters	30	McQueen, William	20
McDonald, Murdoch	18	McRae, John	30
McInnes, Christiana	16		

[Treasury 50, Vol. XXVIII. E. R. 16.]

BIBLIOGRAPHY

This study was written largely from original sources which were found in Canada, Washington, D. C., and North Carolina. The state of North Carolina is almost destitute of manuscript material or source material for the period of the Revolution after 1776, except for that found in *The Colonial* and *State Records*. *The Colonial Records of North Carolina,* which comes down to the close of 1776, contains a greater amount of material than does *The State Records* after that date. England preserved her Colonial records fairly well. During the period of the struggle with England the newly formed state was careless of the preservation of documents, and of those saved, many have since disappeared.

The Bibliography includes only a small number of the works which were consulted (often in vain) for material bearing on the subject. As indicated in the footnotes, *The Colonial* and *State Records* form the basis for the study.

A. MANUSCRIPTS

Duke University Library, Durham, N. C.
  MS of James Fraser, which gives an interesting inventory of his estate, and tells also of his application to the British Government for compensation.

Nova Scotia Historical Society, Halifax, Nova Scotia.
  Land Papers of the early counties of Nova Scotia, which contain the names of settlers from North Carolina.

Archives Building, Ottawa, Canada.
  The Haldimand Papers, a large collection of documents of General Haldimand, Governor of Canada during much of the period of its settlement by Loyalist Americans. Contains the letters between General Haldimand and the British officials and accounts of a large number of Loyalists who migrated from North Carolina to Canada.

North Carolina Historical Commission, Raleigh, N. C.
  Papers of the Confiscation Commissioners for the New Bern, Salisbury, Halifax, Hillsboro, Wilmington, and Edenton Districts. No report appears for the Morgan District. These papers give an account of the property sold by the Commissioners and the amount of money which was turned into the state.

Transcript of the Manuscript Books and Papers of the Commission of Enquiry into the Losses and Services of the American Loyalists held under Acts of Parliament of 23, 25, 26, 28, and 29 of George III, preserved among the Audit Office Records in the Public Record Office of England, 1783-1790. Volumes pertaining to North Carolina Loyalists are in the Historical Building at Raleigh. These papers contain the most valuable information concerning the Loyalists that is accessible to students at the present time. In stating their claims the applicants divulged much information concerning the Revolution in North America, which is not to be found elsewhere.

Henry E. McCulloch Letters. Historical Society, Raleigh, N. C. These letters contain a large number wherein McCulloch beseeches his friends to save his property in North Carolina.

Intercepted Loyalist Letters. Library of Congress, Washington, D. C. A collection of letters written by Loyalists and taken from British ships en route to and from England.

B. Archives and State Records

American Archives: Consisting of a Collection of Authentick Records, State Papers, Debates, and Letters and other Notices of Publick Affairs, the whole forming a Documentary History of the Origin and Progress of the North American Colonies; of the Causes and Accomplishments of the American Revolution; and of the Constitution of Government for the United States, to the final Ratification thereof. Fourth Series. (From the King's message to Parliament of March 7, 1774, to the Declaration of Independence by the United States.) Edited by Peter Force. 6 vols. Washington, D. C., 1837-1846.

Canada. *Reports on Canadian Archives.* Edited by Douglas Brymner. Ottawa, 1883-.

The Colonial Records of North Carolina. Edited by William L. Saunders. 10 vols. Raleigh, 1886-1890.

Ontario, Bureau of Archives. Report for 1904. Edited by Alexander Fraser. 2 vols. Toronto, 1905.

Parliamentary History of England from the Norman Conquest in 1066 to the Year 1803. From which last-mentioned Epoch it is continued in the work entitled *Cobbett's Parliamentary Debates.* 36 vols. London, 1806-1820. Vol. IX.

The State Records of North Carolina. Edited by Walter C. Clark. 15 vols. Goldsboro, N. C., 1886-1907.

Virginia, General Assembly. *Journals of the House of Burgesses of Virginia, 1773-1776.*

C. Memoirs and Diaries

Caruthers, Rev. Eli Washington. *Interesting Revolutionary Incidents: and Sketches of Character, Chiefly in the "Old North State." First Series.* Philadelphia, 1854.

Cruikshank, Ernest Alexander, ed. *The Correspondence of Governor John Groves Simcoe.* 5 vols. Toronto, 1923-1931.

Curwen, Samuel. *Journal and Letters.* Edited by George Atkinson Ward. *First Series.* London, 1842.

Lee, Henry. *Memoirs of the War in the Southern Department of the United States.* London, 1869.

Moore, Frank. *A Diary of the American Revolution.* 2 vols. New York, 1860.

Raymond, William Odber, ed. *Winslow Papers, A. D. 1776-1826.* St. John, New Brunswick, 1901.

D. Newspapers, Periodicals, and Publications of Learned Societies

Annual Register, 1776. London, 1777.

Barringer, General Rufus. "Battle of Ramsaur's Mill," *Davidson College Historical Association Magazine.* Vol. 1, No. 1. Davidson, N. C., 1898.

Battle, Kemp P., ed. "Letters and Documents Relating to the Early History of the Lower Cape Fear," *James Sprunt Historical Monograph.* No. 4. Chapel Hill, 1903.

Boucher, Rev. Jonathan. *Reminiscences of an American Loyalist, 1738-1789: Being the Autobiography of the Revd. Jonathan Boucher.* Edited by Jonathan Boucher. Boston and New York, 1925.

Connor, Robert D. W. "Cornelius Harnett: The Pride of the Cape Fear," *North Carolina Booklet,* Vol. V, No. 3. Raleigh, 1906.

————. "Race Elements in the White Population of North Carolina," North Carolina State Normal and Industrial College, *Historical Publication,* No. 1. Raleigh, 1920.

————. "Revolutionary Leaders of North Carolina," North Carolina State Normal and Industrial College, *Historical Publication,* No. 2. High Point, N. C., 1916.

Gentleman's Magazine, 1776.

Graham, William Alexander. "The Battle of Ramsaur's Mill, June 20, 1780," *North Carolina Booklet,* Vol. IV, No. 2. Raleigh, 1904.

Grey, Colonel Robert. "Observations on the War in Carolina," *North Carolina University Magazine*, VIII, 145-160 (Nov., 1858).

———. "British Invasion of North Carolina in 1780, and 1781," *North Carolina University Magazine*, Vol. I.

Henderson, Archibald. "The Origin of the Regulation in North Carolina," *North Carolina Booklet*, Vol. XVII, No. 4. Raleigh, 1918.

Noble, Marcus C. S. "The Battle of Moore's Creek Bridge," *North Carolina Booklet*, Vol. III, No. 11. Raleigh, 1904.

North Carolina Gazette, 1776-1777.

Waddell, Alfred Moore. "The Stamp Act on the Cape Fear," *North Carolina Booklet*, Vol. I, No. 3. Raleigh, 1901.

Whitaker, Bessie Lewis. "The Provincial Council and the Committee of Safety in North Carolina," *James Sprunt Historical Monograph*, No. 8. Chapel Hill, 1908.

E. BOOKS AND MONOGRAPHS

Allen, William Cicero. *History of Halifax County*. Boston, 1918.

Ashe, Samuel A'Court. *History of North Carolina*. 2 vols. Greensboro, 1908-1925.

Bancroft, George. *History of the United States of America, from the Discovery of the Continent*. Vol. IV. Author's Last Revision. New York, 1882-1884.

Beer, George Louis. *British Colonial Policy, 1754-1765*. New York, 1907.

Boyd, Julian Parks. *The County Court in Colonial North Carolina*. Duke University, Master's thesis, Durham, N. C., 1926.

Boyd, William Kenneth. *Some Eighteenth Century Tracts Concerning North Carolina*. Raleigh, 1927.

Carr, James Owen, ed. *The Dickson Letters*. Raleigh, 1901.

Caruthers, Rev. Eli Washington. *A Sketch of the Life and Character of the Rev. David Caldwell, D. D., near Sixty Years Pastor of the Churches of Buffalo and Alamance. Including Two of his Sermons; Some Account of the Regulation, together with the Revolutionary Transactions and Incidents in which he was Concerned; and a very brief notice of the Ecclesiastical and Moral Condition of North-Carolina while in its Colonial State.* Greensborough, N. C., 1842.

Clewell, John Henry. *A History of Wachovia in North Carolina: The Unitas Fratrum or Moravian Church in North Carolina, 1752-1902.* New York, 1902.

Connor, Robert D. W. *North Carolina: Rebuilding an Ancient Commonwealth.* 4 vols. Chicago and New York, 1929.

Crittenden, Charles Christopher. *The Commerce of North Carolina, 1763-1789.* New Haven, 1936.

Cruikshank, Ernest Alexander, ed. *The Correspondence of Governor John Graves Simcoe, with Allied Documents, Relating to His Administration of the Government of Upper Canada, 1789-1796.* 5 vols. Toronto, 1923-1931.

Draper, Lyman Copeland. *King's Mountain and Its Heroes.* Cincinnati, 1881.

Eardly-Wilmot, John. *Historical View of the Commission for Enquiring into the Losses, Services, and Claims, of the American Loyalists, at the Close of the War between Great Britain and her Colonies, in 1783: with an Account of the Compensation Granted to them by Parliament in 1785 and 1788.* London, 1815.

Eaton, Arthur Wentworth H. *The Church of England in Nova Scotia and Tory Clergy of Revolution.* Second Edition. New York, 1912.

Eckenrode, Hamilton James. *The Revolution in Virginia.* New York, 1916.

Fanning, David. *Colonel Fanning's Narrative of His Exploits.* Toronto, 1906.

Falconer, Sir Robert Alexander. *The United States as a Neighbor from a Canadian Point of View.* Cambridge, England, 1926.

Foote, William Henry. *Sketches of North Carolina, Historical and Biographical.* New York, 1846.

Ford, Worthington Chauncey, ed. *George Washington, Writings, Being His Correspondence, Addresses, Messages, and Other Papers, Official and Private.* 14 vols. New York, 1889-1893.

Fries, Adelaide. *The Moravian Church, Yesterday and Today.* Raleigh, 1926.

———, ed. *Records of the Moravians in North Carolina.* 2 vols. Raleigh, 1922.

Graham, William Alexander. *General Joseph Graham and His Papers on the North Carolina Revolutionary History.* Raleigh, 1904.

Greene, Francis Vinton. *The Revolutionary War and the Military Policy of the United States.* New York, 1911.

Hannay, James. *History of New Brunswick.* 2 vols. St. John, N. B., 1909.

Harrell, Isaac Samuel. *Loyalism in Virginia: Chapters in the Economic History of the Revolution.* Durham, N. C., 1926.

Hawks, Francis L., David L. Swain, and William A. Graham. *A Revolutionary History of North Carolina, in Three Lectures.* Compiled by William D. Cooke. Raleigh, 1853.

Hough, Franklin B., ed. *The Siege of Savannah by the Combined American and French Forces under the Command of General Lincoln and the Count d'Estaing, in the Autumn of 1779.* Albany, 1866.

Jones, Joseph Seawell. *Defense of the Revolutionary History of the State of North Carolina.* Raleigh, 1834.

Lecky, William Edward H. *The American Revolution, 1763-1783.* New York, 1898.

Lossing, Benson J. *The Pictorial Field-Book of the American Revolution.* 2 vols. New York, 1860.

McRee, Griffith J. *Life and Correspondence of James Iredell, One of the Associate Justices of the Supreme Court of the United States.* New York, 1857-1858.

Martin, François-Xavier, ed. *Notes of a Few Decisions in the Superior Courts of the State of North Carolina, and in the Circuit Court of the United States, for North Carolina.* Newbern, N. C., 1797.

Meares, Catherine De Rosset. *Annals of the De Rosset Family.* Columbia, S. C., 1906.

Ramsey, James G. M. *The Annals of Tennessee to the End of the Eighteenth Century: Comprising its Settlement, as the Watauga Association, from 1769 to 1777; a part of North-Carolina, from 1777 to 1784; the State of Franklin, from 1784 to 1788; a part of North-Carolina, from 1788 to 1790; the Territory of the United States, south of the Ohio, from 1790 to 1796; the State of Tennessee, from 1796 to 1800.* Charleston, 1853.

Raper, Charles Lee. *North Carolina: A Study in English Colonial Government.* New York, 1904.

Reed, William B. *Life and Correspondence of Joseph Reed.* 2 vols. Philadelphia, 1847.

Rumple, Rev. Jethro. *A History of Rowan County, North Carolina.* Salisbury, N. C., 1881.

Sabine, Lorenzo. *Biographical Sketches of the Loyalists of the American Revolution.* 2 vols. Boston, 1864.

Schlesinger, Arthur Meier. *The Colonial Merchants and the American Revolution, 1763-1776.* New York, 1918.

Siebert, Wilbur H. *The Flight of American Loyalists to the British Isles.* Columbus, Ohio, 1911.

————. *The Legacy of the American Revolution to the British West Indies and Bahamas: A Chapter out of the History of the American Loyalists.* Columbus, Ohio, 1913.

————. *Loyalists in East Florida, 1774 to 1785.* 2 vols. De Land, Florida, 1929.

Stevens, Benjamin Franklin, ed. *The Campaign in Virginia, 1781: An Exact Reprint of Six Rare Pamphlets on the Clinton-Cornwallis Controversy.* . . . London, 1888.

————, comp. *Report on the American Manuscripts in the Royal Institute of Great Britain.* London, 1904-1909.

Tarleton, Sir Banastre. *A History of the Campaigns of 1780 and 1781 in the Southern Provinces of North America.* London, 1787.

Turner, Joseph Kelly. *A History of Edgecombe County, North Carolina.* Raleigh, 1920.

Wallace, David Duncan. *The History of South Carolina.* 4 vols. New York, 1934.

Wharton, Francis, ed. *The Revolutionary Diplomatic Correspondence of the United States.* 6 vols. Washington, D. C., 1889.

Wheeler, John H. *Historical Sketches of North Carolina from 1584 to 1851.* 2 vols. Philadelphia, 1851.

Wirt, William. *Sketches of the Life and Character of Patrick Henry.* Ithaca, N. Y., 1850.

INDEX

Act of Pardon and Oblivion, 165-166
Agnew, Parson, 66
Albemarle, merchants of, 54
Albemarle Assembly, 4
Alexander, Moses, Battle of Alamance, 45
Alston, Philip, captured by Fanning, 144; falsely accused of loyalism, 104-105; killings enrage Highlanders, 143
Andrews, Samuel, exempted from pardon, 165
Anson County, assures Governor Martin of loyalty, 85; Committee of Confiscation, 170; loyalism, 57; Loyalist guerrillas, 101; Loyalist Military Forces, 59; neutral clergymen, 100; protests against Continental Congress, 84; Regulation, 39; sale of confiscated land, 158; Tory uprising suppressed, 100
Anstey, investigates Loyalist claims in United States, 208
Archbishop of Canterbury, helps Loyalist clergymen, 56
Archibald Hamilton & Co., Loyalist merchants, 53
Arnold, Benedict, receives land in Canada, 198-199
Ashe, John, captured by Craig, 138; collects Patriot forces, 93; committee to win over Scotch, 91; encourages Patriot activity, 105; leader against Regulators, 45; resistance to Stamp Act, 12-13; requests release of Dr. Fallon, 78; Tory danger in Wilmington, 104; court unable to force payment of debt, 179
Assembly, Colonial, censures Governor Dobbs, 36; colonists tried for treason in England, 18; controversy with Governor, 9; creates courts, 27; debates Regulator Revolt, 44-45; declares Governor Martin's courts illegal, 28; dissolved for support of Continental Congress, 32; invokes Tryon in favor of law courts, 29;

joins with Virginia in protest, 28; last meeting, 32; letter from Virginia opposing Townshend Act, 16; members opposed to Stamp Act, 16; paper money controversy, 21-24; powers of, 7; prorogued by Governor, 24, 25, 27, 30; protests subordination to Parliament, 17; representation in, 17; supports Continental Congress, 32; votes house to Governor, 16
Assembly, State, confiscation of property for treason, 154-155; disarming of Tories, 124; divided over confiscation, 164; radicals in control, 164
Assembly, 1779, treatment of Samuel Cornell, 188-189
Assembly, 1781, refuses Fanning's armistice, 151
Assembly, 1782, divided over confiscation, 164
Austin, Solomon, moves to Ontario in 1794, 198

Back country, loyal, 34
Baggs, John, Loyalist refugee, 183
Balfour, Colonel, killed, 150
Balfour, Margaret, letter expressing pleasure at hanging of Frederick Smith, 123
Balls, the, debts paid in depreciated currency, 26
Banishment, of Loyalists by Provincial Congress, 153; for failure to take oath, 156
Banishment Act of 1777, 181
Barrows, David, Patriot merchant, 54
Battle, Elisha, votes on Oath Bill, 156
Bayard, William, correspondence with Allan Jones, 176
Beaufort County, sale of confiscated land, 58
Bedford, Colonel, treatment of his command by Tarleton, 132
Bedford, Jonas, claim partially paid, 212
Bedford, Mary, property restored, 168
Benning, Arthur, Committee on Property Loss, 204
Berkeley, Governor of Virginia, 3

Bertie County, sale of confiscated land, 58

Beverly, Jesse, Tory guerrilla, 102

Beverly, John, Tory guerrilla, 102

Bibby, John, executed after King's Mountain, 132

Black, George, ill-educated committee member, 82

Bladen County, amnesty to inhabitants, 81; Committee of Confiscation, 170; largely Tory, 103, 140; Loyalist Military Forces, 60; opposition to Stamp Act, 14; sale of confiscated lands, 58; Scotch appointed magistrates, 50

Blake, Thomas, Regulator, 40

Bloodworth, Timothy, in favor of confiscation, 164

Blount, Joseph, Patriot merchant, 54

Blount, William, debts paid in depreciated currency, 26, 173; permission given to sue debtors of Thomas Bogg, 167

Blue, Peter, Tory, 122

Board of War, comments on Governor Martin's recruiting, 130

Bogart, Lewis L., speech on Loyalists, 199-200

Bogg, Thomas, property restored to family of, 167

Boote, Benjamin, persecuted by Patriots, 108-109; sent to South Carolina jail for safekeeping, 74; suspected of communication with governor, 71

Booth, Benjamin, censured for Loyalist activity, 64

Booth, Dorothy, claim partially paid, 212

Bourk, William, trial of, 78-79

Boyd, Colonel, recruiting of Loyalists, 105

Bridgin, Edward, property restored, 168

Brimmage, William, Tory official, 56, 104, 159

British Government, expenditures to help refugee Loyalists, 195

Brunswick County, 12; loyalism, 57; not represented at first Provincial Congress, 62; opposition to Stamp Act, 14; sale of confiscated land, 58

Bryan, Captain John, killed, 151

Bryan, Samuel, heads delegation of Loyalists, 85-86; loyal to King, 49; Tory commander at Hanging Rock, 128; Loyalist officer, 61

Burgwin, J., homesick Loyalist in England, 187

Burke County, loyalism in, 60; Patriots become pseudo Loyalists, 130; robbing and murdering of Patriots, 106

Burke, Governor, breaks parole, 147; captured by Fanning, 146; loyalism in colony, 139; prolongs war, 152; receives Fanning's terms of peace, 149-150

Burke, Thomas, 20; letter from Andrew Miller, 66

Burr, Harrison, debts paid in depreciated currency, 26

Burrington, Governor, 5, 7

Bute County, 8; refuses to send militia against Regulators, 45

Butler, General, defeated at Lindley's Mill, 147

Cabarrus County, German immigration, 54

Calston, William, thanks Fanning, 151

Camden, Battle of, 128; captured by Cornwallis, 124

Camden County, sale of confiscated land, 58

Campbell, Colin, jailed by Council of Safety, 82

Campbell, Colonel, King's Mountain, 56, 132

Campbell, Donald, jailed by Council of Safety, 82

Campbell, Dugall, difficulty of owning English property, 100-101

Campbell, Duncan, Bladen County magistrate, 50

Campbell, Farquard, committee to win over Scotch, 91; conduct at Moore's Creek, 97-98; exiled from state, 98; ill treatment by Provincial Council, 79; receives coach of governor, 74; Tory representative to first Provincial Congress, 62

Campbell, Kenneth, heirs of are paid claim, 207

Campbell, Mr., Loyalist merchant, 53

Campleton, not represented at first Provincial Congress, 62

Canada, Benedict Arnold requests land in, 198-199; effect of Loyalist migrations on, 200; end of Loyalist migrations to, 200; government aid to Loyalist refugees, 195-196; haven for Loyalist soldiers, 192; later Loyalists given less aid, 196; Loyalists proud of exile, 199; Loyalist refugees go to, 186; Loyalist refugees prosper in, 194; Loyalists sell land and return to the United States, 199; motives of Loyalist settlers, 197; North Carolina Loyalists attracted to as late as 1794, 197-198; rivalry in the provinces for Loyalist settlers, 195; trouble between refugees and original settlers, 196; Canadian Commission to Investigate Loyalist Claims, analysis of claims allowed and rejected, 207-208; basis for rewarding claims, 207; final report of, 210

Cape Breton, Loyalist refugees settle in, 193

Cape Fear, center of opposition to Stamp Act, 14; merchants here loyal, 54; merchants protest Confiscation Act of 1779, 171-172; only port closed, 12; Scotch emigrate to, 51

Carey, George, British agent, 124

Carlton, Sir Guy, favoritism of Governor Parr, 193

Carr, James, paid debts in depreciated currency, 173

Carr, Captain William, married, 151-152

Carson, Captain John, becomes pseudo Loyalist, 130; votes on Oath Bill, 156

Carter, John, votes on Oath Bill, 156

Carteret County, 8

Carteret, Governor, 3; sale of confiscated land, 58

Caruthers, Mr., praises Fanning, 145-146; blackens Fanning's reputation, 141

Cary, Archibald, indebtedness, 25

Caswell, Richard, committee to win over Regulators, 48, 75; delegate to Continental Congress, 30, 63, 69; disarming of Tories, 106; leader against Regulators, 45; leader in first Provincial Congress, 64; Patriot commander at Moore's Creek, 92, 94-96; speaker of Assembly, 24; treatment of Samuel Cornell, 188-189; weakness as governor, 103

Catawba County, German immigration, 54

Catawba Indians, massacre of Loyalists, 136

Catawba River, Greene and Morgan unite at, 134

Catlett, William, escaped Regulator, 98

Cavendish, Lord John, Committee for Loyalist Compensation, 205

Charleston, Loyalist defense of, 59; North Carolina regiments captured at fall of, 128; refugees from East Florida, 185; surrenders to British, 124

Charlotte, capture of, 129; Patriot stronghold, 93

Chatham County, sale of confiscated lands, 58, 170; Tory uprisings, 57, 103

Cheraw, captured by Cornwallis, 124

Childs, revolt in Granville County, 36

Childs, James, neutral clergyman, 100

Chitwood, Captain James, executed at King's Mountain, 132

Chowan County, news of Battle of Lexington reaches, 69; sale of confiscated land, 58

Chowan River Region, loyalism, 58

Clarke, Alexander, Loyalist refugee, 183

Clarke, Colin, claim rejected, 207

Clarke, John, murdered by Patriots, 121

Clergy, inclined toward loyalism, 55-56; Patriot treatment of, 100; treatment by Patriots, 113-114; loyal to the King, 67

Clergy, Church of England, remain loyal, 186

Cleveland, Colonel, tries prisoners for treason, 133

Cleveland, Mr., Loyalist backwoods leader, 131

Clinton, Sir Henry, blames Cornwallis for failure to rally Loyalists, 137; effects of Moore's Creek on, 96; grants flag of truce to Samuel Cornell, 188

Cobham, Dr. Thomas, refuses to sign Association, 66

Coke, Daniel Parker, investigation of Loyalist claims on Parliament, 203-204, 205-210

Collier, Colonel John, warns governor of Fanning, 151; wounded, 150

Colson's Mill, Battle of, 127

Colvel, Mathew, and family, persecuted by Patriots, 118

Commercial policy of 1660, effect of, 9

Committee of Correspondence, Committees of Safety, 30; establishment of, 28-29; methods of enforcing boycott against England, 65-66

Committees of Safety, boycott of Loyalist merchants, 64-65; control government, 30; co-operation between states, 74; governor ostracized by, 71; importance of, 70-72; important prisoners tried by Provincial Council, 74; nonsigners of Association published, 66; overlapping jurisdiction, 115-116; powers of, 77-78; replaced by Council of Safety, 81; restriction of suffrage and office holdings, 77; some members remain Loyalists, 64; sympathy expressed for Boston, 30; Tory protest against illegal acts of, 66-67; training in government, 83; treatment of suspected Negroes, 71; treatment of Loyalists, 70-73; trial of James Cotton, 109

Committee of Safety of Anson County, arrest of James Cotton, 73; persecution of James Cotton, 109

Committee of Safety of Bladen County, persecution of James Cotton, 109

Committee of Safety of Edenton, 77; activities of, 72; warn of Loyalist officers, 91

Committee of Safety of New Bern, letter from governor denying slave insurrection, 73; prepares to meet Loyalist forces, 92

Committee of Safety of Rowan County, disciplining of Tories, 78; persecution of Loyalists, 108-109; seizes powder on news of Lexington, 69; intimidates Loyalists, 64, 71-72

Committee of Safety of Salisbury, protests against persecution of Loyalists, 108

Committee of Safety of Wilmington, ostracizes governor, 71; persecutes Tories, 70; publication of names of Tories, 65-66

Confiscated debts, paid in depreciated currency, 173; some recoverable, 178; value of, 173-175

Confiscated lands, courts slow in restoring, 169; currency acceptable for, 168; sale of, 166-167; sale of by act of 1782, 162-163; value of sales, 173-175

Confiscation Act of 1776, provisions of, 170

Confiscation Act of 1777, provisions of, 171

Confiscation Act of 1778, provisions of, 156-157; protests against, 157-158

Confiscation Act of 1779, provisions of, 158; protests against, 158-159, 171

Confiscation Act of 1781, provisions of, 172

Confiscation Act of 1782, provisions of, 172-173

Confiscation Act of 1784, sale of Loyalist property, 173-174

Confiscation Act of 1787, sale of British army property, 174

Confiscation of Loyalist property, abuses of, 160; carried out vigorously, 161-162; claims against, 164-165; clemency towards needy Tories, 167-168; distribution of, 180; effect of, 179-180; of all who fail to take Oath of Allegiance, 156-157; of persons convicted of treason, 154; opposition to, 162-164; regulation of by Assembly, 160-161; sale of, 159-160; suspended during 1781-1782, 161

Congress, Continental, delegates to, 30; navigation laws, 116; North Carolina members of urge Committee of Safety to greater efforts, 69-70

Congress, first Provincial, appointment of delegates to Continental Congress, 62-63; declares loyalty to king, 62-63; denounces Boston Port Bill, 63; formation of, 62; forms revolutionary government, 63

Congress, second Provincial, absolves Campbell of toryism, 74; forces merchants into nonimportation, 68-69

Congress, third Provincial, 74-78; amnesty to Loyalists of Bladen County, 81; committee to capture David Jackson, 102; committee to inquire into Loyalist activity, 80-81; committee to win over Regulators, 75; committee to win over Scotch, 91; Council of Safety established, 81; creation of

Provincial Council, 75-76; curbing of county Committees of Safety, 76; declares independence, 96-97; exile of Tories, 98; justification of harsh conduct towards Tories, 80; no quorum, 103-104; summoned by Samuel Johnston, 74; tries important prisoners, 74

Constitution of 1777, militia law, 127

Convention, second provincial, 67

Conway, Mr., 12

Cook, James, ill-educated committee member, 73

Cooke, John, Regulator Revolt, 42

Coor, James, votes on Oath Bill, 156

Corbyn, Mr., revolt in Granville County, 36

Cornelison, Mr., murdered by Tories, 122

Cornell, Samuel, debts and property confiscated, 172; Loyalist merchant 54; treatment of on return to North Carolina, 188-189; recovers property by suit, 178; Tory official, 56

Cornwallis, General, behavior of troops, 137-138; blamed for failure to raise Loyalists, 137; burns baggage to overtake Greene, 134; campaign in North Carolina, 129-130; camps at Winnsboro, 96; effect of Moore's Creek on, 96; Guilford Courthouse Battle, 136; invasion of North Carolina, 124; marches to Virginia, 137-138; retreats to Hillsboro, 135; retreats to Wilmington, 137

Cotton, Colonel, corps deserts Loyalists, 94

Cotton, James, activities of Committee of Safety, 72; arrested by Committee of Safety, 73; claim paid, 207; escapes from Committee of Safety, 73; influential Loyalist, 84-85; persecution of by Patriots, 109-110; recants Loyalist views, 73; Tory official, 56

Coulson, John, property restored, 168

Council of Safety, exile of Loyalist families, 99; persecution of Loyalists, 82

Council, Provincial, able leaders in, 63-64; banishment of John Strange, 79; District Committees of Safety, 76; parole of prisoners, 79; powers of, 76; replaced by Council of Safety, 81; training in government, 83; treatment of Farquard Campbell, 79; treatment of Loyalists, 78-79

Court House Ring, control of counties, 8; undemocratic, 9

Courts, Assembly allows residents to sue nonresidents, 175; Assembly declares Martin's courts illegal, 28; Carolinians sue in English courts, 27; controversy between Martin and Assembly, 26-29; difficulty of collecting debts, 27; inferior courts established, 30; legality questioned, 30

Cowpens, Battle of, 134

Cox, Captain, proclamation of amnesty to Loyalists, 148

Craig, Major James, capture of Wilmington, 122-123; captures many Loyalists, 138-140; expedition to New Bern, 140

Craven County, patriotic, 93; sale of confiscated land, 58; Tory uprisings, 105

Craven, Peter, Regulator Revolt, 38

Crawford, Captain William, 10

Cross Creek, Cornwallis stops at, 137; merchants of loyal, 54; rendezvous for Loyalist forces, 94; horses of Loyalists sold, 175

Crown, purchase of colony, 5

Crown Charter, 5

Crown Officials, loyal to King, 56-57

Cruden, John, Loyalist merchant, 54; nonsigner of Association, 66; with family flees to Nassau, 184

Cruizer, sloop of war, refuge of Loyalists, 72, 73, 84

Culloden, Battle of, Scotch come to North Carolina, 51

Culp, Captain, revenges Piney Bottom Massacre, 121

Culpepper Rebellion, 4

Cumberland County, Committee of Confiscation, 170; loyalism, 57, 140; Loyalist Military Forces, 59; many Scotch immigrants, 51; Tory guerrillas, 101; Tory uprisings suppressed, 106; weak Loyalist forces, 92-93

Cunningham, Robert, Tory official, 56

Curlu, John, Regulator, 40

Currency, South Carolina, 26

Currie, Captain, arranges for truce, 150

Currie, Duncan, murdered by Patriots, 121

Currituck County, Committee of Confiscation, 170; loyalism, 60; refuses to vote for nonimportation, 68-69; sale of confiscated lands, 58

Curwen, Samuel, Loyalist who defends Patriots, 187

Dartmouth, Lord, 11; authorizes Governor Martin to pardon Regulators, 86; promise of arms and soldiers, 86-87; seeks assurance of Loyalist support, 87

Davidson County, German immigration, 54

Davidson, Benjamin, becomes pseudo Loyalist, 130

Davidson, Major George, commands only force left after Camden, 128

Davidson, William, becomes pseudo Loyalist, 130

Davie, Colonel, disputed Cornwallis's march, 129; outwitted by Bryan, 127

Davies, William R., Halifax conservative, 164

Debenture notes, see paper money

Debts, paid in depreciated currency, 25-26

Dent, Captain, first North Carolinian killed, 93

Depreciation of currency, by Loyalists, 99

DeRosset, Lewis Henry, Committee on Property Loss, 204; Tory official, 56-57

Diligence, ship, boarded by insurgents, 13; brings stamps, 12

District Courts, Tories convicted of treason, 119-120

Dobbs County, Patriot county, 93; Regulators, 40; riots, 36; sale of confiscated land, 58

Dobbs, ship, released by king's officers, 13; seized for absence of stamped papers, 12

Dole, James, Loyalists in Nova Scotia, 193

Donaldson, Mr., defies Committee of Safety, 66-67

Dorchester, Lord, Unity of Empire, 199

Doudy, William, killed, 151

Douglas, Captain, captures Owen Griffin, 185

Draper, Lyman C., quoted, 131-132

Drummond vs. Lambert, Regulator Revolt, 42

Dubois, Mr., plunders Patriots, 139

Dubois, Isaac, unable to recover debts, 179

Dubois, Mrs. Jean, and family, exile of, 99; persecution by Patriots, 113

Duckinfield, Nathaniel, land confiscated, 58, 174

Dugan, Colonel, saved from hanging, 120

Duggan, Thomas, thanks Fanning, 151

Dugin, Major, property destroyed, 151

Dummer, Judge William, granted land in Canada, 193

Duncan, Archibald, persecuted by Patriots, 116

Dundas, Colonel, disaffection of Nova Scotians, 194

Dunkards, Oath of Allegiance, 155-156

Dunn, Frances, sent to South Carolina jail for safekeeping, 74

Dunn, John, persecuted by Patriots, 108-109, censured for Loyalist activities, 64

Dunmore, Governor of Virginia, 11; protects Thomas McKnight, 115

Duplin County, opposition to Stamp Act, 14; sale of confiscated lands, 58; turns Loyalist, 139

Earl, Daniel, neutral clergyman, 67

Earle, Reverend Mr., persecuted by Patriots, 113-114

Eastchurch, Governor of North Carolina, 4

East Florida, Loyalist refugees in, 184-185; Rangers, 184

Eaton vs. Hamilton, confiscated debts, 178

Eden, William, correspondence with McCulloch, 174-175; comments on Treaty of Peace, 190-191

Edenton, opposition to Stamp Act, 14; sale of confiscated lands, 162, 166

Edgecombe County, not represented at first Provincial Congress, 62; sale of confiscated land, 58; Tory revolts, 104, 106

Edwards, brig, 188

Eliot, Major John, shooting of, 120
Emory, James, banishment, 82
England, Loyalist refugees go to, 186-188
Eppes, Frank, loyalism, 60
Erskine, Thomas, paroled, 82
Everard, Sir Richard, bribery, 6
Executive, weakness of, 103
Exum, Benjamin, votes on Oath Bill, 156

Fallon, Dr. James, imprisonment, 78; treatment by Patriots, 115
Fanning, David, appeals for recruits, 146; attacks Lapps command, 148; attacks Petersboro, 143; captures Alston, 144; captures governor, 146; captures Greene's supplies, 148; claims partially paid, 212; commissioned Colonel, 142; decides to stay loyal, 141; Elizabethtown, Battle of, 144; exempted from pardon, 165; guerrilla warfare continued, 149-152; importance of, 140-141; loyal militia officer, 61; married, 151-152; men mistreated by Loyalists, 143; militia mobilized, 38-39; persecuted by Patriots, 140-141; raises Loyalist militia, 135; refugee in Florida, 191-192; Regulator Revolt, 41; requests compensation from England, 152; requests peace, 149-152; rules governing militia, 143-144; Wade defeated at Downing Creek, 145; Wilmington captured, 144; wounded at Lindley's Mill, 147
Fanning, Edmund, demands Few's death, 46
Fanning vs. Smith, Regulator Revolt, 42
Ferguson, Major, 130-131
Few, James, hanging of, 45-46
Fields, Jeremiah, Regulator, 41
Fields, John, Loyalist, 50
Fields, Colonel William, and brothers, Regulators who became Loyalists, 48
Fields, William, return of confiscated lands, 179
Fleming family, debts paid in depreciated currency, 26
Florida, Loyalists refugees in, 191
Folsom, Colonel Ebenezer, 98-99; illegal activities of, 99; requested to subdue Tories, 101-102; witness for John McNeill, 122

Forsyth County, German immigration, 54
Fox, Secretary of State of England, commission for Loyalist compensation, 205
Fraser, Reverend James, pressed compensation claims in England, 187-188
Fundamental Constitutions, 4

Garner, William, escaped Regulator, 98
Gaston County, German immigration, 54
Gates, General, Battle of Camden, 128
Gelately, Alexander, Loyalist refugee, 183
George II, Scotch Oath of Loyalty, 51
Germans, estates confiscated, 55; reasons for remaining loyal, 54-55; support Regulators, 54
Gibson, Mr., commission to win over Scotch, 91
Gilbert Town, courtmartial at, 132
Gilkey, Captain, executed after King's Mountain, 132
Glass, James, Loyalist merchant, 53-54
Gorrell, Ralph, votes on Oath Bill, 156
Governor's Council, Loyalists in, 56
Granville County, Regulation, 39, 40, 43; revolt against exorbitant fees, 36-37
Granville, Earl of, trustees claims paid 207
Gray, Colonel, mobilizes militia, 38
Regulator Revolt, 42
Gray, John, 156
Great Deed, 3, 4
Green, Captain, escape from Patriots, 133
Green, James, ship confiscated, 116-117; property seized, 186
Greene County, property restored to Loyalists, 168
Greene, General, Battle of Guilford Courthouse, 136; Southern campaign, 134-135
Griffin, Owen, persecuted under restraining act, 185-186; persecuted violently, 117
Griffin, Major Roger, thanks Fanning, 151
Grimes, Captain, executed after King's Mountain, 132
Guilford County, assures Governor Martin of loyalty, 85; Commissioners of Confiscation, 170; divided allegiance, 93; German immigration, 54; loyal-

ism in, 49, 57; not represented at
first Provincial Congress, 62; Tory
uprisings, 102, 103, 106
Guilford Courthouse, Battle of, 136-137
Guin, Edward, thanks Fanning, 151

Haldimand, Governor of Canada, government aid to Loyalist refugees, 195-
196
Halifax County, Committee of Safety,
64-65; Regulation, 39; sale of confiscated land, 58, 162, 168, 173
Hamilton, Mr., Loyalist backwoods leader, 131
Hamilton & Co., claim paid, 209
Hamilton, Archibald, advised not to return, 176; claim denied and then approved, 208-209; Scotch farms sold
for debts, 177; settles in Canada, 196
Hamilton, John, banishment of, 181;
career in British Army, 182; his regiment settles in Canada, 192; Loyalist
merchant, 52-53; recruiting of Loyalists, 105; Tory leader, 125
Hanging Rock, Battle of, 128
Harne, Mr., Committee of Correspondence, 28
Harnett, Cornelius, captured by Craig,
138; Committee of Correspondence,
28, 29; correspondence with McCulloch, 174-175; enforces nonimportation, 19; leader against Regulators,
45; Patriot merchant, 54; threatens
Governor Tryon, 13
Harris, Tyree, 42
Harrison, Thomas, security for good be-
havior, 170
Harrison, William, debts paid in depre-
ciated currency, 26
Hart, Thomas, beaten by Regulators, 41
Harvey, James, 40
Harvey, John, assures Massachusetts of
support in opposition to Townshend
Act, 17; moderator of Convention and
Speaker of Assembly, 68; President of
first Provincial Congress, 63; votes
for amnesty, 166
Harvey, John, Jr., Regulator Revolt, 45
Hassell, James, Tory member of Gov-
ernor's Council, 63
Hassell, Martin, Tory official, 56
Hawkins, Colonel Joseph, Black Rivers
Loyalist, 139

Hawkins County, property restored to
Loyalists, 168
Henderson, James, Loyalist refugee, 183
Henderson, Judge, Regulator War, 41,
42
Henderson, Richard, property destroyed
by Regulators, 43
Henry, George, persecuted Patriot, 103
Henry, Patrick, 11, 25; debts paid in
depreciated currency, 26; opposes
Townshend Act and Stamp Act, 20
Hepburn, Mr., commission to win over
Scotch, 91
Hepburn, James, accused of raising Tory
troops, 70; persecution by Patriots,
110; recants Tory sympathies, 71
Hertford County, not represented in first
Provincial Congress, 62; sale of con-
fiscated land, 58
Hewes, Mr., delegate to Continental
Congress, 30, 63, 69; Patriot mer-
chant, 54; not re-elected to Congress,
164
Highlanders, disenfranchisement of, 11
Hillsboro, courtmartial of Regulators,
46; not represented at first Provincial
Congress, 62; Patriot stronghold, 93;
rioting, 43; sale of confiscated land,
162, 166
Hillsborough, Lord, paper money con-
troversy, 23; Regulation, 40; warns
Tryon of opposition to Townshend
Act, 167
Hobbs, Augustine, executed after King's
Mountain, 132
Hogan vs. Husband, Regulator Revolt,
42
Hogg and Campbell, Loyalist merchants,
54
Hogg and Clayton, Loyalist merchants,
54
Hogg, Robert, Patriot merchant, 54;
Loyalist member of Committee of
Safety, 64
Holt, Marshall, correspondence with
McCulloch, 174-175
Holt, Michael, beaten by Regulators, 42
Holtron, Commodore, grants flag of
truce to Samuel Cornell, 188
Hooker, Captain William, killed, 151
Hooper, George, Loyalist merchant, 54
Hooper, William, Cape Fear conserva-
tive, 164; delegate to Continental

Congress, 30, 63, 114; leader in first Provincial Congress, 63-64; votes for amnesty, 166

Houston, Dr. William, Stamp Master, 14

Howard, James, protests against Confiscation Act of 1779, 171

Howard, Chief Justice Martin, flees to New York, 183; aid from Parliament, 203

Howe, General, 88

Howe, John, Regulation, 38

Howe, Robert, Regulator Revolt, 45; Committee of Correspondence, 29

Hughes, Joseph, persecution by Patriots, 110

Hunt, Memucian, votes on Oath Bill, 156

Hunter, James, Regulator, 41

Husband, Herman, excepted from pardon, 86

Hyde County, sale of confiscated land, 58

Independence, Declaration of, 96-97

Independence, factors influencing, 50

Innes, Hugh, 11

Iredell, James, Albemarle conservative, 164; condemns Confiscation Act of 1782, 172; correspondence with William Hooper, 175-176; correspondence with McCulloch, 174-175; violations of peace treaty, 202

Irwin, Colonel, Tory uprisings, 101

Isaacs, Colonel, persecutes Loyalists, 148-149

Jackson, David, escaped Regulator, 98; escaped Tory, 101; hung by Patriots, 148; Tory guerrilla, 102-103

Jamaica, exempts refugees from taxes, 185

James, Robert, exorbitant fees, 36

James, William, buys confiscated land, 178

Jefferson, Thomas, 11; English debt payments stopped, 25

Jenkins, John, Governor of North Carolina, 4

John Hamilton and Co., Loyalist merchants, 105

Johnston County, Committee of Safety, 28; loyalism in, 60; Tory revolts, 106

Johnston, Reverend Francis, flees to Jamaica, 184

Johnston, Governor Gabriel, encourages Scotch immigration, 52

Johnston, Samuel, Albemarle conservative, 164; defends wealthy Loyalists, 160; not satisfied with mild protests against Townshend Act, 17; summons Provincial Congress, 74; tells McCormick his property confiscated, 177-178

Johnston, William, correspondence with McCulloch, 174-175

Jones, Allan, correspondence with W. Bayard, 176; hanging of Tories, 104; leader in first Provincial Congress, 64

Jones, Joseph, debts paid in depreciated currency, 26

Jones, Willie, Regulator Revolt, 45; correspondence with McCulloch, 175; Halifax conservative, 164; ignores boycott of Andrew Miller, 20; leader in first Provincial Congress, 64; pays confiscated debt to state, 174

Justices, appointment of, 7; term of office, 8

Kelley, John and Willie, exorbitant prices for powder, 64

Kennedy, Captain, betrays Patriots, 148

Kennon, James, votes on Oath Bill, 156

Kettle Creek, Battle of, 105

Kimick, Captain, Patriot leader captured at Ramsaur's Mill, 126

King's Carolina Rangers, settle in Canada, 192

King's Mountain, Battle of, 131-134; Ferguson gathers Loyalists, 130-131; results of, 134; treatment of Loyalist prisoners, 132-133

Kinnon, Mr., committee to win over Scotch, 91

Knight, William, flees to New York, 183

Kragle, Jacob, Tory guerrilla, 101

Lafferty, Lieutenant, executed after King's Mountain, 132

Land, confiscation of, 58; sale of, 58

Langman, Lieutenant William, escapes from Patriots, 133

Lee, Charles, loyalism of, 60

Lee, Henry, 11

Lee, Colonel, defeat of Colonel Pyle, 135-136

Lees, the, debts paid in depreciated currency, 26

Legislature, biennial sessions, 5; return of confiscated estates, 179

Lexington, Battle of, effect on North Carolina, 69-70

Lillington, Alexander, battle against Regulators, 45; resistance to Stamp Act, 13; Patriot commander at Battle of Moore's Creek, 94-96

Lincoln County, German immigration, 54

Lindsay, James, killed by Regulators, 40

Lindsay, William, battle against Regulators, 45

Linsley, Captain, killed, 150

Littel, John, beaten by Regulators, 42

Lloyd, Colonel Thomas, resistance to Stamp Act, 13; Regulator Revolt, 42

Lobb, Captain, seizes ships, 48

Locke, Mr., committee to win over Regulators, 48

Logan family, two sons on either side at King's Mountain, 132

London Coffee House, meeting place of North Carolina Loyalists, 204

London, John, treatment on return to North Carolina, 188

Lourie, David, votes on Oath Bill, 156

Lowndes, Rawlins, becomes a Loyalist, 125

Loyalism, false accusations of, 104-105; flourishes under Craig, 139; friendship for colonial officials considered grounds for, 74; geographical distribution of, 57-60

Loyalist Claims Commission of Parliament, considers Loyalist claims, 206; establishes rules and classifications of claims, 205-206; precedents for, 205-206; report of, 206-207

Loyalist Military Activities, importance of, 107; summary of, 106-107

Loyalist Military Forces, accomplishments of, 152; anxious for truce, 150; collect for revolt, 89-90; engaged at Moore's Creek, 96; fire on own men, 136; geographical distribution, 59; granted land in Canada, 193; inducements to join, 87-88; large number raised in Upper Yadkin, 127; march on Wilmington, 94; militia companies, 61; needed to support British landing, 87; not supported by regular troops,

89; not to serve out of colony, 88; numbers in, 61; officers of, 90-92; organized by Colonel Ferguson, 130-131; poor discipline of, 93-94; poor leaders of, 94; provincial companies, 61; raising of, 87-88; recruiting of, 105; rules governing militia, 143-144; settles in Canada, 192-193; unable to join Cornwallis, 134

Loyalist officers, encourage loyalism, 91

Loyalist refugees, bring up children as gentlemen, 194; classes of people, 183; defend America in England, 187; destination of, 184-185, 186-187; friends settle together, 194; homesick in England, 187-188; method of departure, 184; mostly loyal from beginning, 183; wanderings of, 184

Loyalist revolts, extent of, 106

Loyalists, claim aid from Parliament, 204; of back country, 34; convicted by district courts, 119-120; distribution of pensions and indemnities, 212; effect of migrations of, 200; encouraged to settle in Canada, 196; end of migrations of, 200; growing bitterness against, 156, 158; guerrilla warfare of, 101-107; hung if captured going to Cornwallis, 123; hunting down of, 98-99; influence of leading men on, 56; investigation of claims by Parliament, 202-204; murdered by Patriots, 121-122; numbers of, 104; number of emigrants, 201; Parliament petitioned for aid, 202-203; peaceful methods of opposing Patriots, 99; percentage of population, 60-61; persecution of, 110-111, 111-113, 122, 140-141; prisoners, 81; property sold to satisfy damages of British armies, 118-119; pseudo Loyalists, 130; revolt prematurely, 125; sentiment towards revealed by correspondence, 174-178; rewards offered for, 114; thank king for liberal treatments, 213; treatment of, 60, 82; trial for treason, 123; trial of, 162; who were they, 34; wives and families experience hardships, 99; wreak vengeance on Patriots, 138-140

Loyalists' claims, cost of to British Government, 212

Loyalists of London, organize to press claims on Parliament, 204
Ludwell, Governor Philip, 5
Lyon, George, persecution by Patriots, 117-118
Lyons, Mr., persecuted Patriot, 102-103

McAllister, Colonel, Bladen County magistrate, 50; committee to win over Scotch, 91
McArthur, Archibald, plantation confiscated and rented, 170
McArthur, Major, joined by Colonel Bryan, 127
McBride, Archibald, Whig, murdered by Patriots, 122
McCormick & Co., property confiscated and sold, 172
McCormick, William, property confiscated, 177-178
McCloud, Murdock, settles on Miramicki River, 194
McCrea, Reverend, Loyalist clergyman, 56
McClain, James, Loyalist refugee, 183
McCulloch, Benjamin, votes for amnesty, 166; pays confiscated debt to state, 174
McCulloch, Henry, confiscation and sale of land, 159-160; claim paid, 207; correspondence with Patriots, 174-175; London representative of North Carolina Loyalists, 204; Regulator Revolt, 40; 60,000 acres confiscated, 174; receives aid from Parliament, 203
McDonald, Alexander, settles on Miramicki River, 194
McDonald, Alexander, and family, persecuted by Patriots, 112-113
McDonald, Allan, Loyalist officer, 90
McDonald, Allen, parole of, 79
McDonald, Daniel, settles on Miramicki River, 194
McDonald, Donald, asks for Loyalist recruits, 91-92; Loyalist commander, 90
McDonald, Flora, daughters of, persecution of, 122; return to Scotland, 184
McDonald, Isabella, persecuted by Patriots, 118
McDonald, John, Loyalist officer, 91
McDonald, Murdock, pensioned, 211
McDonald, Soule, flees to Nova Scotia, 197

McDonnel, John, refuses to sign Association, 66
McDougall, Roger, settles on Miramicki River, 194
McDougal, Colonel, Tory leader, 120
McDowell, Charles, votes on Oath Bill, 156
McDowell, Major, Loyalist backwoods leader, 131; attacked by Moore, 125
McDugald, Archibald, Battle of Lindley's Mill, 147
McEntire, James, ill-educated committee member, 82
McFall, John, executed, 132
McKay, Alexander, committee to win over Scotch, 91; Loyalist refugee, 184
McKay, Archibald, Battle of Lindley's Mill, 147
McKenzie, Kenneth, refuses to sign Association, 66
McKenzie, William, Loyalist clergyman, 56
McKnight, Alexander, returns to claim property, 176
McKnight, Dugald, refuses to sign Association, 66
McKnight, Thomas, Committee on Property Loss, 204; persecuted by Patriots, 114; plantations confiscated and rented, 170; refuses to vote for nonimportation, 68-69
MacLaine, Archibald, advice to Loyalists, 165-166; attacked for defending Loyalists, 177; Cape Fear conservative, 164; correspondence with Iredell, 175-176; letter of, 189; opposed to confiscation, 162, 163, 164; votes for amnesty, 166; votes on Oath Bill, 156
McLaine, Charles, committee to win over Scotch, 91; votes on Oath Bill, 156
McLean, John, gathers Loyalist militia, 90; Loyalist clergyman, 56
McLeod, Colonel Alexander, Loyalist commander at Battle of Moore's Creek, 95-96; murdered by Patriots, 121; second in command of Loyalists, 90
McLeod, Norman, and family, persecution of, 111
McLeod, William, nonsigner of Association, 66
McMaster, William, nonsigner of Association, 66

McMillan, Daniel, murdered by Patriots, 121

McMund vs. Courtney, Regulator Revolt, 42

McNabb, Duncan, claim partially paid, 209-210; persecuted by Patriots, 111-112

McNair, Ralph, unsold property restored, 167-168

McNeil, Colonel, killed at Battle of Lindley's Mill, 147

McNeil, Dan, Bladen County magistrate, 50

McNeil, Dugald, Bladen County magistrate, 50

McNeil, James, property confiscated and sold, 162, 172

McNeil, Neil, Bladen County magistrate, 50

McNeill, John, tried for Massacre at Piney Bottom, 122

McNeill, Mrs., exile of family of, 99; persecuted by Patriots, 113

McQueen, William, pensioned, 211-212

McRae, John, pensioned, 211-212

McRee, William, itemization of Robert Mylene's property, 173

McSweene, Allan, murdered by Patriots, 121

McSweene, Mrs., witnesses murder of husband, 121

Mallette, Peter, exempted from pardon, 165

Manufacturing, scarcity of, 10

Marches, the, debts paid in depreciated currency, 26

Martin, Alexander, beaten by Regulators, 42

Martin, Governor Josiah, acquiesces to colonial courts, 27; aid from Parliament, 202-203; appeals for Loyalist recruits, 129-130; appointed governor, 46; authorized to grant commissions, 86; berates Assembly for using Tryon as intermediary, 29; calls Assembly same time as second Provincial Congress, 67; commands Provincial forces, 87; commissions officers, 90; condemns persecution of Regulators, 47-48; denies plotting slave insurrection, 73-74; denounces action of Council, 63; dissolves Assembly for rebellion, 32; favors pardoning of Regulators, 46-47; forbids New Bern Convention, 30; grants land to Scotch to make them loyal, 88; ignorance of Revolution's progress, 89; instructed to raise Loyalist troops, 87-88; involves Campbell as Loyalist, 74; lack of support from England, 87; Loyalist support of, 61; not popular with friends of Tryon, 46; orders sheriffs to collect taxes despite orders of Assembly, ostracized by Committee of Safety, 71; outlaws first Provincial Congress, 62; outlaws second Provincial Congress, 67; paper money controversy, 23-24; plans defense of colony, 84; position at opening of revolt, 84; property confiscated and sold, 170-171; prorogues Assembly over Court Bill, 27; prorogues Assembly over Tax Bill, 24-25; refugees go to New York, 181; sheriffs leaders in Revolution, 9; succeeds Tryon as governor, 21; supported by interior counties, 85; supported by James Cotton at Cross Creek, 94; unable to stop Loyalist revolt, 89; vetoes Court Bill, 27; won over to cause of Regulators, 46-47; writes of counties, 86

Maxwell, Mr., flees to New York, 183

Maxwell, Daniel, murdered by Patriots, 119

Maxwell, William, harsh treatment of, 99; jailed by Council of Safety, 82

Maybin, Colonel, defeated at Lindley's Mill, 147

Mecklenburg County, protests against Confiscation Act of 1778, 157-158

Medical profession, treatment of during Revolution, 115

Mennonites, Oath of Allegiance, 155-156

Mercer, Commissioner, Stamp Agent of Williamsburg, 20

Merchants, of North Carolina mainly loyal, 52-54; property confiscated during Revolution, 53; Provincial Congress forces them into being Tories, 68-69

Micklejohn, Reverend Mr., persecuted by Patriots, 113

Middleton, Henry, becomes a Loyalist, 125

Military activities, guerrilla warfare 1776-1780, 101-107; *see also* names of individual battles and Cornwallis

Militia, Loyalist, *see* Loyalist Military Forces

Militia, Patriot, behavior of, 128; composition and character, 127-128; refuses to aid Green, 135

Millen, Mr., Loyalist refugee, 183

Miller, Andrew, ignores nonimportation, 20; Loyalist merchant, 52; protests against Committee of Safety, 66; refuses to sign Association, 65

Miller, George, flees to New York, 183; letter to, 187

Miller, Governor of North Carolina, 4

Mills, Colonel Ambrose, executed after King's Mountain, 132

Monroe, James, Committee on Property Loss, 204; property confiscated, 118-119

Montgomery County, loyalism in, 57; sale of confiscated land, 58

Moore County, sale of confiscated land, 58

Moore, John, calls Loyalist meeting at Ramsaur's Mill, 125; escapes to Camden, 126; Tory leader, 106, 125; Savannah defended, 106

Moore, Joseph, persecuted Patriot, 102

Moore, Maurice, committee to win over Regulators, 48, 75; legality of courts questioned, 30; removed from office for opposing Stamp Act, 14; Regulator Revolt, 39; threatens Governor Tryon, 13; urges Governor Martin to call Assembly, 88-89

Moore, William, debt canceled because of British Army damage, 176-177; profits by confiscation of debts, 173

Moore's Creek Bridge, Battle of, 94-96, 152; prisoners of paroled, 79; prisoners of persecuted, 110, 111-113; results of, 96-97

Moravians, Oath of Allegiance, 155-156; take neutral stand, 55; treatment of during Revolution, 55

Morgan, General, Battle of Cowpens, 134

Morgan, Morgan, Tory guerrilla, 102

Morrison, Alexander, Committee on Property Loss, 204

Munn, Alexander, property confiscated and sold, 162, 172

Munro, James, escaped Regulator, 98

Mylene, Robert, itemization of confiscated property, 173

Nash County, sale of confiscated land, 58; Tory revolts, 106

Nash, Abner, battle against Regulators, 45

Nash, Colonel Francis, jailor of James Cotton, 73; Regulator War, 42

Nash, Governor, debts paid in depreciated currency, 173

Navigation Acts, enforcement of, 4-5

Negroes, fear of uprisings of, 71; Loyalists arrive in Canada, 195

Neilson, A., correspondence with Iredell, 175

Nelson, Captain John, 105

Nelson, Robert, claim paid, 207

New Bern Convention, 30-31; Martin's opposition to, 31-32; step toward independence, 31; sympathy for Massachusetts, 30; taxation without representation, 30

New Bern County, opposition to Stamp Act, 14; Regulator Revolt, 43; sale of confiscated land at, 162, 166

New Blessing, ship, 191

New Hanover County, 12; opposition to Stamp Act, 14; Patriot county, 93; sale of confiscated land, 58

New York, banished Loyalists go to, 181, 182-183

Niagara frontier, settlement of by Loyalists, 197

Nicholson, Governor, 5

Ninety Six, captured by Cornwallis, 124

Noay vs. Fanning, Regulator Revolt, 42

Nonimportation, Cape Fear chiefly effected, 19; effectiveness of, 19; enforcement of, 19, 21; Georgia, 21; laxly enforced, 20; led by merchants, 21; North Carolina last colony to enforce, 19; South Carolina, 21

North Carolina, governed by Revolutionary bodies, 83; defenseless after Camden, 128

North Carolina Campaign, Battle of Camden, 128-129; Battle of King's Mountain, 130-134

North Carolina Gazette, protests against Stamp Act, 12; quoted, 182-183; Scotch Loyalists go to Scotland, 184

North Carolina Highland Regiment, composition of, 59

Nova Scotia, effect of Loyalist migrations on, 200; Loyalist refugees go to, 186, 192-193

Oath of Allegiance, of former officials, 155; of pacifist sects, 155-156; required for all over sixteen, 156; text of, 154

Ogden, Thomas, Patriot merchant, 54

Oldham, Captain, massacre of Loyalists, 136

Orange County, Committee of Confiscation, 170; loyalism in, 57; origin of Regulation, 37; Regulator War, 39-41; sale of confiscated land, 58

Orr, Thomas, nonsigner of Association, 68

Osborn, Aaron, Regulator War, 45

Oswald, Mr., British peace commissioner, 202

"Over the Mountain Men," Battle of King's Mountain, 131

Palmer, Robert, unable to recover debts, 179

Pamlico Sound, loyalism in, 58

Paper money, 6; conditions previous to 1764, 22; controversy between Assembly and Governor Martin, 24; debenture notes not legal tender, 23; debenture notes of 1768, 22-23; debenture redeemable by poll tax, 23; Governor and Assembly unable to agree on, 25; need of, 22-23; needed to pay foes of Regulators, 23-24; Parliament forbids issuance of, 22; Virginia, 25-26

Parker, George, property confiscated, 177

Parker, James, leader of North Carolina Loyalists in London, 204; plantation confiscated and rented, 170

Parliament, English, aids Loyalist refugees, 202-203; investigation of Loyalist claims on, 203-204

Parr, Governor of Nova Scotia, accused of patriotism, 193; prosperity of Loyalists, 194

Pasquotank County, Committee of Confiscation, 170; loyalism in, 60; three members of Assembly from refuse to vote for nonimportation, 68-69

Patience, ship, 12

Patillo, Reverend Mr., committee to win over Regulators, 48, 75

Patriot leaders, become Loyalists on Cornwallis's invasion, 124-125

Patriot Military Forces, aid other states, 128-129; deserters of cause revolt, 106; distribution of make North Carolina defenseless, 128-129; formation of, 92-94; number engaged at Moore's Creek, 96; unable to muster men in Bladen and Cumberland counties, 140; used in other states, 124

Patriot seizure of Loyalist property, legalization of, 165

Patriots, become Loyalists to save herds, 130; hunted down by Loyalists, 138-140; lull in activities, 105

Patterson, Daniel, forced to reveal names of Tories, 121

Patton, Hugh, Tory guerrilla, 102

Peace negotiations, Loyalist effect on, 202

Pearson, Thomas, leader of Regulators, 35

Pendleton, Mr., debts paid in depreciated currency, 26

Penn, John, elected to Continental Congress, 164

Pensions, granted for loss of office or profession, 211; granted to North Carolina Loyalists, 211-212

Person, Thomas, leader in first Provincial Congress, 64; Regulator who becomes Patriot, 48

Pickens, Colonel, Battle of Kettle Creek, 105

Piles, John, captured, 99; escaped Regulator, 98

Piles, John, Jr., escaped Regulator, 98

Pinckney, Charles, becomes a Loyalist, 124

Piney Bottom Massacre, 120

Pitt County, Committee of Safety organized, 64; fear of Negro uprising, 71

Pitt, William, bill to indemnify Loyalists, 212-213

Politics, Colonial, undemocratic county government, 8-9

Polk, Thomas, battle against Regulators, 45

Price fixing, 3; Rowan County Committee of Safety, 64

Prince Edward Island, Loyalist refugees settle in, 193

Prisoners, treatment of, after Battle of Moore's Creek, 97

Proclamation Act of 1763, effect on colonists, 10-11

Property owners, difficulties of English, 100-101

Proprietors of North Carolina, 4, 5

Proprietors of Pennsylvania, settlement of claims by Pitt, 210-211

Pryor, John, 39

Pultney, Hornby & Co., land scheme in Genessee Valley, 197-198

Pyle, Colonel, defeat of, 135-136

Quakers, Oath of Allegiance, 155-156

Quebec, French inducements to settle in, 196

Quincy, Josiah, Committee of Correspondence, 29; absence of courts in North Carolina, 28

Quit rents, 3, 4

Ramdon, Lord, British commander at Battle of Hanging Rock, 128

Ramsaur's Mill, Battle of, 125-127; Cornwallis burns baggage at, 134

Ramsay, Captain, receives Fanning's peace terms, 149

Ramsay, John, discouragement of Patriots, 139

Ramsey, Ambrose, votes on Oath Bill, 156

Rand, William, false accusations of loyalism against, 104-105

Randolph County, German immigration, 54; loyalism, 57, 60; sale of confiscated land, 58

Ranes, Major John, Battle of Lindley's Mill, 147

Rowan County, assures Governor Martin of loyalty, 85; Committee of Correspondence, 62; Committee of Safety, 64; German immigration, 54; loyalism, 57, 60, 136; prisoners sent to, 82; Regulators, 54

Reed, Reverend Mr., persecuted by Patriots, 113; refuses to preach for colonists, 67

Regulator Revolt, Assembly considers, 44-45; battle between militia and Regulators, 45; causes, 40, 41, 44; courtroom rioting, 41-43; hanging of James Few, 45-46; illegal practices of officials, 38; leaders, 35; militia called to maintain order, 43-44; mock courts, 42; pardons for Regulators favored by Governor and Crown, 47; reasons for, 31, 32-33, 37-38; rioting at Hillsboro, 41-43; supported by Germans, 54; use of militia, 38-39

Regulators, attempts of Patriots to reconcile, 48; become Loyalists, 47-50; befriended by Governor Martin, 47-48; Continental Congress attempts to win them over, 49; courtmartialed, 46; few become Patriots, 48; grievances of, 35; honesty of, 43; leniency of Governor makes them Tories, 47, 49; pardoned, 46

Restraining Act, no trade between Thirteen Colonies and other British possessions, 185

Riddick, Colonel, arrested by Committee of Safety, 66

Robbins, Michael, shooting of, 120

Robertson, Colonel, Tory commander, 104

Rockfish, town of, occupied by Moore's army, 94

Rogers, Michael, votes on Oath Bill, 156

Ross, Hugh, property restored, 168

Rosur, Captain Joseph, thanks Fanning, 151

Rowan County, assures Governor Martin of loyalty, 85; Committee of Correspondence, 62; Committee of Safety, 64; German immigration, 54; loyalism, 57, 60, 136; prisoners sent to, 82; Regulators, 40; sale of confiscated land, 58

Rowan, Robert, falsely accused of loyalism, 105

Rutherford, General, reports Tory uprising, 106; reinforced to deal with Tory guerrillas, 103; outwitted by Bryan, 127; captured at Camden, 128

Rutherford, Griffith, loyalism in Anson County, 60; McCulloch given advice, 177; Regulator Revolt, 45; votes for confiscation, 164; votes on Oath Bill, 156

Rutherford, John, Tory official, 62

Rutherford, Thomas, Battle of Moore's Creek, 97-98; exiled from state, 98; fails to gain Loyalist recruits in Cumberland County, 92-93; Tory representative to first Provincial Congress, 62

St. John's River, Loyalists settle at, 192

Salisbury, not represented at first Provincial Congress, 62; Patriot stronghold, 93; sale of confiscated lands, 162, 166; value of confiscated property sold, 173

Saltor, Robert, votes on Oath Bill, 156

Sampson County, sale of confiscated land, 58

Sanders, James, votes on Oath Bill, 156

Savannah, defense of, 106

Scotch, appointed magistrates in Bladen County, 50; declare loyalism to Craig, 139; immigration of encouraged, 50-51; join Loyalist Military Forces, 88; loyal to King, 50-52; many flee to New York, 183; monopolize trade of North Carolina, 51; numerous in Cumberland County, 51; reasons for remaining loyal, 51-52

Scotch Loyalists, refugees prefer Canada to West Indies, 193-194; return to Scotland, 184

Searcy, Reuben, 35

Seawell, Benjamin, votes on Oath Bill, 156

Seawell, Samuel, mistreated Loyalist in England, 187

Sectionalism, in state politics, 164

Sevier, prepares to attack Ferguson, 131

Shays, William, Patriot slayer of Warlick, 126

Shelburne, Lord, letter on aid to Loyalists, 203

Shelby, prepares to attack Ferguson, 131

Shepard, Jacob, settles on Miramicki River, 194

Simcoe, Lieutenant Governor of Ontario, attracts North Carolina Loyalists to Ontario, 198; comments on

Pultney, Hornby & Co. land scheme, 197-198; spurious Loyalist refugees, 195

Sims, Mr., leader of Regulators, 35

Slave insurrection, Governor accused of plotting, 74

Slingsby, John, defeated at Elizabethtown, 144-145; nonsigner of Association, 66; plunders Patriots, 139

Smith, David, urged troops for Bladen County, 143

Smith, Frederick, tried and hung for toryism, 123

Smith, Robert, intercedes with Governor Caswell, 183; Patriot merchant, 54

Smuggling, 10

Sneed, Captain, deserts Loyalists, 94

Snodgrass, Neil, aid from Parliament, 199

Sons of Liberty, enforce nonimportation, 19

Sothel, Seth, Governor of North Carolina, 4

South Carolina, North Carolina prisoners entrusted to for safekeeping, 74; Loyalists, 184

Spencer, Samuel, Regulator Revolt, 45; committee to win over Regulators, 91; influential Patriot, 85; threatened hanging of James Cotton, 109

Spicer, John, votes on Oath Bill, 156

Spiney, Mr., revenges murder of Cornelison, 122

Stamp Act, "a dead letter," 13; Patriots oppose, 12-13; opposition to, 11-15; repeal of, 15

Stanley County, German immigration, 54

Stedman, Mr., quoted, 136; reason for Tory failures, 94

Steuben, General, unites with Green, 135

Stewart, Alexander, imprisoned for printing inflammatory articles in *North Carolina Gazette*, 12

Stewart, Black John, Tory leader, 104

Still, Samuel, shooting of, 120

Stokes County, German immigration, 54

Strachey, peace commissioner, supports Loyalists at peace conference, 202

Strange, John, banishment of, 133

Stuart, John, loyalty of the frontier, 59

Sugar Act of 1764, protests against, 10

Sullivan County, property restored to Loyalists of, 168

Summer, Robert, votes on Oath Bill, 156
Sumner, Luke, votes on Oath Bill, 156
Sumter, Colonel, Patriot commander at Hanging Rock, 128
Surry County, assures Governor Martin of loyalty, 85; dominated by Patriots, 148; loyalism, 49, 57, 60; not represented at first Provincial Congress, 62
Sutherland, Ransom, complaints of Tory molestation, 101; proposed treatment of Tories, 114

Tarboro County, Tory uprisings, 101
Tarleton, Lord, Battle of Cowpens, 134; fear of retribution by stops slaughter of prisoners, 133
Tavernkeepers, treatment of, 117
Taxation without representation, South Carolina, 26
Taxes, assessment and collection of, 8; resistance to, 4; on tobacco, 4
Thally, John, suspected Tory, 70
Todd, William, imprisoned for failure to leave state, 182
Tories, protest against illegal acts of Committee of Safety, 66-67; treatment of, 70-71, 72, 78
Townshend Duty Act, 16; opposition to caused by sympathy for other colonies, 20; opposition to in Virginia, 20-21
Trade, nonimportation and embargo, 30-31
Trade Acts, little opposition to, 9-10
Treason, definition and punishment of by Assembly, 154-155
Treaty of Fort Stanwix, 11
Treaty of Peace, becomes law of land, 168; provisions of ignored by North Carolina, 166-167; provisions affecting Loyalists, 189-191, 202
Troops, British, delay of, 89; difficulties of landing, 87; promised to Governor Martin, 86-87; seven regiments to embark from Cork for North Carolina, 87
Tryon County, Committee of Safety, 82
Tryon, Governor, 11-12; annoyed at Assembly for protesting against treason trial in England, 18; appointed Governor of New York, 46; attempt to alter county oligarchy, 9; backwoods against Stamp Act, 14; com-
mon people ignorant of Stamp Act, 15; confers with Hillsboro on opposition to Townshend Act, 16; hanging of James Few; lauded for putting down Regulator Revolt, 46; letter rebuking Wilmington on its conduct during Stamp Act, 15; message to Assembly on Regulators, 44-45; new house given him, 37; nonimportation, 19; prepares militia to defeat Regulators, 45; prorogues Assembly to prevent nonimportation, 18; refuses to release ships, 13; Regulator Revolt, 40, 41, 43; Stamp Act, 11-12; succeeded by Martin, 21
Tryon, William, loyalism in Johnston County, 60
Tyrrell County, sale of confiscated land, 58

"Unity of Empire," Loyalist association in Canada, centennial of, 199-200; organization of order, 199-200

Waddell, Hugh, leader against Stamp Act, 12-13; leader of colonial forces against Regulators, 45
Wade, General, accuser of John McNeill, 122; Patriot revenger of Piney Bottom Massacre, 121; Committee to win over Scotch, 91
Wahabs Plantation, Battle of, 129
Wake County, not represented at first Provincial Congress, 62; sale of confiscated land, 58
Walker, John, enemy of John London, 189; ill-educated committee member, 82; arranges for truce, 150
Walker, John, Jr., nonsigner of Association, 66
Walsh, Major Nicholas, Tory leader, 126
Warlick, Captain, Tory leader, 126
Washington County, restores property to Loyalists, 168
Washington, George, 10-11
Waxhaw Creek, Tories restrained at, 128
Wayne County, sale of confiscated land, 58
Webb, George, debts paid in depreciated currency, 26

Weis, John, Loyalist refugee, 183

West Indies, influence of Loyalist migrations on, 200-201; Loyalist refugees settle in, 184

Whitfield, William, nonsigner of Association, 66

Wilkes, John, subsidized by South Carolina, 26

Wills, John, Loyalist clergyman, 56

William, brig, seized for illegal trade, 181

Williams, family of, persecution by Patriots, 119

Williams, Jacob, recants Loyalist views, 73

Williams, lawyer, receives Fanning's peace terms, 149

Williams, Mr., unpopular lawyer, 41

Williams, Samuel, recant Loyalist views, 73; threatened by Patriots, 85

Williams, Wilson, captured by Patriots, 85

Williamson, William, imprisoned for failure to leave colony, 182

Wilmington, furnishes leaders for opposition to Stamp Act, 14; letter congratulating Tryon on repeal of Stamp Act, 15; Loyalist forces march on, 94; made new capital, 7; merchants ignore nonimportation, 19; release of *Dobbs* and *Patience*, 13; sale of confiscated land, 162, 166; Tories tried for treason, 123; Tory uprisings, 101, 104

Wilmot, John, investigation of Loyalist claims on Parliament, 203-204, 205-210

Wilson, Captain, executed after King's Mountain, 132

Wilson, Andrew, paroled by Council of Safety, 82

Wright, Major, secures land in Canada for Loyalist. refugees, 192

Yadkin, Upper, loyalty of population, 127